Being unemployed in Northern Ireland

Being unemployed in
Northern
Ireland

An ethnographic study

Leo Howe

Department of Social Anthropology
University of Cambridge

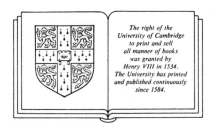

The right of the
University of Cambridge
to print and sell
all manner of books
was granted by
Henry VIII in 1534.
The University has printed
and published continuously
since 1584.

Cambridge University Press

Cambridge
New York   New Rochelle
Melbourne   Sydney

Published by the Press Syndicate of the University of Cambridge
The Pitt Building, Trumpington Street, Cambridge CB2 1RP
40 West 20th Street, New York, NY 10011, USA
10 Stamford Road, Oakleigh, Melbourne 3166, Australia

© Cambridge University Press 1990

First published 1990

Printed in Great Britain at The Bath Press, Avon

British Library cataloguing in publication data

Howe, Leo
Being unemployed in Northern Ireland: an ethnographic
study.
1. Northern Ireland. Unemployment. Social aspects
I. Title
331.13′79416

Library of Congress cataloguing in publication data

Howe, Leo
Being unemployed in Northern Ireland: an ethnographic study / Leo
Howe.
    p.   cm.
ISBN 0 521 38239 4
1. Unemployed–Northern Ireland.   2. Insurance, Unemployment–
Northern Ireland. I. Title.
HD5767.5.A6H68   1990
331.13′79416–dc20   89-70841 CIP

ISBN 0 521 38239 4 hardback

To my Mother and Father

Contents

List of tables	*page*	ix
Acknowledgements		xi
List of abbreviations		xiii
1 Introduction		1
Unemployment, deservingness, and individualism		4
Outline of the book		14
2 The political economy of Northern Ireland and the anthropology of sectarianism		19
Unemployment and the political economy of Northern Ireland		19
Anthropology and the sectarian divide		27
Research setting: Mallon Park and Eastlough		34
The unemployed on means-tested benefits		42
3 Doing the double in Belfast: the general picture		47
Introduction		47
Eastlough		51
Mallon Park		58
Discussion: Mallon Park and Eastlough compared		66
4 Doing the double or doing without		77
Introduction		77
Back to Mallon Park		79
Wages, jobs, and benefits		83
Incomes		91
Some further themes		97
Discussion		101
5 The 'deserving' and the 'undeserving': administrative practice in a social security office		106
Introduction		106
Background		109
The evidence		111
Discussion		128
Conclusion		133

6   Claimants and the claiming process: the reluctant claimant   136
    Introduction   136
    Becoming a claimant   137
    The reluctant claimant   141
    Conclusion   158

7   Claimants and the claiming process: the assertive claimant   160
    Introduction   160
    Orientations prior to becoming unemployed   163
    Mallon Park   168
    Eastlough   174
    Conclusion   183

8   The employed and the unemployed: conflict, discourse,   185
    and ideology
    Introduction   185
    Benefits, jobs, and life-styles   192
    Conclusion   219

9   Conclusion   224

    Notes   236
    List of references   244
    Index   259

Tables

1 Average annual rates of unemployment for United   *page* 22
Kingdom and Northern Ireland

2 Average annual totals of unemployment (excluding school   25
leavers) for United Kingdom and Northern Ireland

3 Belfast totals of unemployment by parliamentary   25
constituency

4 Vacancies at Northern Ireland job centres and   26
totals of unemployment

5 Duration of spells of unemployment for United Kingdom   27
and Northern Ireland

6 Numbers in Catholic and Protestant core samples by age   41
and experience of previous unemployment

7 Supplementary benefit (basic benefit) rates in force   43
between November 1983 and November 1984

8 Numbers of male heads-of-household in employment and   52
unemployment by area and sector of economy (industrial
orders in brackets): Mallon Park and Eastlough

9 Numbers of people experiencing unemployment by age   57
and present employment status, for Eastlough as a
whole, and core samples

10 Eastlough core samples: aggregate totals of previous and   57
present unemployment spells (includes all unemployment
ever experienced), by age and present employment status

11 Number of housing starts for each financial year for east   61
Belfast and Catholic west Belfast

12 Numbers of people experiencing unemployment by age   67
and present employment status, for Mallon Park as a
whole, and core samples

13 Mallon Park core samples: aggregate totals of previous and   67
present unemployment (includes all unemployment ever
experienced), by age and present employment status

14 Mallon Park unemployed and employed core samples: 92
   replacement ratios
15 Eastlough unemployed and employed core samples: 94
   replacement ratios
16 Average replacement ratios for Mallon Park and Eastlough   96
   core samples
17 Total Northern Ireland unemployment (January figures,   225
   1978–89) according to contemporary methods of
   counting
18 Rates of unemployment for United Kingdom and Northern   226
   Ireland for three selected years
19 Duration of male unemployment spells for Northern   227
   Ireland, for the years 1985 and 1989

Acknowledgements

I have not found this an easy book to write. No doubt this is partly due to my own failings as writer, observer, and analyst. It is also due to the large quantity of material I was able to collect and which, at first, seemed chaotic and unmanageable. But for someone trained in social anthropology perhaps the biggest obstacle was the almost complete lack of an established body of anthropological theory and literature on unemployment in Western societies, to which my own findings could be related and which could supply inspiration and guidance. Willy-nilly I was forced into other areas. I scoured the literature on industrial sociology, the psychology of unemployment, the history of the welfare state, the policy process, the sociology of bureaucracy, social security legislation, and so forth. The final version, then, is an inter-disciplinary work which, I hope, will have some appeal to scholars in all of these fields.

Both during the research and while writing I have inevitably incurred numerous debts both to individuals and to institutions. I should first like to acknowledge the generous financial assistance of the Economic and Social Research Council who made available to me two grants over a period of three and a half years. Clearly, without such support the research could never have been done at all.

The study was conducted while I was a Research Fellow in the Department of Social Anthropology, Queen's University of Belfast, between 1982 and 1985. My stay there was a happy one owing largely to the intellectual, moral, and material support of the other members of staff. My especial thanks however must go to John Blacking, even though his energy and dynamism sometimes made the rest of us feel tired by comparison.

My thanks are due also to several Northern Ireland government departments. The Department of Health and Social Security allowed me access to a Belfast social security office whose manager and staff were unfailingly helpful and kind; the Department of Economic Development and the Northern Ireland Housing Executive provided me with various statistics; and the Job Centre at Gloucester House supplied on-site facilities to enable me to make contact with a small number of unemployed men who later participated in a short pilot project.

Of the people who generously gave of their time in reading and commenting on various parts of one or another of the many drafts this work has gone through, I would like to single out Michael Hill, Hastings Donnan, Ernest Gellner, Karen Trew, and Ray Pahl. I am also grateful to Sandra Cullen for some very useful comments on how to improve chapter 5. Particular thanks, however, are due to Chris Hann and Richard Jenkins, who read the entire manuscript and offered much sound advice and encouragement. Whatever faults still lie in the book, and I am sure there are many, these remain entirely my own.

To my wife, Elizabeth, whose patience, tolerance, and good will I have too often taken for granted, and to my parents, whose support and encouragement have never slackened, I owe a very large debt of gratitude.

But I reserve my warmest thanks for the people of Belfast and especially those of Mallon Park and Eastlough. Unbidden, I knocked on their doors, open and unsuspecting they let me in and plied me with cups of tea and pieces of toast. Asking poor and unemployed people to describe their experience and divulge the depressing details of often impoverished lives was never anything other than difficult, though I am sure some obtained a certain, but temporary, cathartic release. Prying (voyeuristically?) into their domestic circumstances in our so-very-privatized society was a constant source of anxiety. The fact that I could do virtually nothing to alleviate the dire situation of such disad-vantaged people (and I am not naive enough to believe that this book will change anything) only compounded my feelings of unease and disquiet. I cannot give these people back what they gave to me. I hope only that what I have to say will not incur their displeasure. It is not possible to name all those who took part in the study, but to Tommy, Sandra, Billy, Theresa, Bill, Gerry, Norman, Pete, Michael, Jim, Alec, Stephen, Janet, Paddy, Seamus, Dominic, John, and Frank, I would like to say thank you for giving not only your time and hospitality but also your much-appreciated friendship.

To protect, as far as possible, the privacy of the people who partici-pated in the project, I have fictionalized both their names and the names of the areas in which they live.

Some of the material contained in chapters 3, 4, and 5 has appeared elsewhere in different form. Cambridge University Press, Galway University Press, and Gower Publishing Company have kindly granted permission for this to be republished.

Abbreviations

ARs	Additional requirements
CAB	Citizens' Advice Bureau
DHSS	Department of Health and Social Security
DUP	Democratic Unionist Party
EEC	European Economic Community
ENPs	Exceptional needs payments
ETS	Employment Training Scheme
FEA	Fair Employment Agency
FIG	Fraud Investigator's Guide
FIS	Family income supplement
HGV	Heavy goods vehicle
IO	Interviewing officers
IRA	Irish Republican Army
IS	Income support
JTP	Job Training Programme
LOSC	Labour-only sub-contracting
LTSR	Long-term scale rate
NCC	National Consumer Council
NHS	National Health Service
RR	Replacement ratio
RRR	Rent and rates rebate
SB	Supplementary benefit
SBC	Supplementary Benefits Commission
SSO	Social security office
VO	Visiting officer
YTS	Youth Training Scheme

Chapter 1

Introduction

Divisions and their reproduction are the themes of this work: divisions between Catholic and Protestant; between employed and unemployed; and, most centrally, between the 'deserving' and the 'undeserving'. We shall see that these divisions operate simultaneously at various levels: social, cultural, economic, and political.

By way of introduction let me point out that such divisions are of somewhat different form. The first two indicate social categories which, for the most part, have readily identifiable and reasonably unambiguous memberships. That is to say there is general consensus not only about the factual existence of these distinctions but also about who is a Catholic and who a Protestant, who is in work and who unemployed.[1]

Such is not the case for the third of these divisions. In relation to unemployment and poverty, deservingness is defined by a set of moral and evaluative criteria. The deserving unemployed are considered to be those out of work through no fault of their own, keen to return to work, and on the whole willing to accept any reasonable offer of a job; they are thus truly eligible for state support. Moreover, they are deemed to be like those in employment since they share with the latter the high values placed on work, independence, individual responsibility, and the family. In this sense they are admitted into the same 'moral community' as those in employment. The undeserving unemployed are defined by an opposite set of criteria and, because they are deemed to espouse a contrary and despised set of values, they are seen as being more or less outside the moral pale.

Two features differentiate the conceptual contrast between the deserving and the undeserving from the other divisions. First, there is no consensus about whether the distinction has any real basis in fact. More correctly, while some people (including some of the jobless themselves) argue that there is a large group of undeserving unemployed, and that therefore the distinction is valid, others take the view that the actual size of such a group is very small and hence the contrast is pernicious. The problem here is to try to explain these differences and the manner in which they are sustained. Second, whilst there is agreement about the validity of the criteria which define the distinction, there is no unanimity concerning the classification of particular unemployed people. That is to say, who is deemed to belong to the one or the other of these classes varies considerably from person to person. When branding others as undeserving it is generally anonymous others who are being labelled; one or two known individuals may be selected for special treatment, but these are used as exemplary cases of a much larger category, the objective existence of which is taken for granted. As far as employed people are concerned, these evaluations include the ideas that a large number of people don't want to work; that many don't bother to look for work; that they are content to live on benefits; and that they are better off than some employed people. As for unemployed people, one of the most interesting features of their derogatory statements about other unemployed is that these are nearly always linked, directly or indirectly, to much more positive descriptions of themselves, particularly their own strong desire for work. Here the point of such labelling is not simply to affirm that the undeserving comprise a large group but also, and perhaps more importantly, to engage in strategies of impression management (Goffman, 1971) to imply positive claims about their own status.

This can be put another way. The categories 'deserving' and 'undeserving' exist as part of the stock of cultural knowledge. Since it is widely recognized that others use such a scheme of classification to organize their understanding of unemployment, individuals who are themselves unemployed feel more or less constrained to invoke similar contrasts to try to secure for themselves deserving status. One of the means of achieving this is to brand yet others as undeserving. Given the disagreement concerning the size and significance of the undeserving group, the anonymity of those designated undeserving, the variation between those carrying out the moral assessment, and the practical use to which the distinction is put, it is clear that there is no simple correspondence between these categories and actually existing social groups possessing the features purportedly characteristic of them, or that they have memberships which can be unambiguously stated and objectively verified. In fact the relation between the distinction and the social correlate is very complex, and much of this book is an attempt to tease out the many themes which compose it. It must be made clear that I am not arguing that there is no such animal as the 'scrounger' or the 'malingerer', only that, from an analytical perspective, what is socially relevant is the *act* of classification; the imputation of their presence counts just as much as which category particular individuals are considered to exemplify.

The importance of the distinction between the deserving and the undeserving should be clear to anyone who has conducted research into unemployment, for it induces in many unemployed strong feelings of private shame, and an almost crippling degree of anxiety concerning which category others are thought to assign them to. Much of what these unemployed do and say can be seen as almost wholly bound up with their efforts to get themselves classified in the deserving category, one result of which is the wholesale stigmatization of others as undeserving. It is this outcome which is partly responsible for the social isolation, fragmentation, and distrust so readily observable among sections of the unemployed. In other words the unemployed are not only divorced from those in work, they are also separated from other unemployed, association with whom may lead to accusations of family neglect, idleness, improvidence, fecklessness, and so on.

The division between the deserving and the undeserving is not only found at the local level, it has also been very influential in shaping social policy. According to certain political ideologies there will always be a need to assist those who cannot help themselves: the sick; the disabled; the old; the genuinely unemployed; etc. These deserving and eligible cases must be distinguished from those others (the 'undeserving') who could make private provision for themselves but prefer to rely on state support. The point is, so the argument goes, state assistance creates dependency (in the modern jargon, it creates a 'dependency culture'), and this in turn saps the will to work, erodes self-esteem and ruins initiative. In trying to ensure that only the 'genuinely' poor receive benefits, Conservative administrations often employ a rhetoric which emphasizes that resources must be 'targeted' or 'channelled' only to those who are most in need. The undeserving must be identified and eliminated, not only to husband scarce resources more efficiently but also so that the former do not demean and stigmatize the service for the deserving.

Although the research on which this book is based was carried out prior to the 1988 social security reforms, it is clear that these changes demonstrate the centrality of the distinction between the deserving and the undeserving in the formulation of social policy. In effect this contrast constitutes a major presupposition underlying a political and economic discourse which dominates the discussion and analysis of issues of welfare support. I hope to show that while of course the distinction between the deserving and the undeserving has a powerful social meaning, it does not refer to those it supposedly describes in any straightforward fashion. The way the contrast is used, by unemployed, workers, politicians, and others, depends on the assumption that the deserving and the undeserving form clearly separated groups of people whose identification is non-problematic. As already noted, however, the correlation between label and group is not simple but very complex. This being so, social policies based on the presumed empirical existence of social groups bearing a simple correspondence to these two cultural categories are therefore seriously flawed. Any such policy will not only fail to achieve its stated aims, but it will continue to reproduce the conditions which appear to render them sensible. Should unemployment remain a significant social problem, further reforms of welfare policy which are based on ideas of this kind can only increase the heavy burden the jobless have to bear.

Unemployment, deservingness, and individualism

Current scholarship suggests that ideas about the deserving and undeserving poor go back to the fourteenth century. The preceding period viewed the poor as God's children to whom personal charitable assistance was an act of merit, and it 'did not make the easy equation between destitution and moral inadequacy' (Golding and Middleton, 1982: 7) that was later to be such a prominent feature of the Poor Law. According to Tierney, 'idleness was condemned and poverty was not automatically equated with virtue . . . but it hardly ever occurred to the canonists that the law should seek to "deter" men from falling into poverty. Want was its own deterrent, they thought' (1959: 11–12).

Rubin (1983) places the emergence of more hostile attitudes to the poor in the late middle ages, and relates it to changes in economic organization and changing demographic patterns. A growing shortage of labour, precipitated by various factors, including the Black Death, produced both a rise in the wages and standard of living of employed labourers, and also a decline in the economic fortunes of landlords, rentiers and employers. As a result, the latter began to attribute their weakening position to the supposed indolence and fecklessness of the labourers. Consequently, the able-bodied unemployed were presented as idle and criminal; putatively they preferred to beg, steal, and lie rather than to work. Even those in employment were charged with failing to work a full day, working only for subsistence needs, and neglecting their social and religious duties (Rubin, 1983: 31; see also Shepherd, 1983). Subsequently attitudes towards the poor hardened into a general denunciation of the less productive members of society.

Viewed as the root cause of economic hardship, labourers and the poor 'were judged for what was seen as wilful withdrawal from the economy and slothful reliance on others' (Rubin, 1983: 293).

Hardly a century earlier the ability to work was marginal to discussions of poverty, but now, in the fourteenth century:

As the test of productivity came to rule in determining social acceptance and moral approbation, the poor, . . . came to acquire a label, to be seen as shirkers or 'wastrels'. In the minds of employers and entrepreneurs struggling with an economy afflicted by an acute shortage of labour, poverty came to be seen more as a choice than an affliction. (Rubin, 1983: 293)

Following the change in the maintenance of the poor from acts of individual Christian charity to a function of the state, the debates about the level, effectiveness, and consequences of material support for the sturdy vagabond, the able-bodied poor or, in to-day's terminology, the unemployed, have been very contentious. The problem has always revolved around the need for policies designed to coerce the unemployed back into work by not making their situation too eligible whilst without work.

The first pieces of legislation concerning poverty, the Statute of Labourers of 1351 and the Poor Law Act of 1388, perceived the fact of people moving around the country in search of work as a problem of vagrancy and social disorder. The legislation sought not only to restrict mobility but, by forcing people to stay in their parish of origin, also to prevent wages from rising (D. Fraser, 1973: 28). Though early Tudor legislation was less harsh in relation to the impotent poor (those who could not work), it was just as repressive in regard to the able-bodied poor (Pound, 1971: 39).

The Elizabethan Poor Law Acts of 1598 and 1601 rooted poor relief in the system of local government. By levying a rate on property, each parish was made responsible for its 'own' poor. Designed to restrict vagrancy (which it generally failed to do), it produced instead a great deal of litigation between parish overseers disputing the rightful settlement of origin of 'vagrants'.

What happened over the next two hundred years is well summarized thus: the Elizabethan Poor Law 'asked overseers to provide money for the impotent, work for the able-bodied and correction for the idle; two centuries of practice created in the Poor Law a tool of social policy of infinite variety and unlimited versatility' (D. Fraser, 1973: 32).

By the end of the eighteenth century, however, outdoor relief (as opposed to the workhouse) in the form of supplements in cash or kind according to income, number of dependents, and the price of bread, came to predominate. But with bad harvests, growing unemployment, and an increasing population, the cost of such relief, considered a national scandal, eventuated in the passing of the 1834 Poor Law Reform Act. The two major planks of this legislation were the principle of less eligibility and the workhouse test. According to the former, support for the indigent and destitute should be at a level below that which an unskilled worker could obtain by private provision. To pass the workhouse test it was simply necessary to enter one. Conditions in the workhouse were made particularly severe so that anyone willing to seek refuge there must be a genuine case. The Poor Law Commissioners thought this a cast-iron method of distinguishing between those in real need and the feckless and idlers.

Pioneering social research into poverty and unemployment, which began in the 1870s, was also much occupied with notions of deservingness and related ideas. This early work (Garraty, 1978) consisted in counting and classifying groups of people under a 'poverty line', and explaining poverty and unemployment in terms both of a surfeit of people and their personal habits, vices, and circumstances. The feckless and improvident were deemed incorrigible, and so nothing could be done for them. But because this group did do some work, of which there was not enough to go round, they competed with the slightly less poor but more industrious type, who nevertheless had small resistance to the alleged deleterious effects of receiving charity and assistance when idle. Consequently, during recessions the perceived problem was the difficulty in discriminating between the truly eligible and the cheats and loafers. Hence the middle-class ambivalence to the poor and needy. Charity as often as not went to the 'undeserving', and when it found its way into the hands of the 'deserving' it merely encouraged the improvidence and dependency that were considered to be the causes of indigence.

As far as social policy was concerned, at the beginning of the twentieth century the overriding objective was to limit unemployment and to ameliorate its effects. Ushered in in dramatic circumstances by Lloyd George in 1911, the principle of state responsibility for aiding the unemployed was, by 1920, when about 75 per cent of the labour force was covered by an actuarially based compulsory insurance scheme, no longer a controversial issue. However, through the 1920s, and particularly after the onset of the Depression, the National Insurance Fund, unable to cope with growing unemployment, went into deficit. Subsequently benefit was cut and one of the qualifying criteria, the 'genuinely seeking work' test (Deacon, 1976), became progressively more restrictive.[2] As a result thousands of workless people were unloaded onto the mercies of the Public Assistance Committees whose harsh means-test caused great misery (M. Cohen, 1945).

In the 1930s the issue of deservingness in relation to unemployment was not a major research priority. The only study to tackle the problem at all was E. Wight Bakke's *The Unemployed Man* (1933). Based on a six-month stay in the London borough of Greenwich, he examined the effect of unemployment insurance on the willingness and ability of workers to support themselves. He found little evidence to suggest that insurance benefits inhibited either the search for, or acceptance of, employment.

Most research during the Depression concentrated instead on how the attitudes of unemployed people changed as their spell without work increased. Looking at the effects of near-total unemployment in the small Austrian village of Marienthal, Jahoda, Lazarsfeld, and Zeisel (1972; originally published in German in 1933) discovered the suggestion of a systematic change in orientations to life (shock – optimism – resignation – despair – apathy) linked to increasing lengths of unemployment and decreasing levels of income.

Only a year later Beales and Lambert (1934) published memoirs of twenty-five unemployed people. These, they argued, disclosed a pattern of attitude change similar to that observed in Marienthal, although the terms used (optimism – pessimism – fatalism) were different. Yet close inspection of the memoirs reveals quite a diversity of reactions and changes only some of which lend any support to the theory of an ordered progression. By 1938, and the appearance of Eisenberg and Lazarsfeld's influential 'The psychological effects of unemployment', this process had almost assumed the status of a general law. In their review of the available literature they concluded that there was agreement amongst contemporary writers concerning the experience of unemployment. Shock is the initial reaction to job loss; this is followed by optimism while the person is looking for work; pessimism supplants optimism when no job is found. Finally 'the individual becomes fatalistic and adapts himself to this new state but with a narrower scope. He now has a broken attitude' (1938: 378).

There was very little social research into unemployment between 1945 and 1970, but due to its increase in the early 1970s interest revived, and through the following decade a substantial amount of work was completed. Many of the studies carried out by psychologists during this period took the phase model as a major focus of inquiry (for example, Harrison, 1976; J.M. Hill, 1977; Briar, 1977; Hayes and Nutman, 1981). Yet with very few exceptions the theory received merely illustrative support rather than stringent analysis (Sinfield,

1981: 37). There were two reasons for this. First, Jahoda's finding that the transitions paralleled a decline in disposable income was largely neglected and second, the extreme circumstances of the Marienthal case were rarely acknowledged. Even though Jahoda herself cautioned against generalizing from her findings, subsequent research failed to take this warning seriously. Moreover, despite the fact that modern surveys of the unemployed (M. Hill *et al.*, 1973; Daniel, 1974) unanimously agree that one of the worst problems faced by the jobless is financial, a major criticism (C. Fraser, 1980; Hartley and Fryer, 1984) of this psychological research was that it failed to take this adequately into account.

It would be inappropriate here to make a more detailed assessment of this research, so I shall confine myself to a few remarks. Generally speaking, research in the 1970s can be classified into three, rather arbitrary, categories. The first comprises the large-scale, cross-sectional and longitudinal surveys and cohort- and area-based studies carried out by social administrators and policy institutes (see Hakim, 1982, for an excellent review). All of these studies are unashamedly empiricist in theoretical outlook, often policy orientated, and designed to 'get the facts'. They concentrated on the financial effects of unemployment, the characteristics of the unemployed (age, sex, race, health, social class, etc.), methods of job search, employment history, effectiveness of government agencies for dealing with unemployment, and similar topics.

The second category, heavily dominated by social psychologists, used one or another type of survey technique. These studies tend to be limited to particular groups of the unemployed (school leavers, adult men, women, professionals, minority groups, etc.) and their main areas of interest concern the psychological effects of unemployment (changes in affective states – particularly mental health – and cognitive abilities, changes in attitudes to work, changes in self-esteem, self-respect, time use, and so forth), and the influence of mediating variables (income levels, attitudes to work , social class, etc.).

There is now a large critical literature on this output (see, for example, Hartley, 1980; Kelvin, 1980; C. Fraser, 1980; Gurney and Taylor, 1981; Hartley and Fryer, 1984) which draws attention to various deficiencies: the general neglect of cultural and economic factors; the lack of interest in the social processes generated by the dependency of the unemployed on welfare benefits; the neglect of the implicit arguments between the unemployed and those still in work and the processes of labelling which arise from these; the indifference to the possible importance of informal economic activity and the 'black' economy; and finally the insufficient attention paid to the unemployed's interaction with wider social institutions within which is embedded a power structure largely responsible for their predicament.

The third category of research, to which the above criticisms apply only in part, comprises a small number of more qualitatively based works (for example, Marsden, 1982; Gould and Kenyon, 1972; Seabrook, 1982) and several general studies of some sociological interest (for example, Crick, 1981; Field, 1977; Hawkins, 1979; Showler and Sinfield, 1981; Sinfield, 1981).

One of the less useful results of this research effort has been the general characterization of the unemployed as largely passive and quiescent. Unintentionally, perhaps, they have often been represented as inevitably deteriorating into apathy, indolence, poor health, and mental torpor. This is a mistake that was pointed out fifty years ago by Singer (1940: 83–4).

Fortunately, the theoretical picture is not as bleak as these criticisms imply because recent ethnographically based research is largely free of such blemishes. This research has, as its primary objective, the study of processes of social and cultural reproduction amongst working-class youth (Willis, 1977), and within this the analysis of unemployment has figured prominently. The particular issue in this literature which I want to highlight is the ideology of 'individualism', since in modern capitalist societies such an ideology has come to be inextricably linked to notions of deservingness. As defined by Jenkins, individualism denotes 'a way of looking at the world which explains and interprets events and circumstances mainly in terms of the decisions, actions and attitudes of the individuals involved' (1982: 88). It typically involves victims being blamed, and often blaming themselves, for their own misfortune (Ryan, 1976).

In their study of youth unemployment in the north-east of England, Coffield, Borrill, and Marshall note the pervasive use of individualistic themes (1986: 83–4). Endorsed by the media, the schools, other state agents, politicians, and employers, individualistic explanations of success and failure become impossible to resist, and the young unemployed focus on their own supposed inadequacies rather than on wider social forces in trying to understand their situation.

P. Brown's study (1987) of the education of 'ordinary kids' in Swansea, and Walsgrove's study (1987) of young unemployed people in Kidderminster, both further demonstrate the centrality of individualism. Such notions, moreover, are not confined to Britain as MacLeod

(1987), writing about both black and white American working-class youth, and Watson (1985), writing about unemployed youngsters in Australia, clearly show.

According to Hutson and Jenkins the prevalent use of individualism should not be surprising: 'Individualism is one of the dominant themes of Western European culture: from the media, from education, from politicians, from our peers, from advertising and the market, the message is the same. Notions about the responsibilities and freedoms of the individual are the foundation stones of modern capitalism and liberal democracy' (1989: 115). An important reason why individualism is so influential is that it is 'commonsensically true' (Hutson and Jenkins, 1989: 115). Individuals are represented as discrete entities; Western capitalist ideology places supreme value on the individual, and subordinates society to the individual. The vocabulary of choice, decision-making and personal responsibility is ubiquitous, and constitutes the taken-for-granted framework for our dealings with other people, and the way we routinely explain how society works. But of course individualism is not something which merely frames our thought; its component themes are of great practical use in manipulating the real world and our place in it. Individualism as an ideology may well conceal some fundamental features of society, but it also reflects very significant aspects of relationships in the sense that it partly constitutes the lived reality of the everyday world.

Ideas of individualism are enshrined not only in the American Dream but also in a veritable battery of maxims and clichés: you can do anything if you set your mind to it; life is what you make it; where there's a will there's a way; etc. Success as a purely personal achievement is validated as much by the startling 'rags-to-riches' stories paraded in the press as it is by trivial, routine examples of it. Because this ideology explains the distribution of rewards and punishments in terms of voluntary, individual activity, it underpins ideas of competitiveness, entrepreneurialism, and the 'managerial ideology' (Abercrombie, Hill, and Turner, 1980: 135). Amongst poorer groups in society such ideologies encourage division and isolation. By thus limiting the possibilities of collective political action the prevailing system of inequalities is both preserved and ratified.

Ideas of deservingness are a fundamental part of individualistic explanations, since they furnish an interpretive framework for the evaluation and labelling of the behaviour of unemployed people. Within individualistic accounts, the undeserving unemployed are those who prefer to scrounge, who choose to remain workless, and who do not make a big enough effort to find work. In this sense unemployment is perceived as a personal affair rather than a public issue (Mills, 1970: 14–15).

It is important to realize, however, that individualistic accounts of unemployment are not the only ones available. Clearly the distinction between the deserving and the undeserving entails that the former cannot be held responsible for their continued unemployment; to be deserving means to be largely blameless. In general the situation of the deserving unemployed is explained by reference to collective or macro-structural features of the political economy. The important task, then, is not merely to describe how and under what conditions different kinds of explanation are used, but to analyse the use and context of these forms of interpretation by linking them to other features of the wider situation.

Some of these themes have been taken up in more recent psychological research.[3] Amongst others Fryer and Payne (1983), Warr (1983), and Fryer and Ullah (1987) have acknowledged that a more realistic understanding of unemployed people requires analysis of their local social and material situation and that they be treated rather less as powerless pawns and rather more as active agents.

Whatever the theoretical framework adopted, however, it is crucial to recognize that long-term unemployment is characterized by a life of grinding poverty and social and psychological distress, and that the constraints within which unemployed people organize their lives are experienced in a more direct fashion, are felt to be more burdensome and less flexible, and impose themselves in a greater array of social situations than do those confronted by people in work. On the other hand, it is just as important to observe that the unemployed are not a homogenous group equally enmeshed by the same set of restricting conditions; they are divided by diverse employment backgrounds, skill levels, ethnic origin, age, sex, etc. and find themselves living in local areas evincing quite different social and economic structures of opportunity and constraint. It is to be expected, then, that within limits the impact of unemployment will differ accordingly.

For many of the long-term unemployed, especially married men with families, the loss of work appears to entail little more than the narrowing of their previous life-styles. Many aspects of their existence are brutally circumscribed, and the time which was spent in work is replaced by individualistic activities in the home. Many admit to feelings of impotence, shame and isolation. In Belfast, as in other depressed industrial regions, the avenues of searching for work are soon exhausted and social life quickly becomes curtailed and may disintegrate. Moreover, this unrelenting material deprivation is mercilessly compounded by the ever-present need to manage the impressions other people (both in work and out) have of them. Their strenuous and sometimes pathetic efforts to get others to see them as genuine and deserving cases is a task which has to be carried out on a routine basis. But not only is this psychologically exhausting, it also brings no lasting guarantee of success.

Nevertheless, some unemployed people ('good copers') immerse themselves into their home life, their gardens, and their families in a constructive fashion, and some wives prefer their husbands to be at home. Others turn to community, charity, and advice work, and occasionally find themselves busier and more satisfied than they ever were in employment. Others (though in the present study only one such case turned up) experience an almost complete role reversal as they remain at home to look after house and children while wives carry on full-time jobs. Finally, some go in for a life of crime, and some get a job 'on the side', in which case they earn money and simultaneously claim benefits.

A curious feature of much of the sociological literature specializing in unemployment is the lack of any consistent and coherent framework with which the phenomenon of mass long-term unemployment can be systematically analysed. As already argued, the options open to the unemployed are fewer than for the those in work, but they do still have choices to make and the range of these, whether in respect to informal work, to the dispositions adopted towards staff who administer welfare benefits, or to other unemployed and employed people in the areas where they live, varies from group to group and area to area.

Whilst I am concerned in this work to show that unemployment is a dynamic process rather than a stultifying, limbo-like state, I also want to demonstrate the evident variation in the experience of unemployment. I have therefore adopted a perspective which requires both the description of the major features of the structures of opportunity and constraint in the area under study, and also the embedding of individual and collective behaviour within wider processes of cultural reproduction, paying particular attention to the importance of the unintended, but systematic, consequences of social action.

In relation to this perspective it is important to be clear what the term 'structure' signifies. Giddens remarks that structure should not be identified only with constraint, since 'structure is both enabling and constraining' (1979:69). Arguing that the idea of social structure as an independent and objective determinant of behaviour is an impediment to analysis, Giddens is concerned to show how social reality is constituted and reproduced by the skilled performance of routine practical activity, the analysis of which involves the interplay of meanings, norms, and power, and actors' own accounts of their experiences (see Bourdieu, 1977: 72–95; Holy and Stuchlik, 1981).

To overcome the dichotomy between 'objective' and 'subjective', Giddens introduces the processual notion of 'structuration' or 'series of reproduced practices'. The central problem of sociological theory is thus to explain 'how it comes about that structures are constituted through action, and reciprocally how action is constituted structurally' (Giddens, 1976: 160–1). In developing a processual theory of structure, Giddens draws a distinction between institutional analysis, that is, the analysis of practices deeply entrenched and perduring, and which are widespread amongst a society's members, and strategic conduct, which is the study of how actors draw upon cultural and structural resources (knowledge, rules, norms, classificatory schemes, material resources) in the everyday conduct of their lives (1979: 80). As Jenkins neatly puts it: 'social structure can only be said to exist in the actions of those people who reproduce and produce it, through the manipulation of its constituent elements, rules and resources, in their everyday transactions'. Accordingly 'institutions do not exist, ontologically speaking, in any sense separately from strategic conduct' (1983: 11). On this reading, structures of opportunity and constraint both shape and are shaped by social action.

Giddens stresses that power relations are at the heart of such a conception of how societies work: 'what passes for social reality stands in immediate relation to the distribution of power' (1976: 113). Accordingly, social action is logically tied to power, and power is therefore a feature of even the most mundane and casual interaction (Giddens, 1979: 88). In this sense power should not be construed as a type of act, but as intrinsic to any act. Moreover power is not a resource, rather 'resources are the media through which power is exercised, and structures of domination reproduced' (1979: 91). Thus command over resources and the ability to bring them into play is of extreme importance. In his account of Belfast youth life-styles Jenkins uses such a framework to good effect. He describes how divisions within the young working class 'can only be understood if they are seen as partially produced and reproduced by the labelling decisions of strategically placed individuals, . . . in the institutions of education, social control, and the labour market' (1983: 11–12). The relevance of this theoretical outlook to the present case will become obvious. The divisions to be described, between employed and unemployed, Protestant and Catholic, functionary and claimant, are characterized by asymmetric power relations. These are relations not only of a moral order; they are also based on a differential ability, based on unequal access to resources (jobs, money, positions and systems of authority, valuable knowledge, etc.) which allow, to one degree or another, the superordinate group to impose its definitions of reality, its cultural distinctions, its agenda of priorities on the subordinate group.

It is important to note, however, that the asymmetry of the command over resources rarely eventuates in one group exercising a complete monopoly. Thus 'even the most autonomous agent is in some degree dependent, and the most dependent actor . . . retains some autonomy' (Giddens, 1979: 93), indicating that even penurious recipients of welfare benefits maintain some, albeit little, control over their lives. However it is important to note that though the poor maintain some choice, the choices they make frequently have the effect of consolidating their lowly position. In this sense the poor can be seen to be implicated in their own subordination.

Central to each of the issues discussed in this book is the analysis of how social categories and schemes of classification are used in daily life and the social processes by which these are perpetuated. Actors' knowledge, ideas, and beliefs constitute frames of reference which function both as guides to behaviour and as the conceptual apparatus through which they interpret and explain the world around them. Of course, account must be taken of broader social forces, but equally collective behaviour can have long-term, unforeseen outcomes which either maintain or change these, and examples of both kinds will be found in the text.

Outline of the book

The study deals with three particular issues. The first, largely left out of account in much other research into unemployment, is the variable degree to which unemployed people take advantage of undeclared, informal economic activity. To what extent are there differences between unemployed Catholics and Protestants in their level of involvement in the black economy in Belfast? What are the factors implicated in the variation; what are the perceived costs and benefits of working on the side; how are such practices culturally represented; what effect does such activity have in changing or perpetuating prevailing conditions and extant divisions? These topics are taken up in detail in chapters 3 and 4, where I address some contemporary debates concerning the role of informal economic activity in industrial society and its relation to the state of the local economy.

The second main area of investigation is the analysis of the effects on the unemployed of the Supplementary Benefit scheme (changed to Income Support (IS) in 1988), the principal welfare support system for married unemployed men.[4] Supplementary benefit (SB) plays a very important part in the lives of unemployed people, and it too constitutes an arena in which claimants are faced with certain options. It is necessary to inquire how this benefit is practically and routinely administered and disbursed, what effects this has on claimants, and whether, and why, different claimants react in different ways to these practices. Thus while the administration of benefit is supposed to be governed by strict regulations designed to ensure equal treatment for all claimants, in practice such administration is influenced both by severe resource constraints and by the value judgements and moral assessments of claimants made by benefit officers. Such evaluations are founded on distinctions between the deserving and undeserving poor, between those who broadly conform to officers' expectations of appropriate life-style and demeanour and those who do not, between those who are perceived to create undue difficulties and those who make the officers' job easy.

In documenting these processes in chapter 5, I show how the schemes of classification employed by staff are reproduced in the very moments of interaction between the former and claimants. I also argue that these processes have the effect of reducing, below the level of legal entitlement, the amounts of benefit many claimants are able to obtain. Here again the emphasis in the discussion is on the cultural mediation of what are supposed to be simple technocratic procedures. In my view, this analysis constitutes a powerful argument against those who seek to formulate social security policy on the basis of the idea that means-tested benefits can be easily and unambiguously targeted so that resources only get to those who 'really' need them.

Chapters 6 and 7 take up the question of why it is that in response to staff practice some claimants react assertively and others reluctantly. Whilst many factors are involved in this issue the principal one is that reluctant claimants are themselves enmeshed by notions of the deserving and the undeserving. Reluctant claimants conceive of the claimant population as divided into the genuine and the ineligible. By engaging in practices of impression management, reluctant claimants seek to gain for themselves entry into the deserving category. Such practices ensure that claimants conform to the role expectations which benefit officers and others seek to impose on them. Claimants should be grateful, subservient, and uncomplicated, and be careful only to claim items deemed essential to welfare. Assertive claimants, on the other hand, emerge out of those unemployed who do not, in this context at least, classify others into deserving and undeserving groups. As such they are less inclined to accept the role of the undemanding supplicant, characteristic of the reluctant claimant, and instead are more disposed to submit claims and to pursue these with dogged persistence. The data, moreover, suggest that reluctant claimants come predominantly from Protestant Eastlough, whilst assertive claimants are more to be found in Catholic Mallon Park (the two research locales) which fact itself is associated with other aspects of unemployment in these areas.

The third issue to be discussed concerns the relationship between those with and those without jobs. Even in the worst-affected regions of the country unemployed people are not residentially segregated from those still in work. This is, of course, an obvious point, but its implications have not always been fully appreciated. Much research into unemployment uses survey methodology, but because this individualizes and fragments social life important types of social relationship often go undiscovered. In my view, a more rounded understanding of what it means to be unemployed can only be obtained by situating individuals in their local contexts. Effectively this means documenting the ideas the unemployed and employed have of each other (including the way the unemployed view other unemployed), and the factors which influence typical forms of interaction between these groups; this is the subject matter of chapter 8.

To anticipate that discussion, let me briefly say here that in the course of analysing the divisions which form the study's focus of research I have found the two related concepts of cultural distancing and symbolic boundary (Anthony Cohen, 1986) to be of considerable value, and particularly in relation to understanding the situation of the unemployed in their local areas.

By cultural distancing I mean the process whereby people seek to draw pertinent distinctions between themselves and others. Individuals (and groups) attempt to persuade others that they should be categorized in the higher of two or more categories seen to be located within a moral hierarchy. Let me explain this. In Eastlough there is a majority consensus (of employed and unemployed) that the jobless consist of both deserving and undeserving individuals. However, unemployed people are never sure to which category others assign them. Therefore they contrive to act and speak so as to convey to others various messages about their personal situation, mode of life, and attitudes to work, benefits, and to other unemployed people.

Such messages bear on long-established and largely taken-for-granted ideas which underpin 'traditional' ideologies of employment, work, individual responsibility, economic independence, and so forth.

That is to say, many of the activities of the unemployed are shaped by a concern to demonstrate that they too espouse the same values as do those in work. This is problematical, since the only evidence which is entirely acceptable to the employed is a return to work. All other strategies the unemployed use to influence those in work are open to doubt and counter-argument. For example, many unemployed make strenuous efforts to persuade others that they are willing to work. However, even if it is acknowledged (and often it is not) that few jobs are available, this is not necessarily taken as an acceptable excuse for not working, since '*not* being willing to work may be hidden behind an argument that work is not available' (Wadel, 1973: 109).

Now work (employment) is a supremely important activity and the distinction between the deserving and the undeserving depends on the ideological verity that work is the source of all rewards. People exchange their labour power for a wage which is subsequently used to buy the goods and services deemed essential in modern society. Underlying this process is the very definite sense of reciprocity which provides the legitimacy for the acquisition of material goods. The long-term unemployed who must claim benefits find it very difficult to conceptualize the receipt of such assistance as a reciprocal, exchange relation. As Wadel explains:

It is through his work in the form of a job . . . that a man earns his living and [thereby] claims reciprocity in relation to society and independence in relation to his peers. Work gives a man . . . a status in relation to the family, the community, the economy and the polity. All these may be regarded as positive values and meanings of work.

However, working for a living also involves costs . . . [W]ork implies one has to stay away from one's family . . .; [many] types of work [can impair one's] health; . . . working is not something one generally does for its own sake but rather something one *has* to do. Work, then, implies a series of negative costs, and it demands moral strength to take these costs.

Because of its positive values . . . the work role tends towards a kind of moral imperative. Work becomes something one *should* do and something that is morally praiseworthy *because* of the costs involved. (1973: 108–9; his italics)

Since work is the foundation for all these statuses, the loss of work for a considerable period entails that their ratification and endorsement by others can no longer be taken for granted. Consequently much of what unemployed people do can be seen as an attempt to shore up an edifice which constantly threatens to crumble under the impact of both real and imagined accusations of scrounging and malingering. The unemployed thus try to persuade others that whilst they are themselves still strongly committed to the 'work ethic' and are continually looking for jobs, other unemployed, from whom they want to distance themselves, are condemned as being unwilling to work and as parasites on state largess.

Cultural distancing, therefore, always involves a dual aspect: individuals attempt to create distance and difference between themselves and others deemed low in the moral hierarchy with whom they fear being confused, at the same time as they seek to nullify a presumed moral gap between themselves and a different set of others considered morally superior and with whom they want to be associated.

Here we shall see that mundane, everyday activities (work, looking for work, spending money, forms of dress, going to the pub, etc.) all begin to assume meanings beyond their usual ones. This is because the social context of such activities, the way they are performed, their frequency, their manner of justification, change when people become unemployed. A community divided by joblessness finds itself imputing further, symbolic, meanings to such practices, because these become critical markers and criteria of differentiation and comparison, inclusion and exclusion. Symbolic boundaries, then, are the set of criteria which are invoked to create and sustain distinctions considered characteristic of supposedly separate and discrete categories. Clearly, in issues such as these processes of management impression, labelling and stereotyping assume paramount significance, and much revolves around the manipulation and negotiation of the meanings of ordinary activities.

Chapter 2

The political economy of Northern Ireland and the anthropology of sectarianism

The first chapter briefly outlined some of the major issues related to the analysis of long-term male unemployment, and the way in which this study is designed to address them. Before moving to the detailed presentation of the material in subsequent chapters, several further preliminary topics remain to be discussed. These deal with unemployment and the political economy of Northern Ireland; anthropology and its treatment of the sectarian divide; and the immediate context of the research.

Unemployment and the political economy of Northern Ireland

In 1600, Belfast consisted of a castle, a few scattered houses and a small market. By the end of the seventeenth century, however, it had become the fourth-largest port in the kingdom (Beckett, 1979: 26).

In what was a purely political move, Belfast became a corporate town in 1613 by charter of James I. The king intended to call a Parliament in Dublin and in order to secure a Protestant majority, he had to create forty new boroughs each returning two members, and Belfast was one of these (Bardon, 1982: 13).

Belfast's subsequent rapid progress stemmed from the fact that it provided one of the main channels through which Scottish (and English) planters entered Ireland (Buchanan, 1982). Although counties Antrim and Down, the boundary between which runs through Belfast, were not included in the plantation schemes of the seventeenth century, nonetheless this area exhibits the highest concentrations of Scottish surnames (Robinson, 1982: 32). With a growing and prosperous Protestant population in the north-east of Ireland Belfast quickly emerged as a centre of trade and commerce. Because of periodic military campaigns the town also housed a garrison; and its port became important as a route for shipping in supplies (Beckett, 1979: 31).

Whilst, then, the origin of Belfast lay in political manoeuvre, its advancement as a significant centre of population was generated by its strategic location and its economic performance. From its inception, Belfast, situated on the coast, became the pivot around which the political and economic fortunes of the north of Ireland raged.

In 1690, after being enthusiastically greeted by the exclusively Protestant population of Belfast, William of Orange marched south to win his famous victory over the Jacobite French and Irish armies at the battle of the Boyne. Each year since, this event has been boisterously commemorated throughout the Protestant districts of Northern Ireland with bonfires and the mass marching of Orange bands. According to Beckett, this battle 'was the critical moment in a long struggle between the Roman Catholic and Protestant interests . . . The "protestant nation" which was to dominate Ireland in the eighteenth century here established its supremacy' (Beckett, 1979: 89), and Belfast was, and still is, very much the heart of this 'protestant nation'.

During the early part of the eighteenth century there were less than 500 Catholics in Belfast, but as the Jacobite threat waned more began to enter the town. However, Kennedy (1967: 53) remarks that Catholics were at the bottom of the economic ladder and inhabited the town's worst slums.

By the close of the eighteenth century the linen and cotton industries were firmly established, and there was also activity in pottery, glass, and rope manufacture. The port not only maintained Belfast's role as the leading commercial centre of the north, but it also generated the nascent industry of ship-building. On the social and political scene, however, things fared less well. Fired by the ideals of the French Revolution, Wolfe Tone and the United Irish movement, 'protestant in its origins, rational in its leadership and radically democratic in its aims' (Beckett, 1979: 117), aspired to expand the franchise and to secure Catholic emancipation. After some initial success in popularizing their ideas, the town's authorities clamped down on the leaders and many were lucky to escape with their lives. The movement ended in bitter disappointment when large-scale sectarian violence flared up in many areas west and south of the river Bann.

In the early 1800s there was a considerable influx of people into Belfast and its population rose from 19,000 in 1801 to 70,000 in 1841 (Bardon, 1982: 66). Such population growth intensified the industrial expansion of Belfast and in the following twenty years the linen industry came into its own (as cotton began to decline in importance): by 1861 there were 593,000 spindles and 4,900 power looms, and Belfast was just about the largest producer in the UK. This was also the period in which ship-building emerged as a major industry and large employer (Glasscock, 1967). Much of the population increase in this period was a result of Catholics escaping the famines and the consequent ruinous poverty engulfing the countryside, by trying to take advantage of new opportunities in the town. By the middle of the century Catholics comprised almost a third of the town's population, and with this dramatic change in the balance of Catholics and Protestants sectarian conflict began to reappear: outbreaks of violence of shorter or longer duration have occurred periodically ever since, culminating in the terrible events of the post-1969 'Troubles'.

In the second half of the nineteenth century Belfast's population increased five-fold, to 349,000. During this period ship-building, textile-machinery manufacture and other engineering work gave skilled employment to men, while the linen industry provided unskilled, low-paid work for women. More significantly, the new engineering factories were heavily dominated by Protestant labour. As Hepburn (1983) has shown, in 1901 Protestants were over-represented in the higher skilled engineering jobs and under-represented in the low-status, labouring, and service jobs. Similarly, according to O'Dowd (1980: 30) the growth of the linen industry provided work for both Catholics and Protestants, many of whom entered the city between 1860 and 1880, whilst between 1880 and 1911 ship-building and engineering supplied large-scale employment for skilled Protestant labour. Paddy Devlin is even more forthright in his analysis of this period. He argues that Protestants owned and controlled most of the factories and mills; that there was segregation in factories along Catholic/Protestant lines, with the former getting the worst jobs; that the Orange Order put pressure on shipyard foremen not to employ Catholics; that Protestant skilled workers acted in like manner; that recruitment to skilled trades was by introduction and recommendation by Orange members; that Catholics could only obtain unskilled work; and that after 1920 the 'policy of the new Government was to provide jobs for its own Protestant people' (Devlin, 1981: 18–51).

In large part the pattern of job/skill distribution existing at the beginning of the twentieth century has been sustained to the present day. However, during this latter period traditional industries declined gradually, and since 1936 unemployment rates in Northern Ireland have been consistently higher than any other region in the UK (Doherty, 1982: 226; see also table 1 for regional disparities in unemployment in recent years). Moreover, as emigration rates testify, Catholics suffered more unemployment than Protestants: Barrit and Carter (1962: 120–4)

Table 1. *Average annual rates of unemployment for United Kingdom and Northern Ireland (percentages)*

	1977	1985
UK	5.8	13.5
NI	10.5	21.0

Source: Regional Trends, 1986.

estimate that some 50 per cent of emigrants between 1937 and 1961 were Catholics, despite the fact that they constituted only one-third of the total population.

After the Second World War it became clear that Belfast's industrial base was in irreversible decline as mass redundancies in both ship-building and linen production occurred. O'Dowd argues that, in response to this deteriorating situation, the Northern Ireland state, in order to maintain its Protestant support base intact, was directly implicated in policies of regional development that were destined to attract new growth industries to the largely Protestant areas on the outskirts of Belfast, while permitting the traditional industries of inner Belfast to decay, particularly in west Belfast: 'major industrial growth was to be concentrated in the environs of Belfast, where Catholics accounted for a highly dispersed 20 per cent of the population, thus avoiding Catholic west Belfast and the west of the province' (1980: 42). And so it happened: new textile and engineering plant opened in Larne, Carrickfergus, Lisburn, and many other areas in the north-east of Northern Ireland. The re-structuring of capital also provided large investments in the major engineering industries of east Belfast (Harland and Wolff, Short Brothers, Sirocco; and predominantly Protestant-manned Mackies in west Belfast) but this could not prevent the shedding of labour in all of these establishments as production techniques changed and the recession began to bite. However, the new firms (ICI, Courtaulds, British Enkalon, Michelin, Grundig, Hughes Tool Co., Standard Telephone and Cable, etc.) along with accelerating growth in the service sector, provided just about enough new jobs to maintain employment levels (O'Dowd, Rolston, and Tomlinson, 1980). The only major innovations in Catholic west Belfast were Strathern Audio and, later, the Delorean Motor Car Corporation (actually sited on Protestant 'territory' but employing considerable numbers of Catholics). Additionally, not only did the Troubles exacerbate residential segregation, as Protestants moved out of the mainly Catholic areas of west Belfast and Catholics from other areas crowded into this region of the city; they also, according to one estimate, resulted in the loss of 20,000 jobs (B. Moore, Rhodes, and Tarling, 1978). Finally, in the textile and clothing sectors capital investment tended again to be in the environs of Belfast, in synthetic fibre industries, and inner city factories either contracted or closed. The overall result was a shift in favour of Protestant over Catholic labour (O'Dowd, 1980: 50–3).

Reports published under the aegis of the Fair Employment Agency for Northern Ireland support this analysis. The first report (Fair, Employment Agency for Northern Ireland 1978), analysing the 1971 census data, shows that Catholics are under-represented in engineering, insurance, banking, finance and business, and gas, electricity and water; and over-represented in textiles, construction, and miscellaneous services. In general the report endorses Aunger's conclusion that: 'Protestants are disproportionally represented in the non-manual and skilled occupations, while Catholics are disproportionally represented only in the semi-skilled, unskilled and unemployed classes . . . the median Protestant is a skilled manual worker, the median Catholic is a semi-skilled manual worker' (1975: 4).

The second report, on attitudes to work (Miller, 1978), demonstrates that the inequalities in the occupational profiles of the two religions cannot be explained by differences in motivation and attitudes to work, since any such differences are negligible; that is, the 'work ethic' constrains Catholics as much as it does Protestants. The third report, on educational qualifications (Osborne and Murray, 1978), indicates that while there are differences in qualifications gained at school, these are not substantial enough to explain the occupational differentials. The fifth report, on the occupational mobility of school leavers and the structure of opportunity in Belfast (Cormack, Osborne, and Thompson, 1980), is perhaps the most interesting. The authors conclude that the geographical distribution of male jobs leaves the west and north of the city at a disadvantage.

Protestants from the west and north suffer less than Catholics from these areas in that they have greater ease of access to those areas [Protestant east Belfast] of greater opportunities . . . The transition from school to work of the boys in this study would seem to be greatly affected by the spatio-structural and institutional elements of the labour market. Protestant boys in East Belfast readily find work . . . Catholics in the East, despite their geographical contiguity to the greater concentration of job opportunities in the city, failed to find work with anything like the ease of their Protestant peers. Boys in Protestant West Belfast, while living in an area of low opportunity, still find work more readily than their Catholic counterparts in the West of the city. The pattern of disadvantage occurred despite the greater propensity of Catholics to work in mixed areas. (1980: 63–4)

Results from a more recent Policy Studies Institute report provide further evidence for these arguments. According to the report, there are two main factors aggravating employment inequality. The first is the failure of most employers to examine current employment policies and practices from a fair employment perspective, and the second is the 'continued reliance on informal methods of recruiting and appointing most notably, but not exclusively, in the private sector' (Chambers, 1987: 250). Since residential segregation of the working-class population by religion is very pronounced in Belfast, and because a disproportionate number of jobs are located in Protestant areas, informal methods of recruitment will clearly maintain and reproduce imbalances in occupational opportunities.

The recession of 1979 to 1984 (and in reality still continuing) obliterated much of the new capital investment. The roll of closures is a depressing one: British Enkalon, Delorean, Strathern Audio, Grundig, Michelin, Courtaulds, ICI, Goodyear, as well as a mass of smaller firms including virtually all the mills and bakeries of Catholic west Belfast. Furthermore all the major Belfast manufacturing industries pushed through large redundancy schemes during this period.

Official statistics endorse this bleak picture. Between 1955 and 1975, unemployment in Northern Ireland fluctuated between 30,000 and 37,000 (6.5 per cent and 7.8 per cent). From 1978 to 1982, however, the total nearly doubled, rising from 57,000 to 102,100 (see table 2), and by 1985 it had reached 121,400 (20.9 per cent). While unemployment in the Belfast travel-to-work areas was 9,913 (3.4 per cent) in 1974, by June 1985 it had climbed to 60,545 (17.8 per cent). These figures of course mask large regional differences. Unemployment in Northern Ireland has always been higher than the UK average and internally the east of Northern Ireland has always enjoyed lower rates of joblessness than the west and south of the province. Once again these aggregate figures disguise large differentials, this time as between Catholic and Protestant unemployment rates (Compton, 1981; Doherty, 1981, 1982; Miller and Osborne, 1983). Thus 'Catholic unemployment rates exceeded Protestant rates in *each* of the 26 District Council areas in [Northern Ireland]; in Belfast [in 1971], for example, 19% of Catholic males were unemployed compared to 8.5% of Protestants' (O'Dowd, 1980: 57). Moreover

Table 2. *Average annual
totals of unemployment
(excluding school leavers)
for United Kingdom and
Northern Ireland
(thousands)*

	UK	NI
1977	1313.0	—
1978	1299.1	57.0
1979	1227.3	57.0
1980	1560.8	68.1
1981	2419.8	91.4
1982	2793.4	102.1

Source: Employment Gazette,
March 1983.

Table 3. *Belfast totals of unemployment by
parliamentary constituency*

	Electorate: June 1983	Unemployment: March 1985
Belfast North	61,128	8,543
Belfast South	53,694	5,494
Belfast East	55,581	4,421
Belfast West	59,750	12,098

Source: DOD's Parliamentary Companion, 1984; and
Employment Gazette, March 1985.

O'Dowd reports that by 1978 unemployment had risen to 31 per cent in
Catholic-only wards of the city (1980: 58; see also table 3, which gives
unemployment figures for the four Belfast Parliamentary constituen-
cies). In short, although Belfast is the hub of the Northern Ireland
economy, Catholic areas of the city continue to suffer unemployment
rates much higher than the Province's average.

Using data from a household survey covering all of Northern Ireland,
D.J. Smith has argued that there are reasons other than religion associated with differential rates of unemployment for Catholics and Protestants. The most important of these are socio-economic group and area of

Table 4. *Vacancies at Northern Ireland job centres and totals of unemployment (thousands)*

	Vacancies	All unemployment
1980	1.0	74.5
1981	0.7	98.0
1982	1.0	108.3
1983	1.2	117.1
1984	1.5	121.4
1985	1.6	121.8

Source; Employment Gazette, January 1987.

residence (1987a: 38). However, we have already seen that both of these factors, but especially the latter, are closely linked to religious denomination. Factors such as age, number of dependent children, and academic qualifications were found to be of only limited use in explaining the disparities in rates of unemployment (D.J. Smith, 1987a: 38). Smith therefore concludes that 'religion is a major determinant of the rate of unemployment', and that 'a large part of the difference cannot be explained except on the assumption that there is inequality of opportunity' (1987a: 38, 59).

Between 1978 and 1983 Northern Ireland gained 17,000 jobs in the service sector but lost 13,000 in construction and 40,000 in manufacturing (Northern Ireland Economic Council, 1984). Redundancies by contraction and closure accounted for most of this loss. In the first quarter of 1982 almost 10,000 such redundancies occurred, although the average for 1980–2 was about 5,000 per quarter (Northern Ireland Economic Council, 1983). Because of the location of many of these jobs, much of the decline in employment has taken place in the greater Belfast region, and so Protestant rates of unemployment have also risen dramatically, and are now beginning to approach rates of 30 per cent in some areas of east Belfast.

Figures on job vacancies and duration of spells of unemployment provide a further dimension to the misery of unemployment. Notified unfilled vacancies at job centres (accounting for one-fifth to one-third of all vacancies) between 1974 and 1979 slumped from 3,500 to 1,100 at the same time as unemployment rose from 30,900 to 60,800 (Trewsdale, 1980: 32); from 1977 to 1985 the situation continued to deteriorate, as the figures in table 4 demonstrate. Equally appalling has been the rise in

Table 5. *Duration of spells of unemployment for United Kingdom and Northern Ireland (percentages)*

	Less than 2 weeks	2 weeks to 8 weeks	8 weeks to 13 weeks	13 weeks to 26 weeks	6 months to 1 year	1 year to 2 years	More than 2 years
UK	5.7	13.2	6.9	12.9	15.3	16.8	29.3
NI	3.6	10.5	4.9	11.5	14.2	16.4	38.8

Source: Regional Trends, 1986.

the numbers of long-term unemployed (defined as more than one year out of work). In March 1973, 28.3 per cent of the jobless were out of work for more than one year. By January 1983 this had risen to 47.6 per cent (Ditch, 1984: 9). Table 5, giving comparison figures for Northern Ireland and the UK as at October 1985, demonstrates that more than half of all the unemployed in the province have been out of work for more than one year. Long-term unemployment is no longer the exception; it has become the rule.

Anthropology and the sectarian divide

Since I am primarily concerned about unemployment what I have to say now about the sectarian divide should be considered as no more than a brief overview.

Sectarianism in Northern Ireland is so called because the two sides to the conflict are identified by religious labels. However, whilst the conflict clearly has a religious dimension, to conceive of it as one which is centrally concerned with religion or religious doctrine is facile and seriously misleading. To expose this misconception, it is enough simply to record that each side is also designated in various other ways. That Catholics are 'Irish', 'nationalists', 'republicans', 'fenians', 'taigs'; while Protestants are 'British', 'Ulstermen', 'unionists', 'loyalists', 'Orangemen' (Jenkins, 1986: 5) demonstrates that the division has both nationalistic and political dimensions. Moreover, between 1921 when the Northern Ireland state was established and 1972 when Direct Rule from Westminster was imposed, the state was politically controlled largely by Protestant elites, and since this has had persistent differential effects, as between Protestants and Catholics, on the distribution and allocation of jobs, houses, and other resources, the conflict is also economic and social in nature. To the extent that it affects where one lives, what kind of school one attends, what kind of job one is likely to get, whom one marries, whom one's kin and friends are, and so forth, the division is virtually all embracing.

The conflict, in fact, was never purely religious. English designs on the territory of Ireland began three centuries before the Henrician reforms set in train the English Protestant Reformation, and the incorporation of Ireland into a British state was, if not inevitable, at least always highly likely.

Ever since the English became embroiled in Irish affairs in the twelfth century, Ireland has never ceased to be a thorn in England's side. However, until the reign of James 1 English colonial ambitions in Ireland were continually thwarted by the strength of the Gaelic clan chiefs, particularly in Ulster. But even during this period there is clear evidence of cultural differences, racial abuse, and extensive discrimination, and of the concern that Englishmen in Ireland had a tendency to 'degenerate' by the adoption of Irish customs, speech, and clothes (Johnson, 1980: 21–5).

It was, in fact, the failure of the half-hearted policies of Elizabeth I towards the subjugation of Ireland that finally eventuated in the major plantations of Ulster shortly after her reign ended in the early seventeenth century. Less than a century later only '14 per cent of the land in Ireland remained in the hands of Catholic Irish, and in Ulster the figure was 5 per cent' (Darby, 1983a: 14).

After the battle of the Boyne, English domination in Ireland became relatively secure, and the exclusively Protestant legislature in Dublin passed a series of discriminatory acts against Catholics (and Presbyterians too to a lesser extent). Over the next century Catholics were excluded from the armed forces, the judiciary, the legal profession, and from Parliament; they were forbidden to buy land from Protestants or to carry arms; Catholic bishops and clergy were banished and the Catholic religion went underground (Darby, 1983a: 15). Such discrimination against Catholics was reminiscent of English discrimination against the Irish in the fourteenth century (Johnson, 1980: 24).

In broad terms what this boils down to was the imposition of a new social order in the north of Ireland. Certainly the period from 1600 saw the introduction into Ulster of a foreign community which spoke a different language, practised a different religion, represented an alien culture, and which suppressed the native Gael politically and economically.

The division between English and Irish, and later Protestant and Catholic (though there is no simple overlap), therefore was never only religious in essence. More accurately, it began as a conflict between two groups which shared very little in common, and as such it was, and still remains, an ethnic conflict.

There are many definitions of ethnic group and ethnicity. Post-war American sociology defined ethnic groups as cultural groups, that is, in terms of 'objective' cultural content (Warner and Srole, 1945). This view of ethnicity embodied the idea that under conditions of contact ethnic groups would assimilate. Most troublesome for this model are the persisting facts of ethnicity and the 'ethnic revival' (A.D. Smith, 1981).

Impressed by the continuing presence of ethnicity in New York City, with its hierarchical ethnic division of labour, Glazer and Moynihan (1963) defined ethnicity as an essentially political phenomenon involving a power struggle among ethnic groups for collective control over material resources. Several major anthropological studies have demonstrated the importance of treating ethnic groups as informal interest groups (Abner Cohen, 1969, Hannerz, 1974; Lloyd, 1974). The difficulties associated with this perspective have been cogently summarized by Epstein (1978: 93–6). He argues, first, that ethnicity can be relevant in circumstances where collective interests are not an issue; second, that looked at over a long period a group's interest may change but the group itself persists; and, finally, that in many situations lines of ethnic cleavage take precedence over collective class interests. In short, for Epstein, to define ethnicity in political (or cultural) terms is to mistake an aspect of the phenomenon for the phenomenon itself. As he sees it, what is central to ethnicity is the notion of ethnic identity, identity being created by the interaction of forces operating both from within the group and from outside it. Ethnic identity assumes tremendous importance because it so often performs an integrating role:

It represents the process by which the person seeks to integrate his various statuses and roles, as well as his diverse experiences, into a coherent image of self. The contemporary sociological significance of ethnic identity is that so often it becomes what has been called a terminal identity, one that embraces and integrates a whole series of statuses, roles and lesser identities. (1978: 101)

This has much in common with Barth's analysis (1969) of ethnic groups as categories of ascription and identification undertaken by the actors themselves. According to Barth, it follows from this that, first, the cultural content of ethnic groups cannot be a defining feature since 'ethnic groups provide an organisational vessel that may be given varying amounts and forms of content in different socio-cultural systems' (1969: 14); and second, 'the critical focus of investigation from this point of view becomes the ethnic *boundary* that defines the group, not the cultural stuff that it encloses' (1969: 15, his italics).

What, then, is common to most contemporary definitions is that ethnicity can only be characterized in relational and contrastive terms. That is to say, ethnicity is a principle of recruitment to a group the salient characteristics of which, as seen by the members themselves, are considered to be different to those of another group with whom some interaction takes place. The parties to an ethnic conflict may define themselves and hence their differences to one another in many ways, but the most significant of these, according to A.D. Smith (1986: 22–31) are usually: a collective name, a common myth of origin, a shared history, a distinctive shared culture (including religion and language), association with a specific territory, and a sense of solidarity and belonging (i.e. an ethnic identity). Whether or not economic and political interests become a component of ethnicity will vary according to circumstances.

The situation in Northern Ireland clearly conforms to this character-ization of ethnicity and it is one in which collective material interests have always played a major role. In fact it could be argued that, since the partition of Ireland into the states of Northern Ireland and Eire, econ-omic and political interests have come to constitute the dominant dimensions of the conflict, because Protestant economic advantage depends on and reinforces Protestant political control. This is why a central issue in the conflict is the contested legitimacy of the Northern Ireland state, or in colloquial terms, the border question.

An implication of this argument is that cultural differences are no longer as important as they once were, especially since Catholic and Protestant now share a common, educational, industrial, and bureau-cratic mass culture, which according to Gellner (1983) are some of the prerequisites of the modern nation-state. However, despite the fact that from an outsider's viewpoint Catholic and Protestant today appear to share some common cultural ground, the two sides nevertheless see themselves as inheritors of distinctive historical, religious, and linguis-tic traditions (although few Catholics speak Gaelic, nevertheless Gaelic culture – language, literature, history, sport, etc. – is held up as an ideal). Continuing economic and political differences, together with the celebration each year of key historical events, during which crucial symbols, identities, and ideologies are paraded, serve not only to emphasize cultural difference over cultural similarity but also to main-tain the integrity of both traditions and therefore the gap between them. The point seems to be that the perpetuation of cultural differences depends on long-term disparities, generated by the conflict itself, in the allocation of scarce material resources, but that equally perceived cultural differences, lack of cross-religion marriages, and residential segregation (and sectarian violence, of course) serve to highlight the separation of the two communities and thus to sustain economic and political differences. In short, once the two communities have been established they are kept in being by the complex interaction of cultural/ethnic, political, and economic factors. These tend to be mutually reinforcing because the cultural differences which act as boundary markers to label and identify the two groups are also used to recruit people to kinship groups, economic roles, and political positions, and this in turn consolidates the separation of the communities.

Anthropological research on the Northern Ireland sectarian divide has been summarized by Donnan and McFarlane in a recent series of articles (1986a, 1986b, 1983). In their discussions of the work of Harris, Leyton, and others, they highlight certain issues which require further investigation and broader theorizing, largely within the terms of reference sketched out above. They argue that anthropologists have usually concentrated their efforts in two related areas: 'on what people *do* with the cultural division in their everyday lives and . . . on the various factors which serve not only to maintain the cultural and social division but also to counteract its negative charge' (1986a: 24; italics in original). They also point to the continuing rural bias of much anthropological research, and note that one of its main findings is the seemingly high degree of integration found in many small communities. Such integration is often explained by researchers as stemming from a diverse set of circumstances: the existence of some collective interests which bind people from both sides of the divide; a sense of regional identity and common humanity; shared views on norms of behaviour; common membership in some voluntary organizations; occasional 'horizontal' class solidarity as against 'vertical' ethnic separation; and so forth (Harris, 1972; Larsen, 1982; Donnan and McFarlane, 1986a). Conversely, these researchers also point to the manner in which mundane activities reaffirm and sustain the division: the dearth of intermarriage between the two sides and the problematic nature of mixed marriages (McFarlane, 1979), and co-operation between kin, who of course come from only one side of the divide (Harris, 1972; Leyton, 1975; Buckley, 1982). Another aspect of this is the important notion of 'telling' which, according to Burton, is 'the syndrome of signs by which Catholics and Protestants arrive at religious ascriptions in their everyday interaction . . . Telling illustrates how . . . history is used in the contemporary society to construct a form of ideological social relations that amounts to an ethnic difference between Catholic and Protestant' (Burton, 1978: 4).

The twin themes of integration and division have in this way come to the forefront of anthropological work. However, the anthropological image of rural Northern Ireland has sometimes tended to stress the importance of the integrative forces at the expense of a proper understanding of the divisive ones. Some writers have argued, for example, that disruptive forces in small communities originate extra-locally and are therefore alien; they come from outside, brought in by hot-heads, and disturb the suspicious but generally peaceful co-existence and co-operation of villagers (Leyton, 1974: 198; Bufwak, 1982: 10). Such a representation of Northern Irish society is thus one which portrays it 'as having some kind of balance at its core, a balance which is periodically disrupted by dramatic events' (Donnan and McFarlane, 1986a: 31). It is clear that this depiction carries a different emphasis to that which has emerged from research conducted in other disciplines and which focuses on the more urbanized areas. Apart from the border regions, it is the cities and big towns which have experienced the worst violence and movements of population, and it is therefore not surprising that the divisive forces have left the deeper impression. Here the representation is that Northern Ireland is riven by a fundamental and irreparable sectarian fissure which often explodes into violence but which for long periods remains dormant 'beneath a veneer of good relations' (Donnan and McFarlane, 1983: 135).

To explain the apparent paradox suggested by these two divergent images, Donnan and McFarlane have argued that research should be more sensitive to the different levels at which the sectarian divide comes into play, and this can only be accomplished by extending the context of community studies to incorporate the wider economic and political forces in Northern Ireland (Donnan and McFarlane, 1986a). It is not enough to portray local cultures as largely independent of historical development and the effects of wider forces immanent in Northern Ireland as a whole. Giving greater prominence to these factors provides a better starting point for grasping how the integrative and divisive aspects of local cultures are both the refracted outcomes of these forces, and also themselves influential in shaping them and contributing to their persistence or change. There is, therefore, a pressing need for research to address more explicitly the wider issues of inequality, sectarianism, discrimination, and the nature of the Northern Ireland state.

The present study also diverges from two other characteristics of the anthropological tradition in Northern Ireland. First, the research has been conducted not in a rural community but in the most urbanized part of the province, in which little ethnographic research has so far been carried out (Jenkins, 1984: 261). Second, the primary focus of study is less the sectarian divide than issues of unemployment and social security, which are treated within the context created by sectarianism. The point is made succinctly by Jenkins: 'social scientists have been mesmerized by the "troubles"', and as a result 'many other routine aspects of social life have been neglected' (1984: 262).

Two fundamental facts of Irish history, then, set the overall parameters for any social research in Northern Ireland. These are the plantation, which generated the ethnic struggle, and the partition of Ireland into two states, leaving a majority of Protestants over Catholics in Northern Ireland. Given the historical background of Catholic nationalism, Protestant loyalism, and various forms of political and economic discrimination within which the imposition of this division was accomplished, it is not surprising that Catholics on both sides of the border have persistently withheld their approval of the legitimacy of the Northern Irish state. The Irish Republican Army (IRA), Sinn Fein, the Irish National Liberation Army, and other para-military associations are the channels through which radical Catholic nationalism finds its outlet. The fact that over 100,000 people voted for Sinn Fein candidates in recent Parliamentary elections indicates a great sense of grievance on their part. This is why Jenkins is correct to argue that:

the systematic non-availability of equality of opportunity to catholics should not be seen as in *any* sense an issue which is separable from the legitimacy of the state. Ethnic domination and the national question are different sides of the same coin: the Northern Irish state, with its roots in the Plantation and its birth in the 'temporary solution' of Partition . . . Inequality of opportunity, if it is to be understood at all, must be understood as a basic feature of the institutional structure of Northern Ireland. (1984: 260; italics in original).

This perspective is of considerable moment in relation to this book, especially in regard to employment practices and the uneven distribution of occupations and unemployment in Northern Ireland which, as already explained, are a precipitate of the way sectarian ideology has shaped the Northern Ireland state and its political economy. One of the major issues in question here concerns the difference between direct discrimination and institutional or indirect discrimination. In the former an individual is denied an opportunity (of employment, housing, etc.) on the basis of his/her known or presumed religious affiliation. The latter denotes long-standing and widespread patterns of allocation of resources which, favouring one side, are themselves discriminatory. Such institutional structures produce outcomes in which discrimination assumes a routine and taken-for-granted nature. For example, after 1945 much new manufacturing industry was located in precisely those areas of the province in which Catholic representation is at its lowest. Catholics therefore secured few of the available jobs, not because they applied and suffered overt, individual discrimination, but because they were not even in a realistic position to apply in the first place. Such distributional imbalances are typically justified by the appeal of Protestants to the legitimacy of the Northern Ireland state and the fact that the Catholic community appears hell-bent on destroying it.

What is problematic about discrimination is the immense difficulty of establishing proof of overt individual discrimination, which the Fair Employment Act makes illegal and of which only a few cases have ever been successfully prosecuted, and the pervasive structure of indirect discrimination, against which the legal apparatus is very inadequate (Osborne and Cormack, 1983). That Osborne and Cormack wish to draw a distinction between direct individual discrimination on the one hand, and on the other to use the euphemistic term 'disadvantage', which is meant to refer to 'circumstances where one community compared to the other is markedly underrepresented given their proportion in the population at large' (1983: 227), seems to me to be symptomatic of the problem (see Jenkins, 1984: 261). The examination in chapters 3 and 4 of employment opportunities and the distribution of unemployment in Belfast clearly indicates that institutional discrimination based on sectarian ideology is at the heart of the under-representation of Catholics in employment and their predominance among the unemployed, and further that such discrimination is ineluctably tied to the contested legitimacy of the Northern Ireland state.

Research setting: Mallon Park and Eastlough

Given the disparities between Catholic and Protestant unemployment rates in Belfast, the inequalities in job opportunities for the two religious sides, and their very different dispositions towards the state apparatus, it seemed reasonable to suppose that their experience of unemployment and their reaction to long-term joblessness might be different in some respects. As research locales, two housing estates were chosen to reflect this general situation.

Mallon Park and Eastlough (both pseudonyms) are public-authority housing estates, the former situated in Catholic west Belfast and tenanted almost completely by Catholics, the latter located in east Belfast and tenanted almost exclusively by Protestants of one denomination or another.

These two estates have much in common in the way of local amenities and services, and the houses themselves are of roughly equal standard. Both estates are on the outskirts of the city and about the same distance from the city centre; both have been provided with a mediocre bus service. They both have a local primary school, churches, a small number of shops, and nearby green areas and parks.

Research in urban areas in advanced industrial societies poses certain difficulties. Research in a society riven by sectarian conflict compounds these, even more so when the study is constructed to incorporate both sides of the religious divide. However, the fact that working-class Protestants and Catholics are geographically highly segregated in Belfast removes some of the researcher's anxiety concerning the ambiguity of role and identity that would be ever present if the two groups lived interspersed in mixed residential estates.

The Catholic community is used to the intrusions of researchers, survey teams, journalists, and others. In terms of what is meant by 'research' they are relatively sophisticated. However, the researcher who returns repeatedly is something of a novelty. But it was precisely frequent visits that allayed suspicions about my credentials and motives.

Several other aspects of my behaviour also helped smooth the way. I arranged with its chairman and secretary to be allowed to attend meetings of the estate's community association. Through its committee of about fifteen people I was able to monitor many of the issues currently occupying residents' attention. More important, since very little of this material has been used in the present work, it afforded me a guarantor in the estate. Any remaining doubts about my activities could then be assuaged by the chairman, who was willing to vouch for me. As relationships consolidated, these too could be used both as entry into new ones (usually on the basis of kin and neighbouring links), and also as further corroboration of my reliability. It was this careful and unobtrusive penetration of the estate which helped to dampen potential hostility. So much was this the case that after several months of research some residents mildly reproached me for not yet having visited them.

Two further factors facilitated my undramatic passage into Mallon Park. The first was the presentation of the research aims. Here I explained the main outlines of the study, emphasizing that a major concern was not simply to find out how the unemployed coped with joblessness, but to allow the unemployed to speak for themselves. Frequently, the voice of those out of work comes from the mouths of politicians, journalists, and others who are in jobs and have vested interests to protect. By allowing the unemployed access, through me, to a wider audience, they could lay bare their worries and problems in the way that they perceived them.

The second factor was my preparedness to provide practical assistance. First, by furnishing the community association with information they required to prosecute their campaigns more successfully; by drawing up a questionnaire used to conduct a survey in the estate; and in other small ways. Second, by explaining aspects of the benefit system to unemployed people and by determining whether they had needs which could be met by the scheme; by occasionally acting as a representative at tribunals; by drafting letters to the Department of Health and Social Security (DHSS); by checking the correctness of the amount of benefit received; and so forth.

It is conceivable that such assistance could have intruded and changed the practices and attitudes of some of the research subjects. Though this might have happened on occasion, it did not materially affect the overall situation in either estate. More important, I felt that any refusal on my part to answer the queries which claimants had was an impossibly untenable position given the alacrity with which they responded to my inquisitions. The saving grace is that information was provided only at the end of interviews after having established a base line concerning their knowledge of and orientation to the benefit system. In any case the detailed probing that is entailed in discovering what information claimants possess, and therefore the gaps that exist, itself elicits valuable data.

Whether my activities in either estate were ever investigated by a para-military organization I do not know. Certainly I was neither accosted nor questioned in an explicit manner. However, I did maintain friendships with one or two men in Mallon Park who had been members of the IRA in their youth, and who had served short prison sentences for membership. It is quite possible that these passed on information that was asked for. At no time was the research overtly impeded by any action of a para-military organization.

A final word on the perception of my role is in order. The sectarian divide is one which separates Catholics from Protestants, but the conflict, as already explained, is not primarily a religious one. It is, therefore, no great impediment to be something other than a practising Roman Catholic when doing research amongst such. When questioned about my religious beliefs I always responded that, though brought up as a Methodist, I no longer attended any church and considered myself agnostic at best. This was always accepted as a satisfactory statement. That I was a nominal Protestant appeared to bother no one. Basically, Catholics are less interested and less threatened by the content of other religions than is the case for Ulster Protestants, some of whom are frightened by the future possibility of hegemonic religious rule emanating from Paisley's 'anti-Christ' in Rome. What some of my Catholic friends were concerned about was my 'Britishness' and hence my stance on the constitutional issue, the legitimacy of the state, the role of the police and army, and discrimination. Here it was possible for me to argue a sincere case which fell quite comfortably within the spectrum of opinion to be found in the estate, namely that I recognize that discrimination takes place, that I abhor it, that Catholics suffer most; that I acknowledge that the IRA and Sinn Fein have, in the eyes of very many Catholics, a legitimate perspective on the status of the border with which I can sympathize, even though disagreeing with their violent tactics; and so forth. It was this combination of sympathy for the unemployed and for the Catholic fight against discrimination, allied to practical assistance and a reasonable knowledge of Irish history and current affairs, that gained me an acceptable, but conditional, status.

One possible source of tension was the fact, which I never hid, that I was doing research in both a Catholic and a Protestant estate. Most Catholics, however, did not explicitly question the propriety of this and people in both areas asked for information about life 'on the other side of town'. This particular issue tended to surface more in Eastlough.

While I made some good friends in Eastlough, I found it more exhausting to work there than in Mallon Park. The estate was socially more fragmented. There was, for example, no community association, whose existence might have forged a community spirit and acted as the centre of communal activity. Moreover, the physical layout of the houses was not conducive to easy familiarity between neighbours, and Eastlough people could sometimes provide only the barest details of neighbours living only two or three doors away. This made a stark contrast with Mallon Park, where most people knew far more about their co-residents. The estate was fragmented for other reasons as well, largely to do with the way in which unemployment was handled and conceptualized; but this is dealt with in the main body of the book.

Eastlough is also, to me, a less attractive place than Mallon Park, being more barren and windswept, and with little visible street activity. Compounding this, I had greater difficulty establishing cordial relationships especially with the employed, some of whom refused to take part in the research on discovering that they would be expected to divulge details of their incomes.

Being myself a British Protestant, it may be thought paradoxical that I experienced more problems finding a viable status and identity in Eastlough than in Mallon Park. On closer inspection this is not so odd. It is, after all, the Protestant communities which consider themselves to be under siege, and their relationship to the British is one of unwavering loyalty to the crown and constitution, but often intense suspicion of its successive representatives (Millar, 1978) who may at any time sell out the loyalist cause (Fisk, 1975; Nelson, 1984; Wiener, 1975); each new political initiative creates further dismay and consternation among many Protestants. Additionally, Protestants are worried and angry about the greater attention usually given to the Catholic cause by 'naive' British and American commentators and 'credulous' academic researchers, and the general failure of the media outside Northern Ireland to give the Protestant view an equal and fair hearing. Not surprisingly, I came across such criticisms in Eastlough and found them rather difficult to counteract. Was I not, when all is said and done, comparing Protestant and Catholic areas? What was there to compare? If more Catholics were unemployed than Protestants (by no means universally acknowledged) this was their own fault; they caused Northern Ireland's parlous economic condition, and if they did not wish to live in Ulster they could leave. Moreover, Catholic grievances, according to Protestants, are hypocritical, since while they decry the state and its institutional set-up, they accept its welfare benefits all too eagerly, benefits they could never hope to receive across the border or in a new all-Ireland state independent of the UK. Put crudely, so far as some Protestants are concerned, Britain's welfare state supports and maintains Republican terrorism.

Despite these difficulties, the tactics of slow penetration, practical assistance to the unemployed, and a genuine sympathy for the plight of working-class Protestants (besieged by Catholics on one side and, on the other, tormented by their distrust of political and economic elites whose interests do not always coincide with those of the former) did help to dispel some of the sources of worry, and eventually some good relationships were created.

As far as the more general problems of urban research are concerned, some of these have recently been vividly and wittily documented by Grillo (1985). Traditionally anthropological research has been conducted in societies which are small-scale and afford easy access to their members. Advanced industrial societies are different, and a great many of the activities in which anthropologists are interested take place in private spheres to which entry is limited and has to be arranged in advance. Outside the home, access to places of work is difficult (it took several months and a series of interviews before I was granted permission to conduct research in a social security office). Within the estates, behaviour is privatized to a great extent and the working day leaves little time for the researcher's requirements. In this respect, meetings with both Catholic and Protestant employed took place mainly in the home, and mainly in the evenings.

The unemployed are generally more accessible. Though much of their time is spent indoors, many welcome an opportunity to escape from drab routines. Conversely, the combination of limited financial resources, fractious home atmosphere, and fragile self-image, often make home visiting a tense encounter.

The fact that I did not live in either estate (both because of the nature of public housing allocation procedures, and because I did not want to subject my family to the rigours of a research project which might have placed them in physical danger and at best would have caused them considerable hardship) further restricted access to the social lives of the people of Mallon Park and Eastlough. As it was, my presence in the estates was largely confined to afternoons and evenings. Research was conducted in the two localities alternately, spending two to three months mostly in one and then switching for a similar period to the other.

When this research project was first formulated, I did not plan a thorough investigation of the activities of the unemployed in the black economy. However, it soon became apparent, especially in Mallon Park where the study began, that this was an issue which, because many of the residents spontaneously referred to it, could not be ignored. Moreover, since the financial circumstances of the unemployed are of the utmost significance, it would have been quite misleading to omit from consideration such an important source of income. The fact that the pattern of such activities is closely linked to other facets of the experience of unemployment made this a crucial area of research. But, of course, writing about illegal activities raises ethical dilemmas. The practice of fictionalizing names of people and places secures protection for the specific individuals who participated in the research. However, published data may be used to formulate policies which then affect other individuals and groups in unpredictable ways.

Ethical considerations do not work in one direction only. Researchers have responsibilities not just to research subjects, but also to the wider society they seek to inform. It has long been my view that the argument concerning the social and economic plight of the unemployed is being lost by the political 'left', partly because of its refusal to address explicitly the issue of informal economic activity. The present Conservative government and the tabloid press rarely miss an opportunity to air their views that a significant proportion of the unemployed are in fact working. Reading between the lines, the implications of their views are quite clear: many unemployed work full-time; they are greedy parasites; they exploit a generous benefit system; they hold jobs which other, honest, unemployed would be prepared to take on a legitimate basis; the few caught are just the tip of the iceberg; etc. (Golding and Middleton, 1982). With little empirical data to go on, the 'left' can only agonize about its own incompetence in the debate and its consequent failure to reveal the actual social reality within which such practices take place: that 'on the side' working is highly irregular and intermittent; that employers collude in the activity; that many of the jobs are not at all viable without the benefit cushion; that the incomes are generally small and used to ameliorate financial problems; that conditions of informal work are often much worse than those of legitimate employment; etc. I hope the material contained herein will be seen as a contribution to the political arsenal of those who are concerned to improve the conditions in which the unemployed have to live.

In each of the estates, two core samples of twenty employed and twenty unemployed working-class married men with dependent families were selected as the major research focus. Initial contact with the research subjects was made by conducting limited surveys. Each head of household was asked to provide basic information on his/her own employment status, age, type of job, previous experience of unemployment, and the number of dependants and their ages and employment status. On the basis of this data the members of the four core samples were chosen according to two criteria: age (20 to 35 years and 36 to 50 years), and experience of previous spells of unemployment (defined as at least one involuntary spell without work, lasting at least four months and occurring within the previous ten years). Both because of the younger age structure of the Mallon Park population and of the difficulty of finding younger men without previous experience of unemployment in Mallon Park and older men with such experience in Eastlough, the samples do not divide equally according to these two criteria (for a breakdown of the samples, see table 6).

Since the unemployment rate in Mallon Park is very high (over 50 per cent) and because most people reacted with enthusiasm, it was relatively easy to secure the two samples. In Eastlough the unemployment rate is about half that in Mallon Park, and with residents apparently more suspicious of the research, greater difficulties were encountered in recruiting both employed and unemployed samples. Given that I had, in certain respects, to take what was on offer, the samples are not directly comparable in either age range, previous experience of unemployment, or length of present spell of unemployment at first contact. The samples are not incommensurate either, and all samples include a broad spectrum of experience and diverse types of people.

Much of the data on the four core samples was collected in the respondents' homes by tape-recorded interviews. A large proportion of

Table 6. *Numbers in Catholic and Protestant core samples by age and experience of previous unemployment.*

	Catholic unemployed		Catholic employed		Protestant unemployed		Protestant employed	
Age in years	20–35	36–50	20–35	36–50	20–35	36–50	20–35	36–50
No previous unemployment	5	4	5	4	4	6	4	7
With previous unemployment	9	2	6	5	6	4	5	4
Totals	14	6	11	9	10	10	9	11

these interviews were of considerable length (up to six hours). Conversations were structured in a limited way; so long as the talk was about unemployment, work, benefits, and social relationships, it was left to follow its own course. The two unemployed samples were interviewed on three occasions, though by a later stage five refused further contact, two had moved away, and a few had obtained jobs. The Catholic employed were interviewed twice and the Protestant employed only once.

This body of information, however, comprises only part of the total research data. Interviews were arranged in advance, but there were many occasions when an interview, for one reason or another, did not take place at the appointed time. These periods were spent visiting other families in the estates (some of which are not in the core samples) on a chance-call basis. Such unplanned visits tended to be seen as social calls, and no tape-recordings were made, notes being written up afterwards. I also used these periods to visit local 'notables' in the estates: community workers, advice workers, local councillors, teachers, priests, etc. In addition, much time was spent on door-steps and in the open chatting to people I met either by chance or when doing the estate surveys. I also attended community association meetings (particularly in Mallon Park where the association was very active) and other types of social gatherings (sports days, street parties and the like), and I often accompanied friends to the pub, the social security office (SSO) and other places. Further, the two surveys of the estates yielded much useful information, and I also monitored local newspapers and job-centre information. Finally, the DHSS in Northern Ireland permitted me to conduct three months' research in a social security office in east

Belfast, and this produced the data on which Howe (1985) and chapter 5 of the present work are based.

The unemployed on means-tested benefits

Ever since its 're-discovery' early in the 1960s (Abel-Smith and Townsend, 1965), poverty in the UK has been a major focus of research. A prominent issue has been the controversial role played by means-tested benefit schemes. The poverty lobby has consistently argued that such schemes have pernicious financial, social, and psychological consequences for those they are designed to assist (Townsend, 1976). They are highly stigmatizing, have low rates of take-up, are a bureaucratic nightmare to administer and leave too much room for informal, discretionary decision-making.

William Beveridge's 1942 plan for post-war social security arrangments envisaged a comprehensive system of social insurance to provide cover against old age, sickness, and unemployment. The benefits, as a return for contributions, and given as of right, were to be unlimited in duration and adequate for subsistence. Because these insurance schemes were supposed to provide sufficient cover, it was considered that means-tested benefits would play only a residual part in income maintenance (Beveridge Report, 1942). National Assistance, enacted in 1947, was the means-tested benefit designed to supplement any other income or benefit that a person recieved up to a 'needs' level prescribed by Parliament. The eventual legislation, however, implemented only part of Beveridge's vision, by setting the rates of support below those recommended and limiting the period of entitlement (Deacon and Bradshaw, 1983). The effect of this, documented many times, has been to transform the role of means-tested benefits from that of bit player to star performer. In 1986, for example, over five million families were receiving a means-tested benefit of one kind or another, a figure which excludes those in full-time work receiving a low-income benefit (Piachaud, 1987: 25).

Studies of the long-term unemployed living on such benefits (Sinfield, 1970; Clark, 1978; Townsend, 1979; Burghes, 1980; Marsden, 1982; Howe, 1984; etc.) are quite extensive, and they paint a picture of unrelenting financial and social hardship. Northern Ireland is a particularly blighted and deprived area and is, by virtually any yardstick one cares to choose, the poorest region in the UK. Within Northern Ireland, surveys such as those by Boal, Doherty, and Pringle (1974), the Northern Ireland Housing Executive (1976, 1979), and Eileen Evason (1976, 1978, 1980, 1985), indicate that the worst conditions (of housing,

Table 7. *Supplementary benefit (basic benefit) rates in force between November 1983 and November 1984*

	£
Married couple	43.50
Dependent child	
aged over 18	21.45
16 to 17	16.50
11 to 15	13.70
under 11	9.15

unemployment, and deprivation) are to be found in predominantly Catholic areas, and that the main factors producing poverty are low wages, single parenthood, and unemployment, with joblessness becoming increasingly significant in the 1980s.

The benefit incomes of unemployed people vary according to circumstances. Supplementary Benefit (SB) scale rates defined a 'needs' level in terms of family composition, housing costs, and other, special requirements (fully explained in chapter 5). The rates applicable during much of the research period are given in table 7.[1] Income Support (IS) calculates basic benefit in much the same way, but housing costs are now met by housing benefit and many of the 'extras' of the SB scheme have either been abolished from the new IS scheme or incorporated into the basic payments.

Income from other benefits (child benefit, unemployment benefit, etc.) was deducted pound for pound from SB. The first £4 of earned income for each spouse was ignored but thereafter benefit was again deducted pound for pound.[2] IS works in the same way, except that the earnings' disregard has been increased to £5.

An effective means of comparing incomes across families in different circumstances is the calculation of a figure for net disposable income per person, per day, after making deductions for essential expenditure. For example Joe Carlin (Catholic unemployed) with a wife and two children under eleven years of age, received weekly £65.90 (plus rent and rates deducted at source). Out of this he had to meet the following weekly expenses: coal (£10), television rental (£2.50), electricity (£5), gas (£1), insurances (£2), washing-machine repayments (£6.40). This left him with £39, or £1.39 per person, per day, to be spent on food, clothes, household goods, entertainment, travel, etc. During the research period, not one family in the two unemployed groups in Mallon Park and Eastlough enjoyed a net disposable income in excess of £1.69 per person, per day. The lowest figure recorded was £1.21 (the Hardings in Eastlough) and the average was £1.52; (there was no significant difference in disposable incomes between the Catholic and Protestant unemployed samples).

Of those families relying entirely on benefit (i.e. excluding those who were able regularly to augment their incomes by one means or another), none found themselves in the stable position in which benefit income equalled or exceeded expenditure. Those families in which either the wife had a part-time job or the spell of unemployment was still of short duration were only slightly better off, and as the period of unemployment lengthened, many of these also began to experience financial difficulties. By the end of the research, not counting those who were back in work (five Protestants and two Catholics), those receiving undeclared earnings (ten, but a group which continually varied in size), and those five not receiving SB (because the wife was in full-time work and the household income exceeded the 'needs' level) only six families did not have at least one debt. The Hardings in Eastlough had the largest debts (to statutory agencies, hire-purchase arrears and to family and friends), totalling over £1,000. Several others had debts well over £100 and the rest had small debts.[3]

To put this in perspective, it needs to be realized that in practice many families, particularly the younger ones, are subsidized in various ways by their parents and close kin, who themselves can barely afford the costs of this aid. Without these hidden subsidies, the poor supporting the poor, life on benefit would be even more intolerable than it already is.

In its Annual Report of 1978 the Supplementary Benefits Commission (now abolished) argued that for claimants with children, and especially the long-term unemployed, benefits are too low, and the large and growing differences between benefits for different categories of claimants are indefensible. Furthermore, the constraints under which means-tested benefit systems labour and the manner in which they are administered (see chapter 5) make it difficult for many claimants to obtain what they are legally entitled to. That is to say, many people do not even receive the full amount of a benefit that is already considered by many to be insufficient.

On the other hand the structure of opportunities is not the same for all the unemployed, and as regards getting work in the black economy some groups are in a more favourable position than others. Here, those few unemployed who receive a regular (undeclared) income, can find themselves in a relatively comfortable position, and even those who only obtain infrequent earnings are at least cushioned against the worst ravages of unemployment. In other words, while in theory unemployed people in generally comparable circumstances should receive equivalent amounts of total income, in practice this does not happen. Varying economic and social conditions in different areas provide more or fewer opportunities to augment incomes. Similarly, the manner in which benefit is routinely administered engenders different forms of claimant disposition, one result of which is that many claimants obtain less than is their full legal due. Patterns of interaction between the employed and unemployed, particularly in Eastlough, tend to consolidate the inclination to underclaim. The desperate plight of the unemployed on benefit is not therefore the principal focus of study, though of course it supplies the essential context for many of the issues to be addressed. Rather, this book is about the processes through which people get more or less than their notional entitlements.

Given this focus, the book does not possess the architecture of a conventional ethnography. In part, as already explained, this is due to the nature of urban research and the fact that much social behaviour is privatized or takes place in highly structured and institutionalized arenas. In part it is due to my concern to present detailed information on certain aspects of unemployment which link it to the major structures of opportunity and constraint. Attributes of the social lives of unemployed people which are not directly relevant to these issues have perforce to be left out of consideration.

In part, finally, it is also a product of the very restricted social lives which most of the unemployed lead. For those who have not been unemployed it is quite a task to grasp just how isolating is the daily existence of the long-term unemployed. Some of the members of the unemployed samples, especially from Eastlough, have so little contact with the outside world that for weeks at a time they talk to no one other than their immediate kin. Even when they leave the home interaction is often perfunctory. Concerned about stigma by association and the problematic nature of interaction, many unemployed avoid unnecessary conversations, cease going to places where their unemployment might prove to be a handicap, and curtail involvement with other unemployed. In trying to present a more complete picture of the social life of unemployed married men, there is often very little to describe other than its breakdown and fragmentation.

Thus, despite the fact that a centre for the unemployed exists very close to Eastlough, not one of the unemployed in the sample ever visited it during the research period (the young, unmarried unemployed did so to a much greater extent). Additionally, hardly any of the Eastlough unemployed group took advantage of concessionary admission rates to leisure centres, and many gave up regular church attendance, and withdrew from football, darts, bowling, and other sports and social groups.

It may be thought that the unemployed can at least take part in activities with kin. However, the processes which influence the interaction between employed and unemployed penetrate to the very core of family life, separating husband from wife, parent from child, and brother from brother. The home and family life are sometimes less a safe haven than an inescapable torment.

I have argued, however, that the unemployed are not a homogenous group. Conditions in Mallon Park are in part different to those in Eastlough. In Mallon Park the unemployed constitute a majority of the active labour force, and they mix more freely with each other and with the employed. Nevertheless, those on benefit experience a marked reduction in social activity. Here, too, the unemployed remain indoors to a remarkable extent; they give up membership of sports teams and other social groups; they rarely use leisure centres and cease regular church attendance. If the interaction with other unemployed and employed is somewhat less of a strain than it is for Eastlough people, tensions within the home are as difficult as those found in the latter estate.

The major division in the unemployed groups is between those who are able to augment their benefit income by working on the side and those who are not. The many advantages of such work are described in chapter 4. Suffice it to say here that this type of work reproduces, to varying degrees – depending on the income derived and the duration and regularity of the work – many of the characteristics of legitimate employment, and assists in re-establishing patterns of consumption and social interaction not dissimilar to those of people with jobs. The real challenge, then, to anyone interested in the study of urban, adult unemployment is not just the depiction of overt patterns of interaction, but, in contrast, the analysis of why so little of it occurs.

Chapter 3

Doing the double in Belfast: the general picture

Introduction

The 'abuse' of welfare benefits by the unemployed takes four basic forms. The first is fraud, properly speaking, and concerns claimants who intentionally withhold information or make false statements bearing on their employment status and/or their net income. A quite different form of 'abuse', defined in moral rather than in legal terms, is constituted by claimants who allegedly exploit the system in a determined effort to obtain, irrespective of 'real' need, any and every available benefit. Malingering or scrounging is a related form of abuse, purportedly identifying claimants who could make private provision for themselves (e.g. by obtaining a job) but prefer rather to be state supported. A final form of abuse involves tampering with the payment instrument (giro cheque, for example), but this is comparatively rare and easily detected.

The issue of 'working while claiming' is addressed in this and the following chapter. Discussion of the alleged exploitation of the benefit system requires an examination of processes of benefit administration in social security offices, which is the subject of chapter 5. Malingering, finally, can only be considered in relation to the labour market and the levels of wages and benefits, topics which are explored throughout the book.

In Northern Ireland 'doing the double' refers to the practice of claiming SB (and/or unemployment benefit) while undertaking undeclared paid work. Conviction for such fraud carries a penalty of a fine or possibly a term of imprisonment. During the research period, benefit regulations included an earnings' disregard of £4 for the claimant and £4 for the spouse's earnings. Earnings above this were deducted pound for pound from benefit (Lynes, 1981). Working for more than twenty-five hours per week makes a person ineligible for SB. Many unemployed consider it futile to declare earnings and see this earnings' rule as a disincentive to working honestly.[1]

Before presenting the evidence, some preliminary and contextual remarks need to be made concerning the black and informal economies. During the 1970s, several sociologists conducted research into various practices associated with these sectors of the economy. Ditton (1977), for example, described the fiddling activities of bread salesmen and christened this 'part-time crime'. Henry (1978) examined the nature of the social relations involved in what he termed 'borderline crime' and 'amateur property theft' (Henry and Mars, 1978). According to Henry, 'hidden-economy' trading is the illicit buying and selling of 'cheap', usually stolen, goods that goes on among ordinary people in honest jobs (1978: 20). Mars described these kinds of practices as 'the normal crimes of normal people in the normal circumstances of their work'; they are the technically illegal, but ubiquitous activities of pilfering, fiddling, short-changing, etc., practised by all kinds of workers over a wide variety of occupations (Mars, 1982: 1). It was left to Henry (1981: 7) to construct a typology of informal institutions differentiated by their legal status and by the degree to which they are integral or alternative to official institutions. Underlying this work is the assumption that most black economic activity is carried out by people in employment.

In the early 1980s, economists ventured to estimate the size of the black economy by using various indirect, macroeconomic methods (Macafee, 1980; Parker 1982a; for methodological criticisms, see Outer Circle Policy Unit, 1980). What counts as black economic activity varies considerably from one definition to another. Minimally, it includes the legal production of goods and services, but for which taxes are evaded. More inclusive definitions incorporate criminal activities and even household production. According to definition and method of computation used, estimates of size vary between 2 per cent (Dilnot and Norris, 1981) and 22 per cent (Feige, 1981) of Gross Domestic Product. However, the fact that these estimates are based on aggregate statistics gives few clues as to who is responsible for the output. When such estimates are linked to levels of unemployment and the supposed effects of the social security system, the issues become politically very sensitive. Some economists on the political right have suggested that the level of real unemployment is considerably lower than official figures represent. They allege that many unemployed are working and claiming benefits. Such accusations are often made during times of economic recession when vast sums of revenue have to be expended to support the workless (Deacon, 1976, 1978). Kent Mathews, for example, has argued that 'if our estimates of the black economy are anything to go by, it is likely that a sizeable proportion of the unemployed in the latter half of the decade [1970–80] represents a monumental statistical illusion'

(1983: 266). Mathews provides a table (1983: 266) showing registered unemployment by year (1972–80) alongside levels of unemployed people estimated to be employed in the black economy, with the clear implication that such people are employed on a full-time basis. Evidence will be presented to demonstrate that this is a gross and disingenuous distortion of the situation.

Of more immediate relevance is the work of Gershuny and Pahl. In a series of studies (Gershuny, 1977, 1978, 1979; Gershuny and R.E. Pahl, 1979–80, 1980; R.E. Pahl, 1980) concerned with the changing structure of the British economy during a period of industrial decline and technological innovation, they emphasized the roles played by the domestic and informal economies, and powerfully criticized the view that a burgeoning service sector would emerge to soak up manufacturing's displaced workers. In some of this work, the two authors described an optimistic scenario by arguing that unemployed people might find rewarding and satisfying work in the informal economy.

More recently, however, Pahl has changed his mind. He now claims that the representation of the hidden economy as a safe haven for the unemployed must be recast because in the 1980s this sector of the informal economy is probably in decline, and he lists five reasons for thinking this is so (R.E. Pahl, 1984: 93–8; Wallace and R.E. Pahl, 1986). One of these is that all household work, do-it-yourself, gardening, etc., is excluded from estimates of the size of the hidden economy, but that it is precisely here that work outside the formal economy has increased. To that extent the attention paid to the hidden economy by such as Henry and Mars has been misplaced.

Pahl's research on the Isle of Sheppey was devoted to all types of informal work, and his major conclusions are, first, that the vast majority of such work is done by household members for themselves rather than for others, and second, that employment and self-provisioning go together rather than substitute for one another. Those who produce a lot of goods and services in the home have access to land, labour, and capital, and this means that they are likely to be formally employed. Contrary to the expectations of Gershuny (1979) and Rose (1983), it is the employed rather than the unemployed who have thriving domestic economies; hence the thesis of polarization between employed and unemployed (R.E. Pahl and Wallace, 1985). It is the employed who have the capital to purchase goods which can be used to produce final services. The unemployed, living on benefits, cannot do this, and while labour is available it cannot be productively utilized.

But do the unemployed engage in informal work outside the home?

Pahl's data show that even the employed did comparatively little outside the household, that only 4 per cent of his sample of 730 households did informal paid work, and that only one unemployed man (out of twenty-six) admitted to doing such paid work (R.E. Pahl and Wallace, 1985: 208–9). The supposed inactivity of the unemployed outside the household also partly accounts, in Pahl's view, for the decline of the hidden economy. He argues that since the unemployed are today under increasing surveillance from both the authorities and their neighbours it is difficult for them to do undeclared paid work (see McKee and Bell, 1986: 147–9). Moreover, they are too poor to work informally, as they lack the money to buy tools, nor can they afford to go to the pubs to make the necessary contacts. Finally, in areas of very high unemployment Pahl argues that even if some have tools to work informally no one can afford their services. However, as will become apparent, there is a greater degree of undeclared paid work by the unemployed (doing the double) in working-class areas of Belfast than Pahl discovered in Sheppey (see Jenkins, 1978; Jenkins and Harding, 1986; Morrissey et al., 1984). Additionally, evidence from Cauldmoss in Scotland (Bostyn and Wight, 1984) and Swansea (Morris, 1984b), indicates that such activity is not altogether insignificant in other depressed regions.

Much previous theorizing carries the implication that activity rates in the black economy are attributable directly to the state of the formal economy. Some have argued that a buoyant economy provides more opportunities for work on the side than does a depressed economy. Others have claimed the opposite, that a weak economy and high unemployment encourage the jobless to divert their energies into informal production (Rose, 1983). What remains constant is the assumption of a simple relation between the formal economy and activity rates of the unemployed in the black economy. The wider theoretical interest of this book lies in the finding that in the same city a buoyant 'local' economy in one area (east Belfast) provides relatively fewer opportunities for work on the side, whilst a much weaker 'local' economy in another area (west Belfast) supplies comparatively greater opportunities. In seeking to explain this, I have had to look more closely at what economists would generally consider to be rather extraneous cultural factors. The data clearly show that cultural elements (in this case religious/ethnic) are of seminal importance. I aim to demonstrate that there is, in fact, no straightforward relationship between this aspect of informal economic activity and the condition of the local economy. In contrast, it is evident that in Belfast ideologies and practices of sectarianism have played a very significant role in the industrial development of the Northern Ireland economy. To this day, people's perceptions of sectarianism and the nature of economic reality continue to influence one another. It is the interaction of economy, polity, and culture which considerably complicates the nature of the relationship in question. In other words, what is usually missing from accounts of this issue is the important mediating role of cultural ideas and knowledge and their attached typical practices. One of the main objectives of this chapter is to situate the economic data in their cultural context.

It is, of course, true that the situation in Belfast, and in Northern Ireland generally, makes it relatively easy to identify the way in which non-economic factors shape both the formal and informal economies. It is also the case that my particular analysis may not be directly applicable in understanding the response of long-term unemployed people in cities such as Liverpool, Lyons, or Naples. Nevertheless, there is a general lesson to be learned, and it is that cultural mediation of economic processes is not specific to Northern Ireland, but occurs everywhere. At bottom the argument is really about whether the distinction between the 'economic' and the 'non-economic' has any validity.

Eastlough

Table 8 indicates the number of male heads-of-household in and out of work, broken down by sector of the economy, for both Eastlough and Mallon Park. The situation in Eastlough will be examined first.

Of immediate interest is the massive reliance of males on the manufacturing sector, which accounts for 50 per cent of all employees and unemployed. Indeed, east Belfast contains 57 per cent of all manufacturing jobs in the greater Belfast region (O'Dowd, 1982: table 4). It was primarily this sector which fared most badly during the 1979–83 recession. Whilst to one extent or another many firms survived the worst ravages of the recession, the late 1980s finds Harland and Wolff and Short Bros. in a very precarious situation. Nevertheless, to those who experienced redundancy from this sector it is manufacturing which is perceived to hold out the best hope of a job in the future.

In the core sample of unemployed, ten lost jobs from manufacturing. Because of age and poor health, two are resigned to 'early retirement'. Two others, unskilled but experienced, are back in work after spells of unemployment of eleven months and nearly three years, both in manufacturing. The rest were still unemployed at the end of the research, all for over two years. Four of this group of ten are skilled (having served five-year apprenticeships) but none has succeeded in finding work.

Table 8. Numbers of male heads-of-household in employment and unemployment, by area and sector of economy (industrial orders in brackets): Mallon Park and Eastlough

Sector of economy	Unemployed									Employed								
Area	Construction (20)	Manufacturing (3–19)	Gas, electricity water (21)	Transport communications (22)	Distributive trades (23)	Miscellaneous services (26)	Public administration, defence (27)	Never worked	Totals	Construction (20)	Manufacturing (3–19)	Gas, electricity water (21)	Transport communications (22)	Distributive trades (23)	Miscellaneous services (26)	Public administration, defence (27)	Professional (25)	Totals
Mallon Park I	13	7	—	3	6	6	—	1	36	11	8	—	8	5	12	1	2	47
Mallon Park II	30	24	—	5	9	10	—	4	82	10	12	3	6	11	12	4	2	60
Mallon Park III	45	28	—	10	13	21	5	9	131	17	14	3	9	16	18	5	3	85
Mallon Park Totals	88	59	—	18	28	37	5	14	249	38	34	6	23	32	42	10	7	192
Eastlough Totals	14	41	—	8	9	9	2	2	85	19	120	9	16	30	29	15	2	240

Notes:

Mallon Park areas I and II were surveyed by myself and are based on 100% samples; area III was surveyed by the local community association and is based on a 50% sample. Eastlough was surveyed by myself and is based on a 100% sample. Response rates are over 85% in all cases. Figures do not include single parent households, or those receiving invalidity or sickness benefits. Mallon Park unemployment rate = 56.4%; Eastlough unemployment rate = 26.2%.

These unemployed men see their future job prospects lying almost entirely within the manufacturing sector, and in the same – or equivalent – firms they have already worked in: 'all you can do is sit and wait till the jobs come back' (Roy Price); 'I just keep pluggin' away, send in the ol' [application] form every six months' (Bobby Marshall); 'the mates down there will get me back in when they can' (Fred Beattie); etc. Discussions with many other unemployed in the estate revealed similar dispositions.

Their reliance on this sector is also demonstrated by their job-hunting activities. The city's main job centre is rarely visited. This is not just because the cost is considered prohibitive, for many jobs are also advertised in a local library and just as few use this. It is because the jobs they want are not usually displayed in the job centre and even when this does happen they are also advertised in the press, or they will hear of them through friends and neighbours. Most of such unemployed people apply mainly for these manufacturing jobs and they continually and ritualistically renew their applications. They know these firms and factories, that is where their experience lies, where they have contacts, and where they feel they have the best chance of a job; they understand what is expected of them, and most of all the wages are higher in this sector than in others (though there is variation across firms). The orientation of this group is very definitely one which directs them to the jobs they have had and which they expect or hope to obtain in the future.

The other ten from the core sample come from a variety of working backgrounds. Three are painters (one skilled; the other two failed to finish their apprenticeships); a further three are skilled craftsmen (mechanic, coach-builder, and cook) and four are unskilled (barman, driver, radio-operator, and garage storeman). Of this group two (the skilled painter and the mechanic) are back in work in their own trades after spells of unemployment of one year and two years respectively. Only the four unskilled can be said to be looking for any kind of job so long as the wages are 'realistic'. Only two of these ten are willing to work indoors, though they do not like the idea. In this respect most of the entire sample initially selected their jobs in terms of an indoor/outdoor distinction, a choice that Blackburn and Mann (1979: 67–87) found to be very significant in the Peterborough labour market.

Doing the double in Eastlough

Of the ten from manufacturing, only one (Tom Haslett) has done the double in any substantial sense (helping to build a house for a friend, occasional work as a barman, work on a building site). As far as could be ascertained the other nine have done very little. Opportunities for such work are thought to be very rare; they have not worked partly because they have never been asked.

Of the other ten, all but two (both unskilled) have done a double at some time during their present spell of unemployment, although much of their activity has been desultory and short term. Only Jim Hughes, the cook, solicited work by advertisement, and in this way was in business for about one year painting and decorating private houses. At one point he had so much work he actually 'employed' two unemployed brothers-in-law to help him out. Things began to go wrong when the latter two withdrew their labour because Jim would not increase their wages.

Whilst some in this category acknowledge that their trades give them an advantage, nevertheless they too claim that opportunities are few, and none of them see doing the double as a viable *long-term prospect*. Hence none are yet prepared to stop looking for a legitimate job. Apart from the cook, those who have taken work tend to see it as an extension of their normal routines when formally employed. Thus the painters and the mechanic all do 'homers' as a matter of course when in work and see no reason to stop simply because they have become unemployed.

From the core sample, then, whilst eleven have engaged in undeclared economic activity for only two has this been substantial in terms of time worked and money earned. Many of these unemployed assert, however, that others in the estate are doing a double on a more or less regular basis, though when pressed they cannot usually provide specific details. The theme: 'I'm not doing it but there's plenty who are' is quite pervasive in both Eastlough and Mallon Park. Nevertheless, such insistence is not entirely without foundation. For Eastlough, information from a variety of sources (newspaper reports of court cases, research in an SSO, my own observations) does indicate that the level of black-economy activity is at least as high as the data from the core sample suggest. One reason for this appears to be the activities of part-time but regularly employed female workers (whose husbands are unemployed) in the service sector (in shops, in school and office cleaning, child minding, etc.). In general however, doing the double for men in Eastlough is not considered as a particularly viable option, for several reasons.

First, the vast majority of jobs in east Belfast are concentrated in large firms and public administration, in which doing the double is imposs-ible; but it is in these establishments that most of the unemployed pin their hopes for future employment. To them the dole still constitutes an *interruption* of work. Legitimate employment is still overwhelmingly that which is sought and desired and which is strongly supported by long-standing attitudes and values.

Second, opportunities for doing the double fall mainly to tradesmen in the construction sector, to those in repair and renovation, to electricians and mechanics, and to women. But those in construction comprise only 10 per cent of the active labour force, and whilst a large number of houses have been and are being built in Belfast contractors are often from out of town and import their own labour.

Third, for most of the unemployed, work on the side is usually of short duration and seen as a means of alleviating immediate financial problems. Such odd jobs are usually acquired through local networks (doing the mother's kitchen, fixing the brother's car, mending the guttering on a friend's house, etc.), and are jobs which arise in the normal course of events. They are often called 'thank-you' jobs, done as favours, and if money does change hands it is rarely conceived of as 'earnings' unless it is a considerable sum. In many cases money is not involved at all, since the recipient of the favour is usually a provider of other goods and services: minding and feeding children, supplying clothes, excessive Christmas presents, loans without interest, bags of groceries, buckets of coal, and so on.

Fourth, in Eastlough there is a widespread belief that people are paid for informing to the DHSS. The fear of informers and of being caught is pervasive, and it probably inhibits people from doing a double. 'If I did get a turn I'd be the one to get caught' was a phrase I heard many times.

Fifth, DHSS fraud investigators probably face fewer threats from para-militaries in east Belfast, and consequently it is believed that they maintain a more visible presence there than in Catholic west Belfast.

Finally, doing the double is an activity commonly attributed to Catholics. Catholics supposedly prefer to exploit the benefit system by choosing not to work at all, and to prefer working the double to working legitimately. These are not merely tactics adopted to sabotage the Northern Ireland state; they are seen to be part of the very nature of Catholics. Doing the double has in this way become part of the stereotypical representation of Catholics. In a sense, Protestants who do the double reduce the cultural distance between themselves and Catholics.

In short, the east Belfast local economy, at least for those living in Eastlough (inner city areas, where the opportunity structure is probably different, might well diverge from this pattern), provides few realistic opportunities for doing the double. It occurs in the margins of the formal economy, in certain skilled occupational categories, and for women in the service sector, and is not considered a viable substitute to formal employment.

Moreover, unemployment in east Belfast has always been low in comparison to other areas of the city, and legitimate jobs have consistently provided the best options. Material on job histories of those working in the 1950s and 1960s indicates that men leaving jobs in one week were often back in work the next, that men changed jobs frequently 'to chase the money', and that long spells of unemployment were comparatively rare and more strongly stigmatized. This situation may be changing. Many of those who have lost jobs in the last four years remain unemployed, and those over forty years of age are beginning to wonder whether they will ever work again. There are, nevertheless, some jobs available, but in the main these are badly paid for long hours. Taking one necessitates the claiming of low-income benefits, resulting in total household income remaining much the same. In consequence unemployed family men tend to reject and even scorn such openings (a theme expanded in the next chapter), and one or two are beginning to take the view that life on the dole supplemented by some undeclared earnings might provide an alternative to seeking legitimate jobs which are increasingly difficult to find. Thus some long-term unemployed assert that, because they are so bored and poor, they are willing to consider doing the double, should opportunities permit and despite the possibilities of being caught. Having said that, the organization of the local economy is not yet producing sufficient jobs in the informal sectors which Eastlough people can take advantage of.

Ray Pahl has characterized British society subsequent to World War II by noting how households have a limited and narrow view of work as factory employment. They are 'completely socialised to the time and work disciplines of industrial capitalism' and have 'lost the means of getting by with a household work strategy' (1984: 57; cf. Kumar, 1984: 210, 218). Although Pahl admits that this description is probably overdrawn for many parts of the UK, it does seem accurately to reflect conditions in east Belfast. Overwhelmingly, male manual workers are wedded to the notion that a realistic wage from legitimate employment (supplemented by the wage of a part-time or full-time working spouse) is by far the most acceptable method of financing households. In sum, the minds of Eastlough male workers are directed to well-paid, skilled and unskilled, jobs in high-status manufacturing and engineering firms. Since long-term and pervasive unemployment is a relatively new phenomenon in east Belfast, working-class men are not attuned to the possibilities of a different mix of 'earning' strategies, and present

Table 9. *Numbers of people experiencing unemployment by age and present employment status, for Eastlough as a whole, and core samples (in brackets)*

	Unemployed		Employed	
	20–35 years	36–50 years	20–35 years	36–50 years
No previous unemployment	14(4)	25(6)	42(4)	88(7)
Previous unemployment[a]	26(6)	20(4)	69(5)	41(4)

Notes:
[a] 'Previous unemployment' defined as at least one involuntary spell without work, lasting four months or more, and occurring within the past 10 years.

Table 10. *Eastlough core samples: aggregate totals (in years) of previous and present unemployment spells (includes all unemployment ever experienced), by age and present employment status*

	Unemployed				Employed			
	20–35 years		36–50 years		20–35 years		36–50 years	
Previous unemployment	8	n = 10	6[a]	n = 10	6	n = 9	4.5	n = 11
Present unemployment	27.75		23		—		—	

Notes:
[a] This figure includes four years of unemployment experienced by a single individual.

conditions do not appear to presage much change in this orientation.

The 1979–83 recession produced a marked change in the working experience of Eastlough residents. The underlying cause of this can be seen in the figures for previous spells of unemployment for two age categories. As the figures in tables 9 and 10 graphically demonstrate, previous experience of unemployment is not only proportionately higher, it is also absolutely higher for the under-35s than for the over-35s, and this is true for those presently in work and for those presently unemployed.

Moreover, the older groups have experienced relatively short spells of previous unemployment (typically between three months and one year), whereas in the younger group many have already been unemployed for over one year and some for over three years, in addition to having suffered previous spells of considerable length. This is reflected in the fact that the older group, having entered the labour market in the period 1945 to 1965 when unemployment was historically very low, see the present situation as one of unusual severity but one which might improve, though the unemployed are less sanguine than those in work. For the younger group, on the other hand, present circumstances are not unduly untypical and many have begun to speak of unemployment as a 'way of life', as an almost inevitable concomitant of growing up. I would argue, however, that the young are not being socialized into jobless-ness, both because the contemplation of very prolonged periods with-out employment is an extremely bleak prospect, and because there is no rational alternative, as a method of obtaining money, to getting a legitimate job. If an alternative exists, it is life on benefit supplemented by undeclared earnings from doing the double. But on balance it is the older groups with the better skills, contacts, knowledge, and experi-ence, who are better placed to exploit this possibility.

There is little evidence, therefore, of any marked changes in the high value placed on paid employment amongst the young. The values of the older unemployed are largely intact, since they still see their salvation as depending on securing a job in the same firms in which they once worked. Benefits provide a subsistence living in unemployment, and doing the double, even for those with marketable skills, is not consid-ered to be a serious long-term option to legitimate employment. Oppor-tunities to do the double arise in the normal course of events and not because they have been solicited. Inferior in status to legitimate employment, morally dubious and dangerous, doing the double is seen as at best a temporary expedient to financial hardship. The unemployed of Eastlough, skilled and unskilled, young and old, from manufacturing or other sectors, continue to endorse 'traditional' employment values and still retain some hope of a recovery. At least there are firms to which they can and do submit application forms; it is still rational to ask kin and friends to keep an eye and an ear open; jobs are still advertised; and friends and acquaintances do sometimes strike lucky. The continued existence of historically famous establishments, their recent capacity to absorb large numbers of the labour force, the substantial numbers still employed by them, and the procedures necessary for gaining entry into them, legitimate, preserve, and reproduce not only the orientations and life-styles of those in work but also those who are seeking employment.

Mallon Park

In many ways the situation in Mallon Park and in Catholic west Belfast generally is quite different. Referring again to table 8, it is obvious where some of these differences lie. It is very unlikely that the unemployment rates for any of its areas are below 50 per cent, and it is not over-dramatic to say, as do some of the residents, that the formal economy has all but disintegrated. Of the 441 male heads-of-household in the estate, only thirty-four still have jobs in manufacturing, and many of these are not actually located in Catholic west Belfast. Of the core sample of unemployed, nine had manufacturing jobs, and while one is back in work as a street cleaner, the other eight remain officially unemployed (all for at least two years). The other eleven of this sample come from a variety of work backgrounds (security, barman, binman, chef, driver, nurse, labourer, and four in construction) of whom only one, the chef, is back in work.

The manufacturing workers of Mallon Park are in a quite different situation to their counterparts in Eastlough, since whereas manufacturing industry is still functioning in east Belfast it has disappeared almost entirely from west Belfast. With the recent fiasco at Delorean (the luxury car maker) and the closure of the mills, bakeries, and other large establishments (as well as many small ones put out of business during the Troubles) there is now no large manufacturing or engineering firm in west Belfast. Mallon Park residents therefore have few of those infrastructural supports to shape and sustain attitudes and orientations to formal employment that still exist for Eastlough residents.

If residents assert that the formal economy of west Belfast has all but collapsed, many also aver that it is those doing the double who prevent it collapsing altogether. If the east Belfast economy is dominated by large-scale manufacturing and engineering companies and public administration, the west Belfast economy is fragmented, with large numbers of small enterprises and numerous small retail outlets. In addition to public services (post-office, hospital, council services, etc.), the area is replete with small clubs, back-street garages, private taxi firms run from homes or temporary cabins, small building firms (less than five employees), office and school cleaners, security guards, street traders, scrap dealers, and many more. Many of the people employed in these establishments are part time, many are female, and many are either registered unemployed or are women married to unemployed men.

Doing the double in Mallon Park

For Eastlough it was argued that several factors restrict the scale of opportunities for doing the double. Whilst there are proportionately and absolutely far fewer jobs in west Belfast than in east Belfast, proportionately more people are able to do a double. This is because a number of converging factors facilitate the practice. First, as already mentioned, the local economy is fragmented, dispersed and unco-ordinated. There are no dominant industries which require a large number of supply firms. Second, there are opportunities for getting work over the border in the Republic of Ireland. Third, there tends to be greater moral acceptance of doing the double by the local population. Fourth, policing of west Belfast by DHSS fraud investigators poses difficult problems. Finally, it is likely that the para-militaries are involved at some level in organizing and allocating certain types of jobs.

From the core sample, of those from manufacturing Dennis Flynn is back in work, four have never done the double, but four have. Of these latter, Danny Chapman worked six or seven days a week for three months in the Republic; Gerry Daly scavenges at a local dump for scrap metal; Matt Davis worked six days a week for six months, whereupon the job ended; and Gerry Murray repairs cars when he wants to. Of the remaining eleven, Billy Stewart is back in work, Joe McCartney has disabled children and spends most of his time with them, Pat Hardy is studying for a university place, and eight are doing or have done the double. Of these, Martin Cavanagh has worked as a street trader and bar doorman, Kevin Hurley assists a friend on a market stall, Frank Connolly has a six-night-a-week job as a private taxi-driver, Brian O'Neil helps on a coal-delivery business, and four work in construction. However, only the taxi driver can be said to have a full-time job in the sense that it could become viable, legitimate employment. In sum, from this sample there are twelve who are or have done a double. This is virtually the same as the Eastlough figure, but the periods worked are longer and the sums of money earned are greater. Of those who have not done the double this is either for practical reasons or for lack of opportunities; only Ray Carlile and Pat McVeigh feel that the practice is corrupt and even these confer only mild opprobrium on those who engage in it, reserving their scorn for the system which produces it.

In addition to these cases I have substantial evidence (corroborated from at least two independent sources) on others in the estate who do or have done the double. Most of these are in service-sector jobs or construction. The service sector in fact provides limited opportunities to all categories of worker. Whilst many of the jobs depend on contacts and personal knowledge, many are also self generated, and carried out on an individualistic basis.

The construction industry is generally considered to be the great provider of 'jobs for the boys', and Mallon Park is no exception. Precise figures for this sector cannot be given, since the situation changes rapidly. Evidence suggests that a significant minority of unemployed construction workers in Mallon Park are actually working at any one

Table 11. *Number of housing starts for each financial year for east Belfast and Catholic west Belfast*

	1980–1	1981–2	1982–3	1983–4	1984–5	Total
East Belfast	113	423	299	255	91	1181
Catholic west Belfast	152	287	183	502	153	1277
Total	265	710	482	757	244	2458

Source: Northern Ireland Housing Executive Research Department.

time. Only a small number of skilled tradesman (electricians, plumbers, joiners, etc.) are in virtual full-time jobs. Some in the wet trades (bricklayers, painters, and plasterers) work a double for sub-contractors or in small gangs of their own doing repair and renovation of private housing. Others obtain work irregularly and some just do odd jobs locally. Aside from those factors, already listed, which affect the structure of opportunities for doing the double in all sectors of the west Belfast economy, there are two which are specific to the construction industry.

First, because of its erratic and seasonal nature, the industry lends itself to casual labour. A reliable indicator of this is the number of public authority housing starts. Table 11 provides figures for both east Belfast and Catholic west Belfast for the five financial years beginning April 1980. The figures for Catholic west Belfast do not include the 1,400 houses built on the Poleglass site. When these are taken into account, housing starts in west Belfast over the last five years are 250 per cent higher than east Belfast, providing construction workers with correspondingly more jobs in that part of the city. This is not to say that only Catholics work on these sites, since many of the houses have been built by firms from other areas of the Province.

The fluctuations in housing starts are clearly evident and influence the kinds of work and earning strategy that construction workers adopt. For example, if an unemployed worker is offered a job for a short period, he may continue to declare himself unemployed. Indeed, the employer may well demand that he remains officially unemployed. In this way the worker obtains a good addition to his benefit and circumvents the process of signing on again, which can result in subsequent benefit being delayed or incorrect. By playing the system to his own advantage (or by being forced into doing a double) the chances of being caught are small, and a considerable sum of money can be made.

Second, there has been a steady increase in the industry of the use of labour-only sub-contracting (LOSC) squads which cannot be controlled in the same manner as the direct employees of a firm. These circumstances led to a situation in the Province in the 1970s of firms finding it difficult to recruit employees directly, despite a large total of registered unemployed in the industry. To investigate this problem, the Northern Ireland Federation of Building and Civil Engineering Contractors in 1977 enlisted a consultancy company to carry out a random survey of thirty of the Federation's member companies (P.A. Management Consultants, 1977). At this time some 35,000 men were employed in the industry and over 13,000 further were registered as unemployed. The survey, based on a questionnaire answered mainly by senior management (its methodology and findings have been the source of considerable controversy), reported that various forms of malpractice were rife in the house-building sector, and particularly in high-risk areas such as west Belfast, Derry, Craigavon, Newry, and Strabane. Without going into details the report points to collusion between main contractors, sub-contractors and employees.

The main forms of abuse can be listed as follows: (1) A sub-contractor recruits a squad of men to supply labour-only to a contractor. The former is paid partly in cash, and he then pays in the same way his own men, some or all of whom are registered unemployed. Thus a sub-contractor may employ legally a small gang for whom he can provide enough work on a year-round basis, but needs to employ extra labour on the double as and when needed. There is therefore a select elite in continuous work in the formal economy and a reserve pool in and out of work in the black economy. (2) A sub-contractor unlawfully acquires (perhaps through a para-military organization) the use of a tax-exemption certificate. When paid, he receives the gross rather than the net (of tax) amount. In this case he can pocket both his own and his employees' income taxes. If he does not pay these taxes he is constrained to use as labour only those willing to do the double. (3) Unemployed tradesmen work for individuals who are willing to pay cash. This may be a private house-holder wanting a washing machine plumbed in or a supermarket requiring its walls tiled. (4) A direct employee takes sick leave and then does work elsewhere in the industry, or for private individuals.

The report concludes by arguing that a minimum of 2,000 of the estimated 7,000 employed in the LOSC sector are working the double at some time during the year. When estimates for those working on their own or in small gangs for private individuals are taken into account, the report suggests that the number of people involved is considerable, rising possibly to 50 per cent of unemployed construction workers in some high-risk areas. I do not have sufficient evidence to corroborate or dispute the accuracy of these figures, but it should be borne in mind that the report itself does not present adequate evidence to support such 'guesstimates', and that consequently they must remain speculative.

The cumulative result of these practices, however, is clearly one which puts legitimate firms at a disadvantage, because by paying statutory taxes and overheads they cannot compete effectively. Smaller firms particularly are constrained to indulge in malpractice. In effect the various practices of employers, sub-contractors, and employees in the construction industry entail that construction workers have just as great a difficulty as workers in other sectors of finding jobs in the formal economy. However, the former group are better placed for getting work in the black economy.

These findings can be supported by statistics from the DHSS. In 1982, for example, when there were 107,000 people registered as unemployed, 6,640 benefit claims were examined by fraud investigators (since only certain categories of claimants, tradesmen mostly, were selected, the sample was a biased one and extrapolations from it are not possible), of which 1,294 were recommended for prosecution (Northern Ireland Assembly, 1984). Of these 990 involved doing the double (either hushand or wife), 764 were prosecuted, and 747 convicted. In addition eighty-four employers were successfully convicted of collusion. Both categories received equivalent forms of punishment: fines ranging up to £100, indicating that the state is unconcerned about the situation. Further, from a sample of 345 cases sent to the Department of Public Prosecution in 1982, 92.5 per cent concerned doing the double (94 per cent were male and 95 per cent married). More significantly, the types of work involved were: building trades (34 per cent), driving (11.3 per cent), labouring (10 per cent), sales and shops (10 per cent), bar work (2 per cent), and farm work (2 per cent).

Overall then, doing the double is the major form of social security fraud in Belfast, and it is mainly to be found in the house-building sector of the construction industry. It must be reiterated, however, that even in west Belfast only a small number of registered unemployed are working on a full-time basis. The great majority of those doing the double are employed irregularly and/or part-time; and the young, the old, the unskilled, and those with few contacts have great difficulty in finding openings. In other words, most of these black-economy jobs do not in themselves provide remuneration which can remotely substitute for social security benefits, and therefore they are not viable alternatives to life on the dole. In most instances they are feasible only because the people doing them are unemployed and have the safety cushion of their benefits. The income derived from these various types of work is in fact conceived of as a supplement, not as a rival, to benefit income. Aside from the low wages this work commands, such doubles are also characterized by their temporary nature, irregularity, unsocial hours, rapid emergence and disappearance, insecurity, and lack of safety.

Given the extent of unemployment in Mallon Park it is small wonder that many describe it as a 'way of life'; only slightly less surprising is the fact that doing the double is similarly characterized: 'the double is the only way to make a living. The way I look at it, it would take me to be coming home with over £100 and there's no jobs like that now' (Tony Madden). As with other marginal ways of life, this one too fosters anecdotes, jokes, and apocryphal stories. There are other indications of its status of a 'way of life': 'Some people are so blatant you don't realize what they're up to. It was only when I went into her house and saw her trying to hide [her husband's] bru card [the unemployment signing-on card] that I found out [he was doing the double]' (from the wife of Pat Ward about one of her neighbours). The lengths to which a few people go to retain both incomes sometimes defy belief. Ray McGrath, a bricklayer, who does the double whenever he can, informed me of a neighbour who has been doing the same on a more or less regular basis. According to Ray, his neighbour recently went to a Third World country on a short-term contract, pipe-laying. Rather than sign off the register, he took the chance of getting a friend to sign on for him while he was abroad.[2]

Some people turn to doing a double very quickly and with apparent alacrity (given opportunities, of course). Frank Connolly and Brian O'Neil, from the core sample, had a double within weeks of being paid off. Two other men, not in this sample, both working for the same sub-contractor, were paid off by agreement with their employer, only to be taken on again the following week on the double. Some, having been doing the double on and off for a long period of time, consider being caught as little more than an occupational hazard. Many, though, are worried about being caught and hence are cautious over aspects of their life. Working routines are varied so that neighbours cannot know for sure whether a person is working or not; claims for grants are less frequently made to avoid having benefit officers calling at inconvenient times; children are schooled to be inscrutable about what their parents do. Given these facts there is a subtle but definite change in the way some people arrange their lives; there is an air of subterfuge about it, a different way of thinking about jobs and benefits, and while 'everyone knows what's going on' doing the double is not usually a topic for open conversation.

With the exception of those few doing almost full-time doubles in recognized trades, such activities are rarely classified as 'jobs'; they are seen rather as means of survival, as enabling people to get by (the terms used to describe it are all euphemistic: 'double', 'a touch', 'a turn', 'the other thing', 'working out of two holes', etc.). According to almost everyone who is unemployed, whether doing the double or not, the 'bru' is thought to be entirely inadequate. Frank Connolly, the taxi-driver, summed up the feelings of many in typically brutal fashion: 'the bru, fucking useless, that to the bru' (embellished with an obscene gesture). The clear message is that benefit income is not a substitute for wages but is something which itself has to be supplemented.

Attitudes to doing the double vary, but distinctive themes are detectable. A small minority in legitimate jobs condemn it virulently. The majority, however, accept it as part of life in west Belfast: 'You're forced into it, what else can you do? There's no legit jobs and the assistance is no fucking good' (Gerry Collins, ex-tiler, now a postman, who used to do a double); '[doing the double] isn't wrong. In the eyes of the law its wrong, but the people making the laws aren't living on the bru. We're supposed to live on it every week' (Danny Chapman).

Another theme concerns the self-imputed stupidity of those in jobs: 'Look at us, Brian's working his guts out, but we can't afford to go out or run a car like them'uns' (from the wife of Brian McCallister, referring to her brother who does a double as a night security guard). And this is echoed by the unemployed: 'I'd say anyone who didn't [do a double] was a fool. Well, like, I'm working for my family, you know what I mean' (Eddie McCann).

Perhaps paradoxically, those doing the double receive grudging admiration; seen as astute and clever they know how to take full advantage of prevailing conditions; they get the best deal by exploiting the situation: 'See, if you're on the bru getting £80, £90 a week, and you touch for a wee turn, say £50 a week, that's £140. You tell me where you're gonna get that in a legit job. Sure, I'd do it if I had the chance' (Eddie Canavan, a school caretaker). Those in better-paid jobs actually commend the unemployed for doing a double since at least it shows a willingness to work, and, although there are exceptions, their complaint tends to echo that of the unemployed themselves, that no one with a family can afford to take the kinds of jobs available as the pay is so low. On one point there is almost unanimous agreement, that the whole system is 'up the left'. It is the 'system' which is to blame, not individuals. In a 'dog eat dog' world it stands to reason that those who are in a position to do so will take advantage of any opening which presents itself, and in Catholic west Belfast a number of converging factors generate significant opportunities.

In discussing the Eastlough situation I noted that the recent (and continuing) recession produced a major change in the working experience of its residents. Data on previous unemployment and on aggregate totals of previous and contemporary spells of unemployment were presented to reflect this (tables 9, 10). For example, in the older, employed category, 68 per cent have experienced no unemployment, but in the younger employed category only 38 per cent have never been unemployed. Again, the older employed group from the core sample (n = 11) have experienced a total of 4.5 years of unemployment during their working lives. In contrast the younger group (n = 9) have already accumulated six years, and the younger unemployed group (n = 10) have grossed eight years of previous unemployment and 27.75 years of present unemployment. Despite this appalling increase in both the rates and the duration of unemployment, little evidence was found of a change in 'traditional' evaluations and methods of how to finance households.

Presented below (tables 12, 13) are equivalent figures for Mallon Park residents. What these demonstrate is a more gradual decline, but from a position that already was a good deal worse than that in Eastlough. Thus in all categories, young and old, unemployed and employed, there are more people who have experienced previous spells of unemployment than have not. In addition, in the core samples Mallon Park residents have experienced more unemployment in total than their Eastlough counterparts in all categories save one, the young unemployed group, who are each enduring on average a present spell of unemployment of slightly under three years. It is such conditions which support the contention that some Mallon Park residents have given up the formal economy altogether and have generated in response new notions of how to get by whilst unemployed. This entails using welfare benefits as a base on which to build by taking, whenever possible, jobs in the black economy. In other words, for many in Mallon Park unemployment is no longer seen as an *interruption* of a normal working life. On the contrary, it is beginning to be seen as a permanent condition imposed externally by a permanently depressed economy.

Discussion: Mallon Park and Eastlough compared

The local economies of west Belfast and east Belfast are, in certain respects, very different. Levels of employment by sector and levels of total unemployment in the two areas clearly reflect this. These two local economies exhibit quite different opportunity structures in both the formal labour market and also for jobs in the black economy. Manufacturing workers in Eastlough appear to be better placed than their

Table 12. *Numbers of people experiencing unemployment by age and present employment status, for Mallon Park as a whole, and core samples (in brackets)*

	Unemployed		Employed	
	20–35 years	36–50 years	20–35 years	36–50 years
No previous unemployment	47(5)	35(4)	39(5)	25(4)
Previous unemployment[a]	111(9)	56(2)	80(6)	48(5)

Notes:
[a] 'Previous unemployment' defined as at least one involuntary spell without work, lasting four months or more, and occurring within the past ten years.

Table 13. *Mallon Park core samples: aggregate totals (in years) of previous and present unemployment spells (includes all unemployment ever experienced), by age and present employment status*

	Unemployed				Employed			
	20–35 years		36–50 years		20–35 years		36–50 years	
Previous unemployment	16	n = 14	6	n = 6	9	n = 11	12	n = 9
Present unemployment	37		15.5		—		—	

counterparts in Mallon Park. But such divergencies do not exist to the same extent in other sectors. In construction, both Catholics and Protestants find it equally hard to secure permanent legitimate jobs. In the informal sector, Mallon Park has more construction workers than Eastlough, but also more opportunities for doing the double. In the service sector, the differences between the two areas are harder to pin down.

The dominant orientation amongst Eastlough workers is the demand for legitimate jobs in the formal sector. Welfare benefits are perceived as a low-status and inadequate substitute for wages from a proper job. For men 'work' is what is done for an employer at his place of employment in return for wages; and it remains one of the most significant factors in producing and maintaining an acceptable self-identity. The argument is that the local economy in east Belfast furnishes the conditions (even in times of depression) within which prevailing attitudes and practices of both employed and unemployed are likely to be reproduced over time.

A reflection of the dominance of the ideology of legitimate employment is the evaluation of doing the double as morally dubious and as a temporary expedient. Presenting few opportunities, doing the double does not constitute a viable alternative for financing households. Here the overriding view is that, although benefits are perceived as wholly inadequate, all that one can realistically do is hang on, tighten one's belt, and wait for an up-turn.

In west Belfast manufacturing jobs are virtually non existent and jobs in other sectors very difficult to obtain. The unemployed in Mallon Park can be divided into three broad categories: the few who enjoy both a benefit income and earnings from a virtual full-time double; the many who have no option but to exist entirely on benefits; and an indeterminate number who have established a mix of incomes (from benefits and from either or both husband's and wife's income from doing a double).

For all the unemployed in Mallon Park legitimate jobs have declined in number, but for some they have also declined in importance and status. The practice of doing the double has attained a fairly high degree of moral acceptance, and some people assert they will never again take a legitimate job. For some of the unemployed benefits are becoming an acceptable source of income, but an income which has to be augmented if dire poverty is to be avoided. Benefit income is, therefore, not a substitute for wages but rather a base on which to build. Though most doubles are viable only because the people doing them are in receipt of benefit, this income supplemented by that from a double can leave some unemployed not only better off than they would be in a (presently available) legitimate job, but better off than they have ever been in any legitimate job. Unemployed people have not lost their commitment to *work*; on the contrary this is very strong indeed. What they are modifying is the notion that households can only be financed by legitimate *employment*. Clearly this is a cultural adaptation to the material necessities of prevailing labour-market conditions, but one that could easily be reversed should these improve. My point is not that they do not want to work in the formal economy – they clearly do – but that present circumstances supply no incentives for maintaining such a desire.

Thus far I have argued that differences in the two local economies, and the consequent differences in their opportunity structures, are important factors in the creation of divergent attitudes and ideas concerning jobs, benefits, earnings, and in general the nature of economic reality. These ideas can be seen as residents' cultural constructions of the way the economy works, historically shaped by forces generated in both the local, and in the wider UK, economy. Whilst this form of explanation provides insight into the present situation such a deterministic analysis is, in itself, inadequate. Although individually the working-class residents of these two estates wield very little control over what happens in the local economies from which they strive to gain their livelihood, nevertheless economic reality is not apprehended directly but is mediated by cultural schemas, some of which are only contingently related to the economy. Thus what they think and do can have long-range, cumulative consequences in shaping the opportunity structures of this economy in particular ways. Thus, taking the long historical view, it is only too clear that the configuration of the Northern Ireland economy as a whole is an outcome of complex relations of power, themselves partly dependent on perceived differences between Gael and Planter and hence between 'native' Catholics and 'incomer' Protestants.

At this point let me, very briefly, recapitulate the industrial history of Belfast, outlined in chapter 2. Despite the fact that there is controversy concerning the precise combination of forces which produced the distinctive shape of the Northern Ireland economy, the main lineaments of its development are relatively clear. Some writers stress how Protestant political and business elites and the Orange Order controlled investment and job allocation and thereby manipulated sectarian divisions (Farrell, 1976; Devlin, 1981). Others note the importance and strength of the Protestant workforce and how it could influence industrialists, against their wishes, to hire only Protestant labour (Millar, 1978; Patterson, 1980). When the famines of the 1840s forced many Catholics into Belfast they entered a city in which much of the industry was already Protestant owned, controlled, and manned. In the formative period of Irish industrialization, but including post-1945 capital restructuring, it was some combination of Protestant elites, the Protestant skilled workforce, the Orange Order, and the strategic location of Belfast, which partly accounted for the flow of investment and jobs along sectarian lines. While this is an over-simplified sketch, nonetheless it is no coincidence that the greatest chunk of industry in Ireland is in the north-east of Northern Ireland, the heartland of traditional Protestant loyalism.[3]

Once consolidated through the nineteenth and twentieth centuries, the economy came to be seen, particularly by Protestants, as objectively constituted and viewed as independent of, and hence outside the control of, most of those who worked in it, but especially those at the lower end of the occupational ladder. For these reasons the type of analysis required is one which stresses that to some degree the beliefs and practices of ordinary working people are situational adaptations to the exigencies of the material conditions of their lives, but one which also takes seriously the view that these material conditions are themselves culturally constructed in patterned ways and are not wholly determined by external forces in any straightforward manner.

In general many features of social, economic, and political life in Northern Ireland are crucially affected by the sectarian divide (Harris, 1972; Burton, 1978). Thus the residents of Eastlough overwhelmingly support and vote for either the Official Unionist Party or Paisley's Democratic Unionist Party (DUP), both of which are staunch loyalist parties, and neither of which has very much to say about the economy or unemployment (Nelson, 1984: 137–9). The Labour Party in Northern Ireland has never been very successful and though it tried to resurrect itself in the 1985 local elections few people in Eastlough voted for it. Mallon Park Catholics vote for either the Social Democratic and Labour Party or, since 1980, Sinn Fein. Generally, politics in the Province is based on sectarian ideology, and economic issues take second place to those concerning north/south relations, Catholic/Protestant relations, and Northern Ireland/UK relations.

It may be repeated here that several of the factors, mentioned earlier, which influence people's perceptions of doing the double are not primarily economic, but are in fact aspects of the sectarian divide. Thus, for example, there is a pervasive belief in Eastlough that doing the double is very risky because the estate is riddled with potential informers who, it is thought, receive a reward for information leading to a conviction. Residents say, for example, that only kin can be trusted not to betray one. Hence people do not tell their neighbours what they are doing in case, out of jealousy and greed, they inform. Most of the unemployed, and many of the employed too, can point to someone who has been 'shopped' (the same cases tend to crop up repeatedly) and to one particular man who has a diabolical reputation for having, at one go, 'squealed' on between thirty and forty people ('he bought a car soon after' so the story goes). Such ideas are current in Mallon Park but are less significant for, as Burton notes, 'the distaste for informing runs very deep in Irish history' (1978: 35). However, in those few cases known to me of people caught doing a double, the victims have always blamed jealous neighbours. Whilst Catholics do not have much to say about Protestants on this issue, the latter are in general agreement that Catholics are less likely to inform on others, and that in some way Catholics are more solidary: 'they stick together more than we do'.

Additionally, most Eastlough unemployed people think DHSS investigators watch them more closely than they watch west Belfast Catholics because, it is assumed, they are too frightened to lurk about in dangerous

Republican areas such as Ballymurphy, Turflodge, and the Falls Road. So, as far as Protestants are concerned, doing the double in west Belfast is a 'way of life'; because they can get away with it, Catholics will do the double rather than work legitimately. In Eastlough people say that DHSS 'snoops' sit in cars, even in trees, keeping a watch on suspects; they take photographs, follow people, and interview them on the dangers of working while claiming. None of this, it is imagined, could take place in west Belfast.

The sectarian divide is also very influential in shaping people's perceptions of the labour market. For many in Mallon Park if a job is not in Catholic west Belfast or close by safe areas, such as the city centre, then it is not in the labour market. For example, it is reported by Cormack, Osborne, and Thompson (1980: 39) that labour mobility figures for Belfast 'reveal that the two sectors which show the smallest out-movement are Catholic West Belfast and (predominantly Protestant) East Belfast' (cf. chapter 2). If large numbers of co-religionists are involved, Catholics will work in potentially hostile Protestant 'territory', as they did in Delorean, although this is very close to the southern edge of Catholic west Belfast.[4]

During the research, the air-craft company Short Bros., in east Belfast, was awarded a large contract by an American firm, provided it tried to improve its Protestant/Catholic workforce ratio. The company advertised widely, announcing it would welcome applications from Catholics. Mallon Park had many unemployed who were potential applicants, but even though the firm reputedly pays some of the highest wages in Belfast, of those known to me only two applied. In discussion, all gave similar reasons for not applying. It was too far to travel (two bus journeys each way), and too dangerous both to work there and to travel there. It was also considered a waste of time since, despite the exhortations, Catholics would not get the jobs, or if they did they would be the worst ones, and they would quickly be intimidated out of those. Protestants, naturally, applied in large numbers (many had already worked for Short's and been laid off in the recession). They argued that not only were there now as many unemployed Protestants as unemployed Catholics, but also that these jobs were Protestant jobs: 'we don't go over there taking their jobs so they've no right coming here to take ours'. Protestants equally do not like to travel outside their own areas to get jobs and certainly will not go anywhere near west Belfast. Somewhat inconsistently, Protestants attest that there are very few legitimate jobs in west Belfast since the bombings have put everyone out of business. Simply, each side wants to work in its own areas and only feels really comfortable when doing so.

That each side feels a proprietary right to the jobs in its own area was starkly revealed in the summer of 1986 when the overwhelmingly Protestant workforce of Short's threatened to strike if the company's management insisted on the removal of Orange emblems, Unionist badges, Union Jacks, and sundry other symbols of Ulster loyalism, which were festooned all over its factories. The workers claimed it was a Protestant firm loyal to the Union and that they had the right to announce this even if it offended the Catholics who also work there (and who live in small Catholic enclaves in the inner city and east Belfast). The workforce, by its vehement opposition, was also implicated in the suspension of plans to set up a supply factory on the old Delorean site, which was destined to be manned by both Catholics and Protestants but the latter argued that those jobs should remain in east Belfast.

What these examples clearly suggest is that the notions of 'local economy' and 'local labour market' are themselves cultural constructions which both reflect and sustain the sectarian divide in Belfast. Donnan and McFarlane (1986a: 26) argue that there is 'a great deal of ignorance and misinformation apparent in the ideas which people in each bloc have about the other' but that these 'are not the causes of the division, [but rather] they are the products of it'. It may be similarly advanced that the ideas these Belfast residents have of their local labour markets are not caused by purely economic forces but are the outcome of sectarian ideology, not merely intruding into, but actively shaping economic life. Working-class Catholics and Protestants construe the Belfast economy as segregated into friendly and hostile zones, that is, into local economies and local labour markets. Once entrenched in this way, each side jealously guards the jobs in its own areas and is frightened, for good reason, to poach jobs in the areas dominated by the other side. This framework then provides the basis for a whole ideology concerning economic life in the city. That most working-class jobs in the city are concentrated in the Protestant parts of east Belfast is not a neutral economic fact, nor is it the cause of sectarianism. Historically the latter precedes by two centuries the industrialization of Ireland, and was and is implicated not only in the location of major manufacturing industry but also in the social, economic, and political infrastructure which serves it. Once industry was established, however, vested interests were created which served further to consolidate the division between Protestants and Catholics. Given such conditions, economic forces unleashed in other parts of the world sometimes affected these zones differently. Prior to the present recession, it was the linen and cotton industries which were badly mauled by periodic booms and slumps. Since the workforce was spread fairly evenly between the two religious blocs, both sides were battered in about equal measure. However, as described in chapter 2, the post-war re-structuring of industry moved manufacturing from the city to the growth towns of the Protestant north-east (i.e. greater Belfast). This is why the 1979–83 recession has had a traumatic affect on this section of the population. In other words, brute economic forces originating externally to the Northern Ireland economy affect it, and therefore its workforce, in ways structured by sectarian political economy. It is in fact true that a few Mallon Park residents do work in east Belfast companies (including Short's). But too many other Catholics have tales to tell of intimidation and physical beatings whilst employed in Protestant areas (before and during the Troubles, when segregation was less pronounced than now) for this to make much difference to prevailing ideas of what working conditions would be like for Catholics in east Belfast.

While Catholics argue that inequality in job opportunities is a function of conscious and entrenched discrimination, based on the Protestant need to defend an illegitimate state apparatus, Protestants reject this view, and even when, on occasion, they acknowledge the statistical imbalance in unemployment rates by religion, they explain it by recourse to other factors. Catholics, by their support of the IRA and its bombing campaigns, are accused of having destroyed their own jobs and the confidence of investors; they therefore have only themselves to blame. Moreover, Catholics, as initiators of the present Troubles, are deemed responsible for the loss of jobs everywhere in Northern Ireland, and thus deserve their fate. Stereotypically Catholics are described by Protestants as lazy, unreliable, and poor workers, which is contrasted to Protestant industriousness, skill, and reliability. These representations thus reproduce in the urban context those that have been widely reported in the literature on rural areas (Harris, 1972; Blacking et al., 1978; Donnan and McFarlane, 1986b). Finally, Protestants assert that Catholics, being lazy, do not want to work and are content not merely to live on the dole but actively to exploit it. But Catholics are also thought to be fond of doing the double. This is not as contradictory as it seems, since which stereotype is invoked depends on the context; the availability of both allows Catholics to be damned whether they work or not.

Furthermore, as I have just mentioned, by no means all Protestants concede that there are imbalances in unemployment rates by religion. This fact is supported by some startling findings from the recent Policy Studies Institute report on equality and inequality in Northern Ireland. D.J. Smith reports that 56 per cent of Catholics, compared with only 9 per cent of Protestants, say that Protestants have a better chance of having a job, and that this contrast is most extreme among Belfast working-class Protestants and Catholics (1987b: 139). Smith concludes that:

a possible explanation of these extraordinary findings is that unemployment has become the symbol of contention between Protestants and Catholics about social justice in the midst of sectarian divisions. For Catholics, the assertion that they have unequal access to jobs has become their cause. The great majority of Protestants oppose this cause by denying that it has any basis in fact. (1987b: 140)

What such data indicates is that Catholic explanations of unemployment are much more likely to take a macro-structural form focusing on discrimination and exclusion created by a Protestant state. In other words, Catholics are likely to export blame for unemployment outside their own areas and away from their own people. Because Protestants can have no recourse to a similar argument, explanations for Protestant unemployment are more likely to rest on ideas of deservingness and individual motivation and effort. In later chapters I will present a good deal of evidence to support these hypotheses.

Catholics of course stereotype Protestants. As Donnan and McFarlane note, 'Catholics contrast Protestant bigotry, narrow-mindedness, discrimination and money-centredness with their own tolerance, openness and interest in culture' (1986b: 386). The practices related to these stereotypes have a real impact on material conditions of existence, not necessarily in a direct and voluntaristic way, but in the sense that they have both immediate and long-term, unintended effects on wider social processes. Thus the conflict in views between Protestants and Catholics concerning the causes and consequences of discrimination was one of the issues which in 1969 sparked the Troubles, and today these beliefs and practices are instrumental in keeping Protestants in Protestant areas and Protestant jobs, and Catholics in Catholic areas and hence probably in unemployment, or if lucky, in a job on the side.

In this way, the actions of political and business elites together with the typical, culturally informed practices of ordinary working Catholics and Protestants have produced a situation in which the larger economy and labour market are divided into segregated zones; in which Protestants enjoy better employment prospects than Catholics; in which there is a higher representation of Protestants in better-paid, higher-skilled manufacturing jobs, leaving Catholics over-represented in the lower-paid, more insecure jobs in service and construction (Fair Employment Agency for Northern Ireland, 1978; Cormack et al., 1980; Aunger, 1983; Hepburn, 1983); and in which there is a greater proportion of unemployed Catholics over Protestants. The fact that during the present recession Protestants have begun to suffer massive unemployment is interpreted by them as showing that they are just as much victims of blind economic forces as are Catholics, and hence they have become even more concerned to protect the jobs that are left in their own areas.[5]

These emergent conditions are conceptualized differently by the two sides. While social and historical data indicate that the beliefs and practices of both communities, and the imbalance of economic and political power between them, contribute to building and maintaining the present situation, this appears to Protestants as an objective and legitimate structure of opportunity and restraint. If an inequality between the two sides is recognized, this is attributed to the personal characteristics of Catholics themselves, and the facts that a disproportionate number are unemployed and that many do the double serve merely to corroborate the stereotypes Protestants have of Catholics. On the other hand, while perceived constraints and restricted opportunities prevent Protestants doing the double to more than a limited extent, the possibility of a return to higher rates of employment, and therefore the prospect of high rates of pay, keeps them oriented to legitimate jobs and hence reinforces their image of themselves as honest, hard-working loyalists.

Catholics differ in their conceptualization of this situation to the extent that they do not confer legitimacy either on the Northern Irish state or on the economic conditions which are partly a product of it, but rather attribute present and past imbalances to naked discrimination which Protestants have to practise to defend this state structure. Nevertheless the majority feel that there is nothing, or very little, that can be done about this, at least in the short term. Whether Catholics' assertions about individual discrimination are accurate or not, they act as though they are and will not in general trespass into Protestant territory to seek work, both out of fear for their physical safety and in their secure belief that anyway they would not be offered work. Such beliefs and behaviour can only reinforce the effects of indirect and institutional employment discrimination. Thus, even though Catholics are unwilling to legitimate this economic situation, and even though the constraints upon them as far as the formal economy is concerned are very burdensome, nonetheless what they think and what they do contributes, albeit indirectly, to their own exclusion from certain types of employment and from areas where employment prospects are better.

In sum, the argument is that sectarianism, involving a relationship of domination and subordination of Planter over Gael, later to be transformed into the Protestant/Catholic divide, preceded the industrial revolution, and hence provided the cultural framework within which the form, structure, and geography of the modern economy was established. Once installed, the economy generated large-scale (largely Protestant) vested interests which were both sustained by and helped to strengthen further the sectarian ideology, and thus deepen the divide. With the progressive physical separation, in greater Belfast, of the two populations, local economies and local labour markets were created. These then served to establish dominant orientations to the kinds of jobs and labour opportunities available to the two sides: construction and unskilled labour for the Catholics, and manufacturing and skilled trades for the Protestants. What happens in the wider economy is then always experienced locally through this cultural apparatus. Brute economic forces originating externally to the Northern Ireland economy affect this latter and thus also its workforce in ways shaped by sectarian conflict. With the virtual collapse of legitimate employment in west Belfast, Catholics have not reacted by attempting to raid jobs in Protestant strongholds, they assume this is 'impossible', but rather have either moved into the 'black' economy, which provides some with good opportunities, or simply remained unemployed. In train with this they are modifying their ideas on the evaluation of legitimate jobs, on the meaning of benefits, and on how to finance households. Eastlough Protestants on the other hand, while doing the double occasionally, have reacted to unemployment by tightening their belts and re-affirming their attitudes to legitimate employment and to the 'traditional' notions of work, wages, and benefits.

Chapter 4

Doing the double or doing without

Introduction

Since they were not designed to collect such information many surveys of the unemployed (Hill *et al.*, 1973; Daniel, 1974, 1981; White, 1984) have little to report on those working for undeclared income and claiming benefits. Data contained in other works are also rather sketchy. Morris argues that in Port Talbot *'occasional* work for undeclared income was relatively common' (1984b: 349; her italics), and that the incidence of such work correlates with patterns of social activity, those with dispersed or collective patterns of social contact being involved more than those with an individualistic pattern. Elsewhere (Morris, 1984a) she records that such additional sources of income tend to reinforce gender roles. Bostyn and Wight, working in Cauldmoss, Scotland, found that irregular work on the side is quite common, that it is not described significantly differently from legitimate work, and that obtaining it depends on social contacts, especially kin (1984: 61–4; cf. Turner *et al.*, 1985). Perhaps the best description available is still that provided by Marsden. According to him 'fiddling' generally starts when unemployed people have exhausted legitimate options and when financial and other pressures begin to escalate within the home. Work on the side removes the man from the house, furnishes constructive activity, and puts money in his pocket. On the debit side, such work is informally controlled by locals unwilling to see anyone do too well out of it. However, even small amounts of earned income, together with benefits, were coming to be seen by some of Marsden's informants as a viable alternative to formal employment (1982: 138–45, 198–200).

In all respects but the last this latter description fits the conditions and practices found in Eastlough. None of the core sample, save John Galbraith (the motor mechanic, who continued to do work for friends), did a double until some time after becoming unemployed. Even Jim Hughes and Tom Haslett, the only two to have done a double to any appreciable extent, did not begin until they had been unemployed at least a year and had endured considerable privation. In general the Eastlough unemployed do not entertain the idea of work on the side until other, traditional, avenues have been explored.

Being still strongly committed to the formal economy, their initial response after losing work was to enter the labour market in an active way. Those having little or no previous experience of unemployment initially envisaged only a short spell on the dole (Sinfield, 1981: 42). Even some of the unskilled had high hopes of obtaining work quickly despite their awareness that the level of unemployment was high and still rising. Such optimism was based on the belief, whilst in work, that those on the dole were scroungers habituated to the style of living they had chosen to adopt. Seeing themselves as deeply concerned with securing work, and therefore as different to those already unemployed, the newly unemployed had a self-image allowing them to think that they were a better prospect for employers. The skilled, particularly, expected only a short stay on the register: 'I thought, well, there's all these years experience I've got and being skilled I thought there'd be no problem. I didn't expect to walk into a job but I thought I'd touch lucky' (Alfie Peters); 'I thought I'd get back in right quick . . . Sure I knew there was a whole lot of unemployed, but to me they haven't the right attitude. They don't seem to want to work' (Roy Price). Consequently these men invested much time and energy seeking work: scanning the newspapers; personally contacting firms; completing application forms; occasionally visiting the city's main job centre. The skilled tended to be more focused in their search, going directly to the firms requiring their skills.

Whilst those still unemployed after six months continued to look for work in a desultory fashion using most of these methods, virtually all have dispensed with the job centre. It might be full of job specification cards, as many workers unfailingly point out, but the unemployed describe these as 'mickey-mouse' jobs: 'The only jobs that the job market is operating for are the people who work in it . . . the jobs that are advertised are jobs nobody wants . . . Anybody I have ever met has never got a job through the job centre' (Galbraith); 'I'm wastin' my time going up and down to these job centres; it's a total waste of time; everything that they have got, have got these written clauses, it seems one way or other to delete me' (Green, coach-builder). This is a litany repeated over and over again, and in even more scathing terms by the Catholics of Mallon Park. Some also have depressing tales to tell either of their own experience or that of their unemployed children, who have been sent to jobs that have already been filled or that in various ludicrous ways have been quite inappropriate.[1]

Those Eastlough unemployed who had already suffered a spell of unemployment were less sanguine about both their immediate and long-term prospects, and few bothered to visit the job centres even once. Two years of unemployment, however, is a great leveller and both young and old, skilled and unskilled, tend to settle down to a routine characterized by occasional bursts of job-hunting followed by long periods of quiescence. Indeed, many long-term unemployed had not applied for any job in the eight weeks prior to first contact, and some could not remember their last application (ignoring repeat applications to firms like Short Bros. or to the post office and bus companies). Some unemployed people apply for jobs only when prompted by friends or relatives revealing a possible opening or pointing to an advertisement in the press.

There is little point in detailing the double jobs which the Eastlough unemployed have done as they are, with a couple of exceptions, rather trivial. Most of those having done work on the side have only been engaged for short spells (three weeks at most) at long intervals and for comparatively little money. Such income, used mainly as collective expenditure, enables these families to subsist at a slightly higher level than others, and to keep debts down to manageable proportions.

Back to Mallon Park

Gerry Daly, married with two children, has a good working background. Although unemployed on previous occasions he has always managed to find a job. His last one, the best he had ever had, was in Delorean. But since redundancy he has given up looking for jobs in the formal economy:

I was always handy at getting a job, and I hunted and hunted for about weeks on end, application forms went everywhere and anywhere, and I says 'frig it, there just isn't any'; and from there I've just resigned myself to the fact there's no way there is going to be any.

Others in Mallon Park speak of job-hunting in much the same way, a frenetic burst of activity that serves merely to reveal the dreadful state of the labour market, followed by intermittent responses to other people's promptings. Some were already well aware of what was happening and knew that the job they had lost was likely to be the last for some time: 'In this country anybody over 30, 35, – no jobs, fuck all. They may as well hand you the pension book now' (Ray Carlile, unskilled, but wide experience in manufacturing). Despite having different ideas at the point of job loss, within a short time of becoming unemployed many entertain little prospect of getting another job. While some continue to be completely unemployed, some gravitate slowly to doing a double, and some make a beeline for it.

Some cases of the double

When Frank Connolly was sacked in 1983, he began his first spell of unemployment. Within weeks he was feeling desperate: 'There's no way I'm staying unemployed, no way. This supplementary is useless, there's no way I can make ends meet. I'm not going to stay unemployed. There's no money in it.' All the money coming into the house went to his wife, he had nothing for himself. He was bored, irritable, and surly. Very keen to work, he was uninterested in any job that did not pay a premium above the dole: 'I mean what's the use of me going out to work for the same as I'm getting on the dole, that's the whole point of going out to work, to earn money.'

Five weeks later, Frank, having purchased a second-hand Cortina with a loan from his mother-in-law, was taxiing for a private firm six nights a week. The organizer, living nearby, had been on the double but was now working legitimately. Eight of the seventeen other drivers were doing the double and came from all over west Belfast. 'The guy came down and said, "Frank, get yourself a motor and go taxiing." Why not? They're all making money so I just went ahead and did it. The common way of earning your living on the Falls Road is to do the double. It seems the only way to make money.'

Frank planned to remain on the dole until he had repaid the loan, obtained a Public Service Vehicle licence and could afford the high insurance premiums. But six months later Frank was driving a Granada, working days, earning around £100 a week and still signing on. Frank's case should not be taken as evidence that anyone with a car can manage a smooth entry into this profession. Most firms expect their drivers to have a driving background (which Frank had), and good personal contacts are needed to be hired by an existing firm. Additionally, west Belfast is now probably saturated with taxi firms, and the business has become so cut-throat that it has been known for a firm's control cabin to be bombed.

So long as Frank was out of the house and bringing in money his wife was not concerned about its origin. Frank too seemed unworried about being caught, as many of his neighbours knew what he was doing, despite his never telling them, and none of them had yet informed on him. And why should they, since some of them are on the double? Just across the street lives Mike Slattery who received £2,200 redundancy pay on losing his job. After a few weeks of unemployment he used this money to start a business, following his own trade (which cannot be identified), but this time on the double. Like Frank, he planned to become legitimately self-employed, but after eight months he was not earning enough to manage without the safety net of his benefit income. He is certain that at his age he will never get another job in his line of work, and equally sure that life on benefit is no life at all. Basing his view of the world largely on jungle metaphors, Mike sees life as a battle for survival and himself as the prime provider for his family. If he cannot get a job in the official economy and if benefits are so low as to make life intolerable then:

you're forced into doing the double. Its a dog-eat-dog world. I think life is like a jungle, and it's up to every individual to look after himself and his family, and if the government don't provide him with the opportunity to do it – especially when he's willing to work – I'd say 'yes, by all means, its morally OK'.

Brian O'Neil is another who quickly entered the black economy on becoming unemployed. A scaffolder by trade, he is used to frequent lay-offs due to the seasonal nature of the construction industry. Within weeks of registering as unemployed, a friend, who runs a legitimate coal-delivery business, asked Brian if he wanted some work driving the lorry. The wage of £40 a week was conditional on him doing the double. Brian agreed readily, as he needed the money to finance a holiday already booked. The next time I saw him he explained that his friend was considering the possibility of a full-time legitimate job which, while it paid less than scaffolding, would be more secure. On the basis of this, and to the disgust of his wife, he turned down an offer of an eight-week job in his usual trade. Two months later, now in the warm summer weather, he was working only two days a week for £20 and the chances of a permanent start were receding. They disappeared altogether when he was stopped by the police for driving while under the influence of alcohol.

Opportunities to do the double do not always come so easily, nor are they all so lucrative. Ray McGrath and Eddie McCann are in construction trades, both are in their late twenties, and both have been unemployed for more than two years. Neither has got anywhere near a legitimate job during that time, though both do the double irregularly. Ray is a standby worker for a self-employed man who uses Ray, on the double, for about £75 a week, whenever he needs an extra worker. Ray has never worked more than three weeks at a stretch in this way. Eddie McCann is a tiler who has had several small jobs tiling people's bathrooms and kitchens and once did a rather large supermarket. The fourth construction worker in the core sample, Joe Carlin, obtained his first double after a year's unemployment. This was through a friend who arranged for him to work in a squad of three men building yard walls and small domestic extensions in the Falls Road area. From this he has obtained nearly four months' work, the income from which has enabled him to decorate his house.

Danny Chapman, a welder by trade, got his one and only double nine months into his first spell of unemployment. One of his unemployed neighbours had been recruited to a squad of men to work on a building site in the Republic. As more men were needed, Danny and a second unemployed neighbour were asked to help out. They were all given transport to the south and each returned to Belfast the evening before their signing-on days (every fortnight) travelling back, expenses paid, the next evening. Working six or seven days a week, the job lasted three months and netted Danny over £1,500, much of which Danny spent on himself to relieve the boredom of living on a building site.

Gerry Daly, redundant from Delorean, did not work for a good while and then started to help pensioners with their gardens to combat boredom. Finding himself good at this, others asked him to do odd jobs for money. Just when he decided to buy new tools, the work dried up. He then joined forces with one of his brothers-in-law to collect scrap from a local dump. He has been doing this enthusiastically for several months, even buying wet-weather overalls so as to work every day. He can often be seen trudging home in the twilight, filthy from head to toe with a large heavy sack slung over his shoulder. He collects and sorts the scrap in his back yard, and at the end of each week borrows a van to take it to a scrap dealer in Belfast's Protestant Sandy Row area. The return on this work is not princely, rarely more than £35 for a sixty-hour week.

Because short-time working left him with take-home pay of under £60, Matt Davis accepted voluntary redundancy so he could pay off several outstanding debts. After five months of unemployment a neighbour told him of an opening in a new firm in Matt's line of work, and gave him a telephone number to call. He was hired straight away and asked to train a squad of inexperienced men, all of whom were cautioned that the jobs depended on their remaining on the dole for the first six months, to allow the venture time to succeed. Consequently, in addition to his supplementary benefit, Matt received £20 a day, six days a week, for nearly six months. For reasons unclear to Matt, the business collapsed just before he and the others were to go legitimate. Out of work again but with a new fireplace, new carpets, and money in his pocket, Matt could at least while away the afternoons in the snooker hall or the betting shop.

Martin Cavanagh, barman by trade, has been unemployed for four years. Two years ago he began street trading in the town's shopping centre, starting six or seven weeks before Christmas. The first few weeks saw a relatively small but increasing profit which he re-invested. By the last two weeks he would be selling ten hours a day, making up to £100 a week. Unfortunately, each year Martin has worked he has received an increasing number of small fines for trading without a licence. The fines themselves are not a major disincentive, but the charges come after repeated warnings from the police to move on and cease trading: 'the bastards come at you from all sides; I don't know whether I'm coming or going'. Additionally, earlier in the year he was offered, on the side, a part-time job as a bar doorman at a bar in which he once worked. After some months, however, his benefit was stopped and he was questioned at his local social security office. He is certain that a neighbour informed on him, but does not know who.

Wages, jobs, and benefits

Several themes shape the unemployed's ideas about the relation between jobs, wages, and benefits. When unemployed married men either in Mallon Park or Eastlough say there are no jobs, what they mean is that there are no jobs, reasonably available, in their own or related fields, in their own or nearby areas, and which pay enough to make it worthwhile for them to return to work. Many claim that they could probably get a job tomorrow, but it would not pay them. They argue forcefully that the only jobs on offer would leave them no better off than they already are on the dole. Simply, unemployed men with dependent families will rarely admit that they are willing to take a job that does not provide them with an income significantly greater than their benefits. The central aspect in their reasoning, stated very frequently, is that a wage must cover more than benefits:

I don't see why you should go out and pay tax, pay insurance and end up with the same as you're getting on the dole. I want a job where I can go out and I can come in and my wife says to me, 'The kids need a new pair of shoes', and I can turn round and say, 'Right, there you are, there's the money.' Or, if I haven't got it this week, 'Give me till next week and I'll have it ready.' I would like to be able to say to the wife, 'I'm starting to save up. The kids and us will go away on a holiday next year.' You couldn't do that sort of thing if I was working and getting the same as I'm getting on the dole. (Tom Haslett)

Others complain of the lack of financial incentive in relation to the manner in which their wives respond to low incomes:

She was complaining about the bad wages, you know, me handing her £50 on a Friday night, but now if you're arguing the wife would say to youse, 'I wish you'd go out and get a job', . . . but sure you're still in the same boat. She's complaining about very little money now. It was still the same when I was working. (Matt Davis, before he obtained his double)

(Cf. Dennehy and Sullivan, 1977, and Turner *et al.*, 1985, for similar data from Liverpool and Cauldmoss respectively.)[2]

Of nine Protestants and five Catholics who stated a willingness to work in low-paid jobs, six Protestants and one Catholic have wives in part-time employment. In such cases two earners can usually generate a total household income higher than benefit income, since while the husband is unemployed the wife's income (because of the earnings' rule) is worth only £4. For these men it is economically rational to take low-paid work because then the wife's income attains its full value.

The seven others (none of whom had ever obtained a double) to state a willingness to take low-paid work were generally older men suffering their first major spell of unemployment for many years, mostly from a manufacturing background and those feeling very ill at ease in the home. In their cases it was clearly the lack of work and activity that weighed on them, and hence the absence of what Jahoda (1979: 313) has called the latent functions of work (that employment imposes a time structure on the working day; that it implies regularly shared experiences and contacts with people outside the nuclear family; that it links an individual to goals and purposes which transcend his own; that it defines aspects of personal status and identity; and that it enforces activity) was more salient than the financial incentives. Such men also felt strongly that they should work, that it was wrong to be unemployed, and felt very uncomfortable about it.

The stated unwillingness not to take low-paid jobs might be a rationalization of the fact that even these jobs are beyond the reach of the long-term unemployed. It might be a claim that they still have a choice to exercise, that they still have a modicum of control over the course of their lives. After all, during the whole research period I met only one person who gave up a low-paid job precisely because he had calculated he would be better off unemployed, and this was a very unusual case. Moreover, of those who expressed a willingness to accept low-paid jobs only Dennis Flynn actually obtained one. A further two (Dave Martin and Billy Stewart) returned to their own trades, and another is on a one-year temporary job. None of the others have managed to secure any work, which indicates that even low-paid employment is very difficult to find.

On the other hand, four of the unemployed were offered low-paid jobs but refused them (they were very badly paid), and many more could have applied, with some chance of success, for low-paid jobs but nevertheless did not. For example, in Mallon Park the local community association obtained funds to enable it to employ four men for one year as street cleaners. These jobs, at £85 a week, were available only to those who had been unemployed for one year. However, not one of the men in the core sample even applied for the jobs, arguing that the wages were far too low for a married man to support a family. Many also did not like the idea of such a low-status job.

Approaching the problem from another angle, the language of their argument is not one of deception or dissimulation, but rather of anger and frustration. Many express passionately that with so much unemployment wages are depressed, trades unions are useless, employers can pick and choose, and job specifications are outrageous. It is an argument from the heart as much as from the head; inarticulately, perhaps, it voices a resistance to an economic system which impoverishes them in work with low wages and high taxes, and punishes them when unemployed with low benefits and high prices. Those who, despite hating their previous jobs, cannot wait to get back into similar ones because life on the dole is so unbearable are, sad to say, the most pathetic and the most vulnerable.

That the economic equation appears to be the rationale for those disdaining low-paid jobs does not necessarily mean that the unemployed 'behave as rational economic maximizers, responding and adapting their behaviour to changes in the relationship between work income and benefit income' (Showler, 1981: 45). Clearly the economic calculation is very important but, as already suggested, it is difficult to disentangle the influence of this from the powerful pressures and informal sanctions which sustain the 'work ethic'. As Marsden says, so strong are these that 'some of the workless cling to the desire to work to a much greater degree than our society has a right to expect, in view of what they had experienced through work and unemployment' (1982: 210).

Clearly the unemployed want jobs, but they do not want just any jobs. Unemployment is a great financial, social and psychological burden, but so too is work when it is low-paid and has to be endured for long hours and in bad conditions. There is plenty of evidence that people at the bottom end of the occupational ladder have very ambivalent feelings towards the work that they do.[3] There is evidence also that most working-class jobs do not utilize the skills, capacities, and talents of the people who hold them (Blackburn and Mann, 1979). Marsden makes the eloquent point that the 'social contract' which the state offers to people such as these fails them both when in work and when unemployed (1982: 181–210).

Additionally, it may be noted that differential status is conferred not simply in terms of whether one works or not, but also in terms of what kind of job a person has and what its rewards are. Since there is an occupational hierarchy (Parkin, 1972), status can be claimed for one's own job by devaluing other types of occupation. In a depressed economy suffering the total disappearance of whole categories of jobs in some areas (manufacturing in west Belfast, for example), the unemployed can find that the only available openings are of the kind which, when in work, they would have poured scorn on. If this is the case, then one of the few options the unemployed have for protecting their self-esteem is to continue to distance themselves from such jobs. That there is virtually no financial incentive for married men to take jobs like these merely aggravates the dilemma. Yet another element in this unpalatable situation is that should the unemployed lower their sights (as indeed many do) they might well experience rejection from employers for even low-paid jobs. Realizing that this may be psychologically demoralizing, escape is possible only by not applying in the first place.

Basically, then, the unemployed would seem to be engaging in a very complex cost–benefit exercise which pits the financial, social, and psychological pros and cons of available jobs against those of continued unemployment. Of course, if all the unemployed in Belfast decided that work at any cost was preferable to unemployment there would not be enough to meet even a fraction of the demand. As it is, there has been no shortage of examples in which the most ordinary of jobs have attracted very large numbers of applicants.

Intensifying the agony of the decisions the jobless have to make about whether they should even apply for jobs they evaluate as inferior to those they once held, is the realization that society at large only confers positive assessments of worth on those who can prove that they really want to work. In short, the unemployed find themselves in a doubly difficult situation. On the one hand, to be considered as genuinely unemployed they have to show willingness to work, but this can only be achieved by a continual demonstration that they are looking for work. On the other hand, since unemployed people find that repeated rejection makes it psychologically difficult to persevere in what is obviously a forlorn and tormented search (Cohen, 1945), many long-term unemployed tend to withdraw from the labour market at times when it provides very few openings (Hill et al., 1973; Daniel, 1974), and then they run the risk of being branded as scroungers and malingerers.

As a result of the stagnation of the Belfast labour markets, it becomes impossible to decide whether the derision heaped on low-paid jobs by many of the unemployed is a tactic to bolster a self-image that would be damaged if it had to be admitted that one was reduced to applying for jobs once seen as beneath contempt; or whether it is because such a position allows them to feel they still have a degree of choice and control over their lives; or whether it is because the prospect of failing to get even the worst jobs is too awful to contemplate; or, finally, whether it is because acknowledging that there are not enough jobs might destroy any vestigial hope of an early return to work. Given the complex social and psychological backdrop to this issue and given that public opinion expresses contradictory attitudes, I doubt very much whether the unemployed themselves see the situation in a clear light.

The contention that wages must cover more than benefits is related to other themes. Most men feel that wages should stand on their own, that is, there should be no need to claim low-income benefits (family income supplement [FIS], now changed to family credit; rent and rates rebate [RRR], now changed to housing benefit). Wages which require supplementing by benefits are deemed exploitative. Consequently the jobs are seen as offering no prospects, little opportunity for overtime, and likely to be dirty and boring. One might just as well be on the dole as in employment such as this. For those less concerned about the social pressures of the work ethic, taking such jobs is tantamount to moving from the unemployment trap to the poverty trap, and the latter is perceived to be hardly any better than the former. In short, many see very little difference, financially, between being unemployed and supported by one set of benefits, and being in low-paid work requiring a different set of benefits to underpin the wages.

One of the major items a wage must cover is the earner's 'pocket-money'. Few employed men in the samples, and especially the higher-paid ones, hand over the whole of their wage packets to their wives. The most common form of allocation is to supply the wife with 'her wages' (i.e. a sum of money for the upkeep of the house), retaining the rest for a variety of purposes (pocket-money, purchase of consumer durables, settlement of bills, holidays, and so forth). Although there is wide variation in who pays for what, typically the husband divides the cake and keeps some for personal use (see J. Pahl, 1983; Ashley, 1983: 106–11).

The (male) ideology shaping this distribution is that those who receive a wage *earn* it, that is, *deserve* it; they have *worked* for it, it is the exchange for what they do in their place of employment.[4] Part of this money is ear-marked for the financing of the household, but part is kept to be disposed of in any way the earner sees fit. This explains why working wives almost always maintain control of their own wages and why, if husbands do not tell their wives how much they earn, the latter respond with similar reticence. What is important, to the man of course, is what his wage enables him to do. In Northern Irish working-class culture this generally means liberal use of pubs, clubs, pool rooms, betting shops, and nowadays, leisure centres.[5]

This premium over the dole is sorely missed in unemployment and low-paid jobs, for it is precisely in such circumstances (see Morris, 1984a: 501) that household income is passed *in toto* to the female. However, this way of phrasing the issue is ambiguous, because possession and control are quite different matters. McLaughlin (1987) has argued that mens' relationship to household income is changed by unemployment. In Belfast, men in work delegate responsibility to their wives for the short-term upkeep of the home, that is, for recurrent collective expenditure, while retaining responsibility for long-term planning and major decisions concerning the acquisition of costly household purchases. Even in low-income households, where collective expenditure leaves little surplus, this pattern is maintained. In unemployment, on the other hand, benefit income is not perceived as 'earned' (even by the men) and is normatively conceived of as purely for the financing of the household. Thus a majority of unemployed men pass on the whole of the benefit to their wives, and in several cases the wife herself cashes the giro. In addition, large items have to be obtained through claiming supplementary benefit single payments rather than from earnings and this renders the husband's right to control household decisions more ambiguous (McLaughlin, 1989). In this way patterns of domestic authority, so clearly tied to male-earned sources of income, come under potential threat, since it is difficult for the male to assert his dominance as head of the household at a time when the basis of that authority is being whittled away (McKee and Bell, 1985; Jackson and Walsh, 1987). A dilemma for the men is that by not withholding some of the benefit for themselves they cannot fulfil certain typical role expectations and, moreover, find themselves housebound. On the other hand if they do take some benefit for personal spending money, then they risk being condemned by others for their greed, selfishness, and consequent neglect of the household, and being branded as scroungers. These contradictions are just as acute for the wives, for they have (usually) less money to manage on, have to battle against their husbands' demands on it, and have to endure their relatively indolent presence in the house all day. In this sense the conditions created by unemployment and the benefit system conspire to bring into contradiction different sets of role expectations which when in work are more usually perceived as complementary.

Nevertheless, in unemployment, while it would be inaccurate to argue that just because money is transferred from husband to wife the husband loses control, it would be equally incorrect to assume that the female never gains control of such spending power. In a not insignificant number of cases, men in low-income jobs and unemployed men yield actual control of wages or benefits to their wives. In at least eight cases (five employed in low-paid jobs and three unemployed) the husbands have very little influence in financial matters and are clearly dominated by their wives. These latter not only hold the purse strings but make most of the more important decisions, including in some cases which jobs the husband should apply for; and in one case a constant threat of eviction for the husband if he could not find a job. Several other families seem to work a joint-partnership arrangement in which all or most financial matters, especially major decisions, are discussed without either the one or the other clearly dictating policy. However, in the majority of cases, even where men allow the money to be held by their wives they still attempt to exert control over its disbursement. In those cases where unemployed men also try to claim a portion of benefit as personal spending money, marital relations become very fractious and frequent altercations take place.

In conversation, unemployed men often argue that they have very little control over their benefit, that benefit income is nothing to do with them and does not belong to them: 'As soon as [the giro] comes through the door, she gets it. I sign it and she cashes it. That's the only time I ever see it' (Eddie McCann); 'I never see it, don't get no pocket-money at all. I've never took any pocket-money out of the bru. There's little to survive on without me doing that' (Danny Chapman). Despite these protestations, however, it is clear from other aspects of life in such households that even these men exert a great deal of pressure on their wives. The latter have to account to their menfolk for how the money is spent, husbands prescribe a set of spending priorities, and decisions about long-term planning, loans, and so forth are taken largely by the husband. In sum:

Whilst a woman's relationship to the control of household income remains largely constant whether her husband is unemployed or not, the man's does not. The change is sufficient to create feelings of degradation, depression and private 'shame' among men on benefits. The change is not, however, necessarily sufficient to alter the inequality of husbands' and wives' relationships to household income. (McLaughlin, 1987)

It can readily be seen that any income derived from doing a double will off-set many of the difficulties precipitated by the change from work to unemployment. The income, first of all, is earned by work, usually outside the house, and therefore in a location conceptually equivalent to a place of employment; it is, in short, a partial return to the sphere of employment. The move back into the world of work (Kumar, 1979: 13–14; 1984: 218), however far removed from the 'real' thing, re-defines the person not only as someone who can work, who has skills, who has contacts and friends, but also as someone willing to work, someone not content to sit on his backside doing nothing. This therefore re-establishes him in a viable status with a role that provides a valuable identity (Kelvin, 1980: 301; Kelvin and Jarrett, 1985: 42–8).

Further attention will be paid in later chapters to how unemployment affects a person's identity and self-image. All that need be said here is that the state of being unemployed is, generally speaking, more accept-able and more tolerated in Mallon Park than in Eastlough. In the latter estate, a majority of employed (and into the bargain many unemployed as well) perceive the jobless as scroungers who are idle and feckless. There is therefore a greater pressure on these to persuade others that they are actively looking for work and are not entirely delirious about having to live on benefits. But of course this must be work in the formal not the informal economy, and this in itself means that doing the double in Eastlough cannot establish a (partially) valid working status in the way that can happen in Mallon Park.

The move into 'employment' is simultaneously a move out of the domestic sphere, where in large measure the unemployed man is an unwanted intruder who disrupts household routines; for non-employed women the loss of work for their husbands often leads to an unacceptable invasion of their day-time space and privacy. The mere separation of the spouses can serve to enhance their relationship, but a separation based on the man working the double actually reproduces the sought-after complementarity and interdependence associated with a legitimate job. He goes out in the morning to a job of work and returns in the evening tired, hungry, but satisfied. They have things to talk about, experiences to swop, worries to share. That this rather romantic picture does not quite fit the empirical situation is not entirely relevant, for the idealistic image is the conceptual framework within which reality is interpreted, and anything which gets the man out of the house all day, especially if he is clutching £20 on his return, is evaluated as approximating the ideal much better than if he remains indoors.

In general, doing the double provides, even if in an attenuated fashion, some of those latent functions of work described by Jahoda

(1979) and already mentioned. If the double is done for an employer, the worker has a time structure imposed on him, and even if he works for himself, as many do, he still must work to a schedule which requires planning and organization. Working, of course, enforces activity, and this undoubtedly counteracts the listlessness and depression that so many complain of. The double may not entail regularly shared experiences and contacts with people outside the home, but it often does, and this supplies the worker with a new and changing fund of stories with which to regale family, kin, and friends. In order to buttress a work identity slowly slipping away as the time since the last job inexorably increases, the man doing the double no longer has to fall back on stale oft-repeated experiences gained from that job, but can now tell jokes and relive events that happened very recently. While Billy Reid (unemployed for three years) can only recount experiences of his last job in a jaded, dispirited, and monotonous voice, with long silent intervals, Gerry Daly can have me, and assorted friends collected in his living room, roaring with laughter as he unfolds what it is like scrabbling through a dump in the pouring rain hoping to find copper and lead, or about the time he and several others, shouting warnings to each other, scattered in different directions as two men, assumed to be DHSS snoops, appeared slowly walking towards them over the heaps of scrap, rubble, and hard-core. While Frank Connolly can forget about the dismal and depressing problems of life on a supplementary shoe-string, and instead explain to me in meticulous detail the taxi business, overheads, radios, crystals, frequencies, jamming, and so forth, others – both Protestants and Catholics – can spend hours itemizing the miseries of seven-day benefits that only stretch to five or six, of borrowing and lending, of hand-me-downs, of endless waiting at the local social security office, of nothing to eat when the money runs out, and of how two people, man and wife, can see each other all day long yet not speak.

Incomes

Doing the double then provides various intrinsic rewards: it reduces boredom and depression; increases activity; allows working skills to be exercised; widens horizons; creates and maintains contacts outside the home; re-establishes working status; and therefore bolsters a self-identity and self-image, one of whose major elements in working-class culture is the performance of hard, physical work. Additionally, of course, it brings in much-needed income. To assess the impact such amounts make, it is necessary to present data on replacement ratios.

The replacement ratio (RR) is the ratio of income in work to that when

Table 14. *Mallon Park unemployed and employed core samples: replacement ratios (RR)*

Members of unemployed sample (number of children in brackets)	Income in unemployment £	Income in work £	RR %	Members of employed sample (number of children in brackets)	Notional income in unemployment £	Income in work £	Notional RR %
T. Madden (2)	83.50	86.50	96.5	M. Graham (1)	78	102	76
D. Chapman (2)	84	112	75	B. McCallister (1)	77	98	76
J. Nolan (2)	84	112	75	S. Devlin (1)	76	104	73
P. Hardy (2)	82.50	82.50	100	G.Boyle (2)	88.50	112	79
M. Morgan (2)	83.50	94	89	T. Armstrong (2)	84	98	86
J. Carlin (2)	83.50	142	59	F. Wilkinson (2)	85	132	64
G. Daly (2)	85	150	57	L. McGarry (2)	84	107	78
M. Davis (3)	92.50	87.50	106	G. Collins (2)	86	116	74
F. Connolly (3)	95.50	114	84	D.Loughran (3)	99	141	70
P. McVeigh (3)	106	111.50	95	L. Hunter (3)	96	114	84
K. Hurley (3)	95	110	86	C. Harper (3)	92	111	83
R. McGrath (3)	98	128	76	K. McCarthy (4)	103	126	82
B. Stewart (3)	102	114	89	J.Duffy (1)[a]	76	116	66
R. Carlile (4)	117	133.50	87	P. Ward (1)[a]	82	118	69
B. O'Neil (2)[a]	92	200	46	M. Slattery (2)[a]	101	147	69
D. Flynn (3)[a]	105	123.50	85	B. McGonnell (2)[a]	137	198	69
G. Murray (5)[a]	122	160	76	J. Cochrane (2)[a]	102	190	54
M. Cavanagh (3)	95.50	—	—	S. Donaghy (4)[a]	115	134	86
E. McCann (4)	112.50	—	—	M. Franklin (4)[a]	116	173	67
J. McCartney (5)	120	—	—	E. Canavan (6)[a]	138	176	78

[a] indicates wife in work.

unemployed. Here, expressed as a percentage, it is defined as the ratio of total net household income, from all sources, when the head-of-household is unemployed, to total net income, again from all sources, when the head-of-household is in work.[6]

Tables 14 and 15 supply information on the four core samples from Mallon Park (table 14) and Eastlough (table 15). The figures for the unemployed give benefit income at the time of the first interview, and work income for the most recent job. In some cases this latter figure is unrealistic, as it refers to jobs held up to two years previously. In seven cases jobs were lost over two years previously and hence the RR is not recorded, as it would be meaningless. Moreover, some of the other RRs may be unreliable, as people could not remember precisely their wages or whether they claimed a low-wage benefit.

For the employed, actual net incomes are given; and notional incomes, were the head-of-household to become unemployed, have been computed, as have notional RRs. Because the two sets of figures for the employed are contemporary, they are more accurate and realistic than those for the unemployed. On the other hand, whilst only nine of the unemployed have wives in a job, seventeen of the employed have working wives. The notional RRs of these latter groups have been calculated on the assumption that these women would remain in work should their husbands lose theirs. However, as only the first £4 of such income is disregarded in assessing SB, some women would cease working, either of their own accord or because their husbands would 'persuade' them. Of those presently unemployed, nine have working wives. Eight of these are in jobs they had when their husbands were in work, whilst the other obtained a job recently. However, a further six had jobs when their husbands were employed but gave them up or lost them after their men lost theirs.

There are further problems with evaluating these figures. When questioning both the unemployed and the employed about their incomes in work, it was quite obvious that several were/are eligible for low-income benefits but were not claiming them, either because of ignorance or because of a conscious decision not to claim 'hand-outs'.[7] In this respect some of the in-work incomes, for both samples, could be higher. However, the out-of-work incomes are in many cases also an underestimate, for they exclude both the value of free school meals for children and the value of goods obtained through SB single-payment claims.

Another distorting factor is what many people refer to as the 'cost of working'. Both the employed and the unemployed (though the latter more vehemently) stress that being at work has costs. Transport costs,

Table 15. *Eastlough unemployed and employed core samples: replacement ratios (RR)*

Members of unemployed sample (number of children in brackets)	Income in unemployment £	Income in work £	RR %	Members of employed sample (number of children in brackets)	Notional income in unemployment £	Income in work £	Notional RR %
J. Galbraith (1)	73	116	63	S. Evans (0)	65	100	65
F. Beattie (1)	78	109	72	T. Smith (1)	76	93	82
A. Peters (2)	90.50	108	84	D. Cordell (1)	77	116	66
M. Lawrence (2)	81.50	101	80	C. Jackson (2)	82.50	110	75
G. Lynn (2)	83	81	102	M. Wilson (2)	88	98.50	89
J. Harding (2)	84	104	81	R. Moody (2)	85.50	111	77
H. McGregor (2)	86	109	79	A. Martin (2)	91.50	113	81
J. McHale (2)	85.50	105	81	G. O'Farrell (3)	97.50	122.50	80
D. Irvine (2)	86	108	80	T. Oliver (3)	99	139.50	71
R. Price (3)	103.50	131	79	D. Ross (3)	94	126.50	74
T. Haslett (4)	104.50	144	73	J. Fraser (4)	104.50	130	80
J. Robinson (2)	90.50	—	—	M. Givens (1)[a]	91	151	60
B. Reid (2)	86	—	—	H. Osborne (1)[a]	81	135	54
J. Hughes (4)	102	—	—	K. McCormick (1)[a]	96	177	54
N. Kincaid (1)[a]	96	151	64	A. Matchett (1)[a]	92	138	67
W. McCoy (2)[a]	97	132	73	H. Lyons (2)[a]	116	178	65
D. Martin (2)[a]	101	157	64	H. Kerr (2)[a]	86.50	172	50
B. Marshall (3)[a]	103	149	69	F. Hill (2)[a]	94	162	58
B. Green (4)[a]	119	143.50	83	V. Rogers (3)[a]	104.50	167	63
E. Ogle (1)[a]	83	—	—	W. Long (3)[a]	111	151	74

[a] indicates wife in work.

often the major item, can be as high as £10 a week. The effect on RRs of these various factors is impossible to compute, but overall they tend to favour the out-of-work incomes, so that in general the RRs are on the low side. Incidentally, because of such complexities it is virtually impossible for the low-wage earner to calculate whether, financially, he is better off in work or out.

With these remarks in mind, it can be seen that the RRs for the Mallon Park unemployed are high, with one over 100 per cent, three over 90 per cent and a further six over 80 per cent. Looked at another way, seven have present incomes within £15 of their previous in-work incomes and five of these have been unemployed for less than one year. While the notional RRs of the employed group are indeed lower, nevertheless five are over 80 per cent. Furthermore, of those with the highest in-work incomes (Slattery when he was employed, McGonnell, Cochrane, Franklin, and Canavan) three have working wives and each man does more than twenty hours' overtime each week.

For the Mallon Park groups, it is low pay which characterizes these figures. Male, manual workers in Northern Ireland have consistently had to work longer hours for less money than their counterparts in Great Britain (Black *et al.*, 1980: 7), and even if wages and salaries in Northern Ireland have recently grown relative to those in Britain, net disposable income per capita is still substantially lower: in 1978 it stood at 81 per cent of the UK average (Gibson and Spencer, 1981). It is, then, not high benefits that are keeping the unemployed out of work but few jobs and very low pay. For there to be some financial incentive for unemployed married men to go back to work (always assuming there are some jobs to go back to), most would require net household incomes similar to those 'enjoyed' by many of the employed group. However, those in this latter group with the lowest RRs all have working wives and some work extraordinarily long hours. Several of this group therefore actually argue that they are no better off than the unemployed (they point to the shabbiness of their homes, the fact that they eat the same kinds of food, that they have no video, do not go on holiday, and can rarely go out in the evening, etc.). Basically, because they have large families and are in very low-paid jobs, they are forced into working long hours to make ends meet. Because of the overtime worked they rarely claim FIS or RRR, and so their children are not eligible for free school meals. On top of this, they become rather animated when the discussion turns to the furniture and other items allegedly flowing into the houses of the unemployed which the 'bru' pays for out of their taxes. Finally, of the twelve Mallon Park employed whose wives are not working, seven are claiming low-income benefits.

Table 16. *Average replacement ratios (RR) for Mallon Park and Eastlough core samples (percentages)*

	Unemployed	Employed
Mallon Park	86	74.3
Eastlough	76.7	69.3

The figures for the Eastlough groups are somewhat different, in that the RRs for both the unemployed and the employed are lower than for their Mallon Park counterparts, which means they derive greater financial benefit from working (see table 16). This is because Eastlough residents are more highly skilled and so when in work are usually in higher-paying jobs.

Given these facts, there is little doubt that the unemployed groups would take the kinds of jobs that the employed now have, but it is precisely these kinds of jobs, especially for Mallon Park residents, that are not available in the local labour markets. This is another reason why the latter look for opportunities to work 'on the side'.

In the absence of satisfactory wages from reasonable jobs, many Catholics in Mallon Park will do a double whenever they can, and the income they obtain gives them the premium they require. Thus Gerry Daly's £35 a week recycling scrap takes his income to £120. For two months his wife was also doing a double, earning £20 a week. Frank Connolly earns nearly £100 a week taxiing, taking his income to nearly £200 a week. Even if Ray McGrath only does three or four three-week stints through the year, this has the effect of raising his average weekly income from £98 to £115. Martin Cavanagh's earnings probably add on average £20 a week to his income. The occasional job that Eddie McCann gets takes his income to around £125–£130 a week. Those not in the core sample who do a virtual full-time double (for example, one of Gerry Daly's brothers, a neighbour of Gerry's who is a joiner, a neighbour of Mick Franklin's who is a tiler) all have net incomes approaching or exceeding £200 a week, that is, similar to what an averagely paid estate agent might make.

Apart from those few officially unemployed earning realistic wages on the double, none of this work would be worth it if the income from it were declared to the DHSS. What would be the point of Martin Cavanagh standing in the cold and rain for up to ten hours a day selling wrapping paper if in earning £70 in the week he lost £66 of his benefit?

He only does it in the first place to provide a decent Christmas for his wife and children. And the same may be said of all the other doubles in this category. Similarly, because these men have virtually given up hope of the formal economy producing viable jobs in the near future, they no longer look seriously in this direction. As argued in the previous chapter, they now see their benefits as a good, solid base which can be supplemented by doing a double to a point where they enjoy household incomes nearly as high, and in some cases higher, than those in legitimate jobs (cf. Mingione, 1985: 42). They also argue that they are not scrounging, since they put so much effort into the work that they do: as Gerry Daly says, who in his right mind is going to spend so much time on a dump for so little return.

It needs to be reiterated, in case of misunderstanding, that the unemployed, whether doing the double or not, have come to consider jobs on the side as a viable way of financing households, largely because they have simultaneously become accustomed to seeing their local economy in a permanently depressed condition and their local labour market offering only the very poorest-paid jobs. Were the economy to begin providing jobs of the kind they once had, there is little doubt that they would return to them, giving up the doubles in the process. Danny Chapman, for example, discusses the choice of a legitimate job as opposed to a double in terms of their probable duration, their security, their relative pay-offs, and concludes that he would always go back to a welder's job like the one he lost, but in default of that he is prepared rather to look for doubles. Gerry Daly, Matt Davis, Brian O'Neil, and Eddie McCann speculate in much the same terms. The Protestants of Eastlough, because they still invest hope in their local economy, despite its precarious state, and have a good deal to gain if it begins anew to generate jobs, have not yet oriented themselves to the black economy in the same committed way as have west Belfast Catholics.

Some further themes

Into the black economy

Ray Pahl (1984: 96) has argued that in the 1980s 'unemployed people are too poor to work informally: they cannot go to the pubs to make essential contacts, and they cannot afford the tools and equipment to do such odd jobs as decorating or car repairs'. The evidence from Belfast places doubt on this generalization. With one exception (Cavanagh's part-time job as a barman), none of the doubles so far described was the result of a pub contact, fortuitous or otherwise. Of those who have done a double, three (Daly, Cavanagh, and Slattery) are entirely cases of individual enterprise and no contacts were involved. Of the others, all obtained their jobs through neighbours or friends either living in Mallon Park or in nearby areas: 'I've never been offered a job in a bar' (Tony Madden); 'I've a much better chance sitting here waiting on the phone or somebody calling' (Eddie McCann); and so forth.

Of the Protestants, Jim Hughes, the cook, had 100 cards printed and pushed them through letter boxes. John Galbraith just carried on doing the car repairs he used to do when he was in work. Tom Haslett obtained part-time work in a bar because he was a good friend of the owner, and received several week's work on a building site through another friend already working there. Dave Martin, out of the blue, got a phone call from an ex-employer who asked him if he wanted a few weeks work on the double.

None of this, of course, means that doubles are never acquired by contacts in pubs, but the notion that the pub is the arena *par excellence* for making such contacts cannot be sustained. The point is that job information and allocation flow along already existing networks, and so long as these are maintained and serviced, they are likely to pay dividends. Those who have failed to get doubles tend largely to have few contacts and to be housebound. Ray Carlile, Jimmy Nolan, Tony Madden, Michael Morgan, Pat McVeigh, and others have no relatives at all living in Mallon Park, and indeed come from small families. That they have few marketable skills outside factory employment is a further disadvantage. Those who have obtained jobs either have large families with many relatives in local areas, or have a wide circle of friends and acquaintances, or both.

Of course, people can ply their trade only if they have the requisite tools and equipment. But many tradesmen acquire such minimum tools as are necessary whilst at work. Plumbers, electricians, joiners, plasterers, mechanics, etc. usually build up a stock of tools over the years, and the jobs they may obtain when unemployed assist them in maintaining this stock. Moreover, there are many jobs requiring no tools. An unemployed person does not need any resources, save time and a large social network, to be a child-minder, a bar doorman, a scrap collector, a night security guard, a cleaner, a shop assistant, and so forth.

Just because an area is suffering high chronic unemployment, this is no reason to think that local demand for goods and services will be completely suppressed. In an area such as Mallon Park, where over 50 per cent of the economically active are unemployed, life still goes on. People want TVs on the cheap, second-hand washing machines, a neat fireplace, a higher dividing wall, a sofa re-upholstered, an old car fixed up, some tiles put into the bathroom, etc. These goods and services can be provided by local people at prices lower than legitimate firms can afford. In fact, it is precisely because many people have so little money that they will often use the services of the unemployed before those of legitimate firms, since the former will be cheaper. And the money that the unemployed earn helps in maintaining demand. With some of the extra income Gerry Daly obtained, he asked one of his friends, on the double, to build him a new brick fireplace (with bricks 'off the back of a lorry'). With the money Joe Carlin earned building extensions along the Falls Road, he had his upstairs carpeted and his kitchen re-tiled, and the man who did this was an unemployed floor tiler living close by. Mike Slattery provides a service to between ten and fifteen people on the estate. There are many other cases of this kind, which not only sustain those doing the double but also, to some degree, tie in others who are not but who do benefit from it. It is not the case therefore that the unemployed are, in general, too poor to work informally. Those doing the double, especially in Mallon Park, remark that it is their abject poverty which provides them with the incentive to search for and solicit informal work. What makes the difference between one area and another are particularistic cultural values about the morality of the double and the prevailing structures of opportunity and constraint, and these are not, it would seem from the Belfast case, related only to the performance of the larger economy. What needs to be taken into account are the mediating social and cultural processes, and on this particular score Pahl's study of Sheppey remains sketchy.

The final point to make in relation to the demand side of the equation is that, even though there is massive and chronic unemploment in many areas of Belfast, there are still many people in work. Middle-class areas of the city, for example, have very little unemployment and these areas offer fertile ground for those tradesmen who are unemployed.

From the black economy to the formal economy

Jobs 'on the side' can occasionally lead to legitimate jobs; they may thus be a route, through the back door as it were, into the formal economy.

Matt Davis' job was conditional on his remaining on the unemployment register. This did not worry him, since he was overjoyed that such a lucrative offer had finally come his way. However, had Matt not accepted the condition he would not have got the job at all, and had he declared the income to the DHSS he would have placed the other workers in jeopardy, two of whom were his unemployed uncle and brother.

Both Mike Slattery and Frank Connolly began doing the double again as a way back into the formal economy, this time to self-employment. Frank has so far made a success of it, but having got used to the high income he has decided to keep going until he is caught, reasoning that the fine for a first offence will be so small as to make it worth his while continuing (those caught are only prosecuted for the days it can be proved they were working, and generally the DHSS seem happy when they have evidence for just several days). Mike Slattery, however, has found it very difficult to build up his business to the point where he could afford to sign off. Gerry Daly, meanwhile, has ideas of full-time scrap dealing. His plan takes him to a van of his own with which he will be able to make larger profits than at present, and so to an even larger van, enabling him to move the scrap to England, where the prices are higher. However, these are pipe dreams, for little of the extra income is saved.

Of the Protestants, Jim Hughes felt at one time that he might have been able to get enough work to go out on his own. However, various events intervened and he had to sell his car. Having reduced his mobility he had to cancel work and at the end of the research was not doing anything at all. Jim Harding, a painter by trade, once obtained a double for a fortnight during the summer, cleaning and painting part of a bakery. He worked all hours of the day and night in the hope that his enthusiasm and flexibility would see him into a full-time job. He was broken-hearted when, despite glowing praise, the manager said they could not afford to keep him on. David Martin, another painter, did however make the breakthrough. Some eleven months after being paid off from his last job because of lack of work, an old employer phoned him up to see if he wanted a few weeks' work on the double at normal rates of pay. He jumped at the chance. While he was there new work kept coming in and the boss decided to keep David on legitimately. The last time I saw him he had been with this firm for nearly six months.

Low returns but high rewards

It should now be clear that jobs on the side come and go quite quickly, with many only lasting a short time. The income derived from these jobs is rarely a substitute for full-time employment in the legitimate economy.

None of the four construction workers in the Mallon Park core sample have ever worked on the double for more than a few weeks at a time, and complain bitterly that it is virtually impossible to get a legitimate job because employers will not use them in this way. Because the construction industry is depressed, employers cannot afford to keep workers on their books when they have little work, and it pays them, in a variety of ways, to employ people on the double when they need extra labour.[8] In short, many of those doing the double feel forced into it, since it is the only way to make a living; but having become accustomed to such a mode of life, it has come to be seen by some as an attractive alternative to formal employment.

It should be equally clear that the returns from many doubles are quite low. It is often, though not always, the case that the wages are lower than those paid to legitimate workers. This is justified by the fact that such payment is not reduced by taxes. Nevertheless, some jobs carry extremely low rewards. Daly, Slattery, Cavanagh, Hughes, and others make (or made) no more then £30 to £40 a week on average, despite investing very large amounts of time and effort. One man, not in the core sample, has a double working in a fish-and-chip shop, six days a week, for £5 a day. In this sense those doing the double may be commended as reliable, hard workers: despite the many constraints on their lives they are willing to do almost any type of work to increase their income.

In Northern Ireland, the great difficulty of making ends meet on a benefit income explains why the unemployed who are lucky enough to find a niche are willing to work for such apparently low returns. For them the extra income appears substantial and the time cost is seen as comparatively small. As there are few other demands made on this time, it is no longer perceived as a scarce resource. Aside from providing many of the latent functions of work, and reducing marital tensions, the income enables the household to resume comparatively normal patterns of expenditure. By removing people from the no-choice, penny-pinching existence of life on basic benefits, work on the double reproduces some of the conditions of 'normal' life.

Discussion

There is a complex problem concerning the contextualization of social security abuse, of which doing the double is a major form, and this problem is not entirely eliminated by pointing to the much vaster sums of money that are lost to the Revenue through the non-payment of taxes on undeclared income received by those in work (29th Report from the Committee of Public Accounts, quoted in *New Society*, 1980). The fact is that most people receive various benefits, as of right, without acknowledging their origin, their effects, or even that they are welfare benefits at all. The original work on this subject is contained in Titmuss' essay,

'The social division of welfare' (Titmuss, 1958: 34–55), in which he argued that collective interventions to meet the needs of the individual and/or to serve the wider interest of society may be divided into three broad categories: social welfare, fiscal welfare, and occupational welfare. Of these three, social welfare (in the form of unemployment benefit, supplementary benefit, legal aid, rebates, low income benefits, etc.) is the most visible, the most stigmatized, and the most criticized. The transparency of social welfare, the assumed character of the type of people who claim it, the conditions under which it is obtained, together with various Victorian biases concerning the work ethic, individual responsibility for one's own circumstances, and the ideology of self-help, have generated notions that welfare is for the working-class and that it is paid for by the better-off sections of the community. Fiscal and occupational income supplements are generally not conceived as welfare benefits at all, perhaps because they are often received automatically and are enjoyed to one degree or another by the majority of the population.

What Titmuss brought out was that fiscal welfare benefits (relief on mortgage interest, personal and other tax allowances) and occupational benefits (private pension schemes, company cars, subsidized school fees, private health insurance, etc.) though conceptualized as essentially different to social welfare in fact perform similar functions and produce similar effects. Field has pointed out that the main beneficiaries of these forms of welfare are those on high incomes (1981: 129–35).

The initial points made by Titmuss have since received more detailed treatment (Kincaid, 1975; Field, Meacher, and Pond, 1977; Sandford, Pond, and Walker, 1980), while theoretically the argument has been extended by Sinfield (1978) and Field (1981). These analyses argue that welfare benefits of one kind or another are received by virtually every member of society, that the tax system does not, in general, re-distribute income and wealth equitably, and that the economy unloads its social costs on to the state. There is therefore a systematic bias which spotlights social welfare whilst concealing other categories of welfare benefit. This is quite clearly exhibited in the way the media focuses on and vilifies social security abuse at the same time as it either ignores or even glorifies stories of tax avoidance and evasion (Golding and Middleton, 1982: 99). Equally significant is the euphemistic terminology used when speaking of social security, social services, benefits, and welfare. For those with little direct experience of the working of the welfare state, such terms tend to evoke the notion that the needs of its customers are fully and satisfactorily met. However, rather than preserving security and enhancing welfare, so-called 'benefits', Titmuss argued, rather:

represent partial compensation for disservices, for social costs and social insecurities which are the product of a rapidly changing industrial–urban society. They are part of the price we pay to some people for bearing the cost of other people's progress . . . They are the socially caused diswelfares; the losses involved in aggregate welfare gains. (1968: 133)

There exists an economic relation of interdependence between the three categories of welfare, in the sense that resources devoted to one cannot be spent on either of the other two.[9] By regarding them as conceptually distinct and hence as essentially different, this relation has become hidden and its significance lost. This makes it possible to decry growth in public welfare at the same time as the expansion in fiscal and occupational welfare is condoned. By conceptually re-connecting social security abuse to other forms of fraud, and social welfare to occupational and fiscal welfare, practices such as doing the double may be seen in a much more reasoned and sympathetic light.

The working-class unemployed described in this study were poor when in work and are even more indigent in unemployment. Their only legal route out of this trap is to secure a high-paying job. But even low-paying jobs are scarce, and they are far more scarce in Catholic west Belfast than in east Belfast. The only other avenue is to do the double when opportunities avail. If, in doing this, some find it more lucrative than waiting in vain for a legitimate job to turn up, then it is not they who are to blame, but rather the manner in which the involuted and anachronistic system of taxation and benefits is linked to wages. Simply, these people are taking advantage of the opportunities which such a system throws up, just as those in work take advantage of opportunities that come their way, and which are every bit as illegal as doing the double. Given the kinds of working (and workless) backgrounds many of these unemployed have had:

we have no right to be surprised or annoyed if some of the workless are less trusting, less diligent, more aggressive or more apathetic. Nor should we be censorious of individuals to whom employers and the State have shown little responsibility should they in turn break regulations about working while they are unemployed, or even try to avoid the commitments of regular secure work and the payment of tax and insurance. By criticizing the workless for behaving with a narrowly economic motivation, our society seems to be trying to have its cake and eat it. (Marsden, 1982: 210)

It has been clearly demonstrated that the response of Mallon Park Catholics to the recession and the collapse of industry in west Belfast has been to engage in doing the double whenever possible, and this they are able to do more than the Protestants of Eastlough because of certain favourable circumstances. These practices and material conditions have had an effect on their ideas concerning formal jobs, and the status and role of welfare benefits. Given the almost total lack of viable, working-class jobs in Belfast it is no surprise that unemployed married men and women, particularly in west Belfast, seek to augment their income in any way they can. The relatively small amounts that are earned individually are unlikely to add up to more than a small fraction of the total of goods and services comprising the 'informal' economy, the major part of which is probably accounted for, as Pahl rightly argues, by those already in legitimate jobs. But to the unemployed individuals concerned, such amounts can make the difference between living and mere subsistence.

It has long been known that a supplementary benefit income can reduce the long-term unemployed to a life of abject poverty. The men and women of Eastlough attempt to cope as best they can on benefit, on assistance from relatives, and on the occasional double. The unemployed in Mallon Park have to do this as well if they cannot obtain work on the side. But they look for it more actively, have a more positive evaluation of it, and enjoy conditions which favour its existence. However much they may worry about being caught, working on the side is not a matter for quaint discussion on the legal niceties embedded in the distinctions between 'doing the double', 'homers', 'moonlighting', 'perks', 'fiddles', 'tax avoidance', 'tax evasion', etc. It is, quite simply, a case of grabbing any opportunity that presents itself, of carving out a little niche from which they can augment their income to a level which begins to approach a decent standard of living for themselves and their children.

And of course, as has been seen, it is not only the unemployed who benefit. Many employers prefer to use this kind of labour, for they reap a number of advantages: they pay no National Insurance contributions, no sick pay, no holiday pay, no redundancy money, no compensation for industrial injuries; they often pay lower wages, as these are not subject to the usual deductions; they can lay off workers at a moment's notice and know they can hire them quickly; and they can ignore the trades unions. Because of this many employers will only take on workers if they are prepared to remain officially unemployed. This is particularly the case in the house-building sector of the construction industry, but it is found in all other sectors as well. Many of the jobs described in this chapter could not have been worked other than on the double; unemployed people trying to get jobs, especially short-term ones, are expected by their prospective employers to remain on the register and to continue to draw benefit, and if they are not prepared to do this there are others who are. Since there are so few legitimate jobs, since the income is always welcome, since the vast majority enjoy being active, and because a double job may be a route back into the formal economy, few unemployed are willing to pass up opportunities which may only occur at very infrequent intervals. I have already remarked that the state does not appear to be too bothered about the situation; the fines for employers colluding in this practice are no higher than for the unfortunate 'employees' who have no alternative but to comply with a system they help to reproduce, but from which they gain so little in the long term.

For many of the unemployed in Mallon Park and west Belfast generally, doing the double is about the only way of circumventing what they perceive to be a deeply entrenched and discriminatory system of industrial wage labour. Hedged in by a hostile state apparatus, a dearth of jobs, exploiting employers, low wages, and what are considered to be iniquitous taxes, inadequate benefits, and high prices for fuel, food, transport, and clothing (Jefferson and Simpson, 1980) these unemployed conceive that they have little option: they either do the double or do without. The results of such activity, though, are that the Protestant image of the Catholic as a poor worker, unless he can do the double, and as a benefit scrounger, if he cannot, are validated and reinforced, at the same time as this activity maintains the constraints on the production of jobs in the formal economy in west Belfast.

The situation of the unemployed might not be so bad if in claiming supplementary benefit they were able to obtain, without undue effort, their full, legal entitlement. All too frequently however, as the following chapter demonstrates, claimants encounter severe and depressing difficulties in their attempts to do this.

Chapter 5

The 'deserving' and the 'undeserving': administrative practice in a social security office

The two previous chapters described how some unemployed people are able to take advantage of opportunities to increase their incomes. Here I wish to document a reverse process, namely, how it is that the routine administration of the Supplementary Benefit system leads to many claimants being unable to obtain their full legal entitlement. As already mentioned, I intend to retain the present tense when discussing this issue even though SB has been replaced by IS. This is because, although the recent reforms have changed various aspects of the scheme, I shall argue, in chapter 9, that many of the processes to be documented here still appear to be present in the new system.

Introduction

Although Max Weber can be credited with laying the foundations of the study of bureaucracy, it cannot be argued that he greatly advanced our understanding of the real functioning of such organizations. As many commentators have since pointed out, after having delineated the important features of the ideal-type (rigid hierarchy of officials, measurement of performance by objective criteria, promotion by merit or seniority, the link between career and duty, application of rules according to the book, strict control of information, etc.), Weber did not go on to show how empirical cases of bureaucracy compared to this.

Later studies (for example, Blau, 1963; H. Cohen, 1965) have demonstrated that the working of real bureaucracies differs markedly from the formal and depersonalized model developed by Weber, so that alongside the formal system of administration one finds various informal structures and office cultures. These emerge for many reasons, for example to circumvent problems thrown up by the rigidity of the cumbersome formal structures; to take care of the individual and collective needs and aims of personnel; and as a reflection of wider social norms and values.

This kind of analysis also has implications for the study of social policy. If bureaucracies do not perform in the manner of the Weberian ideal-type, clearly the policies they are expected to execute will also undergo modification in the very process of implementation. The gap between official policy, as developed at higher levels of administration and government, and the actual bureaucratic implementation of this policy at the grass-roots level has therefore received increasing attention in recent years. Much of this literature deals with the policy process in general, treating implementation of policy as a stage in that process rather than as a distinct and separate issue from that of policy formulation (M. Hill, 1981; Rein, 1983). It is thus very interested in the reasons why policies implemented at local level often differ from those devised by planners (Blau, 1963; Lipsky, 1981; Higgins, 1978); in the impact of discretion and judgement in decision-making (M. Hill, 1976; Adler and Asquith, 1981); and in the effects of the unintended consequences of policy at various levels of implementation (H. Cohen, 1965).

But there is another dimension to all this, which is the relationship between the state and the individual. Since the development of the modern state has entailed a great expansion of its powers and spheres of activity, it is evident that a substantial portion of people's everyday life is bound up with relationships with the state's vast army of functionaries. As Grillo notes, these 'relationships are of special significance when . . . they coordinate the distribution of, access to, and decisions about basic resources: jobs, housing, education, welfare, health, the environment, development' (1980a: 20). His own work on North African immigrants to France and their position in the fields of housing, welfare, education, and employment highlights the importance of the functionary–client relationship (Grillo, 1980b, 1985). The work of Lipsky (1981) on the general characteristics of 'street-level' bureaucrats in the USA, Flett's (1979) study of public-housing allocation in a large English industrial city, and Saunders' (1979) work on the allocation and distribution of resources in Croydon powerfully substantiate the relevance of this perspective.

A variety of common themes link all these works: the presence of informal processes; the centrality of the differential command over resources and the asymmetrical power relations stemming from this distribution; schemes of moral classification intruding into the supposedly impartial workings of administration; and so forth. In what follows I aim to show not only how these themes shape interaction between functionary and client, but also how the process of interaction results in the reproduction of prevailing cultural categories and systems of classification.

I deal here, then, specifically with research carried out in an SSO in 1982.[1] The analysis attempts to demonstrate, first, that officers do not implement all aspects of DHSS policy in regard to the SB scheme; second, that in certain crucial respects local-level practice deviates sharply from official policy guidelines; and third, that this local 'model' sustains and reinforces the distinction between the 'deserving' and the 'undeserving' at the same time as the beliefs and practices which constitute this model are considered by the officers to be influential in vitiating the distinction.

The contrast between the 'deserving' and the 'undeserving' has shaped the character of much legislation concerning poor relief, especially the Poor Law Amendment Act of 1834. Within the SB system it manifests itself in the reluctance of successive governments to grant the long-term scale rate (LTSR) of benefit to claimants unemployed for more than one year (for a married couple this represents about £11 over the ordinary scale rates), since it is considered that this increased rate would further erode incentives to return to work.

In the SSO under discussion, the contrast has a somewhat different sense. At the broadest level it is used to distinguish between those claimants who, in the view of officers, seem to obtain more than they are (morally) entitled to and those who are thought to get a reasonably fair deal. Many officials argue that some claimants abuse the system to get out of it as much as possible (Berthoud, 1984: B11). This is accomplished, according to staff, in a variety of ways. First, by fraud, pure and simple (working while claiming; claiming items already possessed; making claims on the basis of false statements which it is difficult for officers to disprove; etc). Second, by claiming items deemed inessential to welfare but to which there is a legal entitlement. Third, by making claims for benefit when it is considered by officers that such claimants could make private provision for themselves but prefer to be state supported ('malingering', 'scrounging'). The problem as officers perceive it revolves around the need to impede and reduce such practices and to restrain claimants' appetites.

By contrast, leaving aside those actually committing some form of fraud, I shall argue that the so-called 'undeserving' comprise, first, claimants who are knowledgeable and assertive and who therefore pursue their claims with persistence; and second, claimants who, because they are considered to deviate in some way or other from a set of 'traditional' moral values (concerning the work ethic, individual responsibility, etc.) endorsed by benefit officers, should not really be eligible for benefit in the first place (the unemployed who could get a job if they only tried harder; the single mothers who should be married and be supported by working husbands). Although these two classes of the 'undeserving' are conceptualized in somewhat different fashion, the effect of their claiming, in the view of staff, produces a dual outcome, namely, an increase in the work load of already overworked officers, and a consequent demeaning and deterioration in the service available to the 'deserving'. Finally, I shall demonstrate that 'deserving' claimants are those who are compliant, deferential, and undemanding on the one hand, and on the other those who are deemed to conform to the same set of moral values endorsed by staff and thus considered to be in 'real' need of assistance. Nevertheless, to gain entry to this category, such claimants must not be seen to be importunate, assertive, or overly knowledgeable.

Background

The history and gradually expanding role of the SB scheme have been ably described by several authors (e.g. Atkinson, 1969; Deacon and Bradshaw, 1983), whilst the background to the 1980 reforms has been documented by Walker (1983). More recently the Policy Studies Institute has completed research into the SB scheme (Berthoud, 1984). This includes a very interesting survey, based on participant observation, of ten local offices (Cooper, n.d.), which in large measure corroborates the present analysis.

Benefit income is determined on the basis of scale rates laid down by Parliament, the size of the claiming unit, the number and ages of children, housing costs, and so on, with appropriate deductions for net income from other sources. Amongst many other provisions the scheme allows for 'additional requirements' (ARs) to cover 'abnormal' but regular expenditure, which are integrated into weekly benefit, and for 'single payments' which cover irregular events (Lynes, 1981).

Prior to 1980, single payments (then known as 'exceptional needs payments', or ENPs) were made almost entirely on a discretionary basis (that is, in terms of perceived need). This generated a passionate debate between the Supplementary Benefits Commission (now abolished) and various pressure groups (Child Poverty Action Group in particular). The latter argued that claimants at different offices and different claimants at any one office were being treated in quite different ways (Lister, 1980; Foster, 1983: 123). Guidance, which could be ignored, was provided in the A-code, a very complex, badly organized manual not available for inspection by the public.

To rationalize the decision-making process in ENP claims and other aspects of the scheme, new legislation was introduced in 1980. This provides a firm framework so that, in theory anyway, a single payment can only be awarded as long as the case falls within the provisions of the Regulations. However, the legislation is by no means definitive on every issue and room for discretionary decisions remains (Foster, 1983: 125). Moreover, the new Regulations have severely circumscribed the circumstances within which single payments can be granted, so that awards for shoes and clothing, some of the most regularly claimed items previously, can now only be made under very specific conditions. Such restrictions on single payments have not been balanced by any corresponding increase in the scale-rate monies, so it is possible to argue that the new legislation has left many SB claimants worse off (Walker, 1983: 91, 126–8).

To elaborate further the new legal basis underpinning the scheme, attention may be drawn to a neglected aspect of both present and previous legislation (Colin, 1974: 123). In the Social Security (Northern Ireland) Order 1980,[2] it is stated that:

It shall be the duty of the Department [DHSS] to make arrangements with a view to ensuring that benefit officers . . . exercise their functions in such manner as shall best promote the welfare of persons affected by the exercise of those functions. (Article 33, part II, schedule 2)

The legislation makes clear that the onus for welfare promotion lies squarely with the DHSS, and the Department's own circulars provide a very similar interpretation. For example, internal memos state that officers must give courteous and prompt attention to all claimants, be patient and attentive in listening to requests, be prompt in replying to correspondence, avoid jargon, give proper consideration to exceptional circumstances and needs, provide an explanation to every claimant of the scheme and of his rights and obligations within it, and give proper consideration to special circumstances which might affect payment arrangements. Staff are exhorted to 'adopt these practices irrespective of claimants' manner or circumstances' and are told that 'the first consideration for the welfare of claimants is to ensure that they receive their full entitlement under the Order including any AR or ENP which may be necessary'. Additionally, interviewing officers (clerical-officer grade) are expected to 'ensure that their enquiries cover any possible needs', to supply relevant leaflets, and to explain the various exemptions from National Health Service (NHS) charges. Here again, official policy emphasizes welfare promotion, and the burden for determining claimants' needs is placed unambiguously on the Department's officers.

Since the 1980 legislation has changed the basis of decision-making and because it is rather complicated, officers receive guidance in the form of the revised A-code, now known as the S-manual (which is available to public inspection on request), and also from Departmental circulars. However, although officers are expected to follow this guidance with a view to making consistent decisions on a country-wide basis, the advice is in no sense legally binding. To reinforce this, an internal memo states that such guidance is no substitute for the Order and the Regulations, and that therefore officers 'should familiarize themselves with the legislation'. It is worth noting that throughout the research period, no copies of either the Order or the Regulations were kept in the ground-floor public office of the building.

In the remainder of this chapter it is argued that important aspects of official policy are rarely implemented in full; that the greatest deviations concern the granting of single payments and the provision of information; that discretionary decisions remain an integral part of administration; and that the new legal basis of the scheme has had little impact on welfare promotion (Foster, 1983: 111–30).

The evidence

At the time of the research, the SB section of this office had 6,723 claimants on its books (comprising mostly pensioners and the unemployed), although the building was constructed to enable staff to deal with less than half this number. The ground-floor office which deals with queries and interviews is managed by a supervisor, six clerical officers, and one clerical assistant.

Reasons for interviews fall into three broad categories: the lodging of new claims; notification of changed circumstances; and claims for single payments. The time allotted for each interview is fifteen minutes, with a similar amount of time set aside for assessment. This is, simply, quite inadequate for official policy to be implemented. Lack of time therefore is a major constraint which, while it does not in itself determine the kinds of changes in the official model to be described, does create conditions for these changes to take place, since decisions have to be made concerning which aspects of policy will be practised and which will have to be ignored. In consequence, a local-level model is generated. This has evolved gradually by the accretion of numerous decisions, but decisions taken in the context of national legislation, resource constraints, peer-group pressures, and purported claimant categories, themselves shaped by internal working requirements and external social values and influences. It is in this sense that, as Lipsky points out, street-level bureaucrats 'make' policy (1981: 83–4). Such a model is a set of beliefs, attitudes, and derivative working practices structured by fairly constant and interrelated ideas, which has certain systematic consequences for both officers and claimants. In other words, given the parameters of the framework within which this form of poor relief is administered (and this can change dramatically from time to time), an office culture is constructed. Some aspects of this culture are very stable: the categories of the deserving and the undeserving are centuries old and were used by the Poor Law Committees and officers of the National Assistance Board. Other aspects are much more volatile and come and go quickly. It is not possible to demonstrate the creation or demise of any aspect of this culture, as the research period was too short. However, it is possible to indicate how schemes of classification and cultural categories are maintained and reproduced in everyday practice, and as I see it this is one of the main problematics of social science.

Supplementary Benefit is a scheme of last resort and therefore claimants cannot go elsewhere for assistance. Constrained in part by a legal framework, benefits are allocated and disbursed by staff. However, because there is considerable room for manoeuvre within this framework, claimants find themselves at the mercy of how staff perceive and carry out their duties. Staff/claimant interaction is thus characterized by an asymmetric relation of authority and power. To one degree or another, this relation allows benefit officers to impose their definitions of reality and their cultural schemes of classification on the claimant group. I will show that the different responses of claimants to staff practice serve to validate the categorizations of them that officers use. In this way analytical notions such as 'social structure' and 'institution' are seen to be both context to and outcome of the strategic conduct of interacting persons.

The data on which the following analysis is built derive from seventy-five staff/claimant interviews at which I was (silently) present. It is supplemented with information gained from talks with staff, observation of staff at work, and by the many interviews with unemployed claimants in Eastlough and Mallon Park, only some of whom were registered at the SSO in question.

Of these interviews, nearly half concerned fresh claims. In not one of these was the complete official policy model implemented. Those aspects most frequently omitted were: the explanation of the scheme, the claimant's right of appeal, and items covered by the scale rates; information concerning the 'passport' benefits; the provision of leaflets; and the determination of entitlements to ARs and single payments.

So as to make payments at all, much biographical and financial information has to be recorded, which leaves little time to delve into other, less immediately obvious, aspects of a case. For example, in twelve cases in which either the claimant or his wife had an income, the £4 disregard was always recorded, but in only four of these was information bearing on job expenses brought up. In two the claimant broached the subject and in the others the officer elicited the information. Thus in only two of twelve cases did the interviewing officer seek to obtain information on allowable job expenses, even though these have the force of law behind them. Often, such expenses do not amount to much but they can be crucial to a family living on SB. Interviews, then, are so short that, having collected and documented essential information, the officer has little, if any, time left to explain the scheme or to inquire into any special circumstances that may exist. Unless claimants make an explicit request for information or for a payment for an 'exceptional' need, they will, in many cases, depart without it. Overwhelmingly, interviews are used to collect information rather than to impart it.

Single payments

By virtue of their extremely selective nature, single payments have an importance out of all proportion to the amount of money involved, and without them many families would be in serious trouble. Moreover, it is acknowledged that continued dependence on SB requires a higher weekly benefit so that personal and household items which become worn out can be gradually replaced. Hence most SB claimants receive the LTSR either immediately (pensioners) or after one year (e.g. single parents). The one group that is excluded from such entitlement is the unemployed. Their dependence on these grants is therefore all the greater (Evason, 1980; Burghes, 1980; D.J. Smith, 1980). One of the main differences between official policy and local practice is that whereas in the former responsibility for meeting needs lies with the Department's officers, in the latter this is reversed and the onus is placed on the claimant to declare a need and request a payment to meet it. A summary of twenty-three staff/claimant interviews concerning single-payment grants follows.

Four cases (A, B, C, D) involved a move from furnished to unfurnished accommodation, in which the claimants came in to notify a change of address and present the rent book as evidence, so that the weekly payment could be adjusted. In one instance (A) a separated woman was also claiming bus fares to visit her children (one in hospital and two in a foster home) and a single payment for advance rent, whilst in a second (B) a mother and daughter were also claiming a grant for bedding. In none of these four cases did the interviewing officers (IOs) inquire about any other needs the claimants might have had, nor did they broach the subject of removal expenses, which would have been necessary had the claimants possessed furniture of their own. In two cases (C and D), the claimants mentioned that they had very little furniture only when the IOs were about to terminate the interviews. The response (which in both instances was brusque) was simply to ask what was required, only noting items which the claimants specifically requested. At no time did the officers volunteer any information as to what could and could not be claimed. For these two cases the IOs stated that a visiting officer (VO) would call to determine other needs – though that would have been too late to do anything about removal expenses. In cases A and B no such promise was made or requested, and the topics of household equipment and removal costs were never mentioned at all.

Case B is interesting for another reason. The bedding allowance granted was for one blanket, one pair of sheets, one pillow and one pillow case each (a total of £47.80).[3] In fact, official guidance stipulates a minimum stock of three blankets, two pairs of sheets, one pillow, and two pillow cases per person (a total cost of £106) although, as has been pointed out, such guidance is not legally binding. Moreover, the prices for bedding items list costings for different qualities of materials. In this case the claimant was awarded money for nylon sheets at £7.50 a pair rather than flannelette at £11.25 or cotton at £13.

There were five claims for various pieces of household furniture brought about by moves to unfurnished property, and all these were granted. However, in each case the officer made no attempt to list claimable items not mentioned by the claimant; in only two cases were the costs of removal brought up (once by the IO and once by the claimant) and granted; in two of the three cases in which the move was precipitated by the birth of a first child, claims for maternity needs were lodged, but in neither of these did the IOs seek to determine what else the claimants might have required, dealing only with what was asked for; in only one of the five cases was a leaflet supplied.

Two men claimed (independently) working boots for a new job (at the same place) and both these claims were awarded. However, whilst one of the men claimed, and insisted on getting, the cost of return bus fares for the first week's work, the other man made no such claim and did not get it.

Of six further claims for maternity needs, the IOs listed some of the claimable items in only two cases, and leaflets were provided to only one claimant who asked for them.

Of five further claims, one single parent was awarded money for a new cooker (the IO made no further inquiries); one claimed and obtained bus fares to enable her to visit her husband in hospital (she had to keep her tickets); one claim was refused because it turned out that the person had more than £300 in savings, thus making the claimant ineligible for single payments; a claim for children's shoes was rejected on the basis that, since the 1980 reforms, such items are covered by the scale rates; and finally there was a claim for assistance with funeral costs, the outcome of which was still in the balance when the research ended.

It will be helpful to describe one case in more detail. It concerns a young unemployed man and his wife who, on the birth of their first child, had moved from his parents' home into an unfurnished council house. The man had already claimed two single payments: one for cooker, sofa, and cutlery (£125) and one for floor coverings, chairs, and curtains (£122). Prior to the interview two VOs had been to the house to assess these claims. On this occasion he had come to claim a single-payment grant to cover the purchase of a cot and pram. The IO took the claim, but did not investigate the possibility that other maternity needs might exist. On being questioned, he said that the claimant had not mentioned anything else. According to the SB Order, officers must allow claims for 'the purchase of such items as are necessary for the immediate needs of the child'. These should normally include clothing, nappies, feeding bottles, cot and mattress, pram or carry cot, blankets, sheets, baby bath, and anything else which may be necessary (subject to what the claimant already possesses). The Order and Regulations do not stipulate quantities, so this is left to Departmental guidance, and to the discretion of individual officers.

Although the second VO knew that the wife was in hospital and the baby already born, he too did not inquire about possible maternity needs. He argued that the first VO had told him to deal only with the floor coverings, and had therefore assumed (he had not consulted the case papers) that a claim for maternity needs had already been lodged. Similarly, the IO excused himself by saying the second VO should have told him to look into further maternity needs, whilst the latter complained that as the IO it was his responsibility to acquaint himself with the facts of the case by referring to the documentation. Whoever should have taken care of it is a moot point, but the fact remains that all three knew of the baby's birth but none took the necessary steps. Moreover, the second VO admitted that he should have taken some action but, he reasoned, the claimant did not draw his attention to it. He further argued that the family was not in urgent need, as they had already received £250 in payments, and that if they were in need they would have made a claim. It has to be said though, first, that it has nothing to do with the parents' needs, but with those of the baby; second, that the earlier payments were for essential items properly claimed; and third, that officers have a statutory duty to expose claimants' needs by sympathetic inquiry.

A reasonably clear picture of claimant processing and need assessment emerges from the evidence embedded in both single-payment and fresh-claims cases. Local practice uncompromisingly transfers the onus for welfare promotion from the Department to the claimants: by largely ignoring its duty to determine entitlement to benefits other than the scale rates; by generally failing to give proper consideration to so-called 'exceptional' circumstances; by often neglecting to spell out the various rights of the claimant; by regularly failing to supply full explanations of the scheme; and by inadequate provision of the kind of information needed to make such claims.

It might be objected that, since many single-payment claims are dealt with by home visits, these conclusions are premature. However, increasingly there are fewer and fewer staff available for home visits. Additionally, evidence suggests that by and large the structure of the interaction between claimant and VO parallels that between claimant and IO. Thus data from the core samples of the unemployed in Mallon Park and in Eastlough demonstrate that while many characterize their encounters with officers (either at the SSO or at home) as reasonable or satisfactory, on closer questioning it regularly emerges that they have rarely been given any information concerning the scheme, other than that which has been explicitly requested, and that the typical form of such encounters revolves around the claimant making the request and the officer responding only to that request. In only a minority of cases have officers voluntarily suggested items that might be claimed, or provided unsolicited information on other aspects of the scheme.

It is necessary to point out, however, that VOs are more generous in their disbursement of information than office-bound interviewers. Whether this is because the former have more time, or because, being in the claimant's home, they feel greater pressure to respond in a more sympathetic manner; or because it is only in the home that a claimant's circumstances can be fully appreciated; or because VOs tend to be more experienced than IOs, is a problem worth extended study. Whatever the reasons, occasionally a VO does make unsolicited inquiries into the possible existence of unmet needs. The general picture from the data collected in Mallon Park and Eastlough is as follows: from the thirty-five people in the core samples eligible for single-payment grants, three people claimed on five occasions, six people claimed on four occasions, seven claimed on three occasions, eleven on two occasions, five on one occasion and three not at all, making a total of eighty-seven claims involving a VO. Of this number, twenty cases are not well documented, leaving a total of sixty-seven.

As far as the general tenor of these encounters is concerned, claimants, both Catholic and Protestant in about equal measure, portrayed the VOs as pleasant, reasonable, helpful, etc. Only a minority described the VO as in some way abusive, rude, or insensitive. However, as far as can be ascertained from claimants' descriptions of the events, in only twenty-six cases did the VO voluntarily suggest specific additional items which could be claimed, or provide specific, detailed information on some other aspect of the scheme in an unsolicited manner. It is true that in more than these twenty-six cases claimants did eventually obtain extra items, but this was because they asked questions during the visit about other things they might be entitled to claim. In the other cases, the VO simply dealt with what the claimant originally asked for either in a personal visit to the SSO or in a letter to the office.

When asked if VOs volunteer information, far and away the most typical response was some variant of: 'no, they tell you very little, you have to ask them; and if you don't know what it's all about, how do you know what to ask for?' This is how George Lynn put it: 'See when the assistance man come out he said, "is there anything else you want to claim for?" I looked at him and he looked at me, and I says, "well, I don't know really"'; Theresa Madden related her experiences thus: 'Instead of her telling me whenever she came out what I could put in for, I was frightened. She knows what she's here for, for [my husband] wrote it in the letter, but she says, "What is it you want?" They always ask me what it is you want.'

The following cases further illuminate the form of these encounters. First, Pat Hardy cannot remember making a claim for single-payment grants during his first spell of unemployment; he asserts that he knew nothing about them. In his second spell of unemployment, his wife was told something about them by a close friend. So they wrote in to their office claiming beds and bedding for themselves and their children. The VO called the following week and not only allowed them for these items, but also awarded a grant for extra kitchen cupboards, which Pat had no idea could be claimed. Similarly, Jimmy Nolan and his wife, on advice from a neighbour, put in for a fireguard, a stair gate, a bed for themselves, and a baby buggy. The VO was 'great' and suggested they needed carpet for two rooms and bed linen for the bed. Finally, after Billy Stewart had been unemployed for a few months, Sinn Fein workers leafleted Mallon Park urging residents to claim everything they could. With the explanatory leaflet came a form listing a host of items that could be claimed on single-payment grants. All Billy had to do was complete the simple form, tick the boxes of the items he thought he was eligible for, and post it to his local office. The VO who came out was very helpful and friendly, and not only awarded them what they had asked for, but a couple of other small items as well. Betty Stewart was delighted.

All three of these cases demonstrate that VOs can do a very good job, but what is also obvious is that the original information concerning single payments came from elsewhere, from neighbours, friends, or pressure groups of one kind or another. In general claimants acquire information from a variety of sources, in a piecemeal fashion, over a long period of time and in a quite unsystematic manner. They therefore have a very fragmented and confused picture of the system, and so one which is difficult to use and difficult to complete. Furthermore, in the cases of Nolan and Hardy, they were entering their second year of unemployment before they received these grants. Finally, it is sobering to report that even though the VOs in these three cases sought 'to promote the welfare' of the claimants, each family still has unmet needs not noticed by the VO (gardening tools, pots and pans, guard rail for cooker, draught excluders, etc.). There is no doubt that a scheme which has guidelines on how many knives and forks, how many shirts, underpants, nappies, etc., a family should have has clearly passed beyond the ludicrous. The point to be made most forcefully is that it really does not matter how good the VOs are: without a clinical dissection of a family's total possessions (which would make the cost of administration astronomical), they can never do a completely satisfactory job.

To conclude this section, let me add that the case evidence at my disposal includes many long-term unemployed who are only just beginning to find out about their entitlement to, *inter alia*, gardening tools, draught excluders, stair gates, fireguards, travelling expenses to visit relatives in hospital, removals expenses, laundry additions (Ray Carlile, for example, in penury for eighteen months, eventually discovered he could obtain an allowance towards laundry costs as two of his children are chronic enuretics), help with hire-purchase commitments (under certain conditions), and so on. Additionally, many of these unemployed do not know the level of the earnings' disregard, and very few know that job expenses (bus fares, union dues, child-minding fees if required, etc.) can be set off against earnings; and I have still to meet someone who has heard of the LTSR, although a few are aware that single parents and pensioners appear to receive a higher rate of benefit. Finally, a large majority of claimants do not even know how to check whether their basic weekly benefit is correct or not. Few members of either sample could confidently describe, step by step, how a benefit entitlement is calculated, although several were aware of the underlying formula (so much for a couple, so much for children, so much for rent, minus various deductions, etc.). What many do is compare their benefit with that received by others in similar circumstances, and if the two are about the same amount, it is accepted as broadly correct. If there is underclaiming of additional requirement grants (which are integrated into the weekly benefit) then this form of checking totals is likely to have the indirect consequence of perpetuating such underclaiming.

It is in this context that a recent survey by Briggs and Rees of SB consumers can be criticized. They note that: 'Comments [in the area of information and explanation] were not particularly frequent' but 'over-all twice as many respondents praised the information and explanation they had been given as made critical comments about them' (1980: 70–1). However, on their own evidence (supported by other studies: Bond, 1975; Ritchie and Wilson, 1979; Evason, 1980), claimants' knowledge of the general scheme was 'low' and of its details 'very low' (1980: 129). Given this latter finding, a large majority of claimants would have few reliable criteria against which to judge the adequacy, completeness, or veracity of a piece of information or explanation they had been given. Such blatant empiricism does not advance our understanding very far (see Howe, 1989).

Although many factors play an important role in the shaping of local practice and the consequent reversal in official policy, lack of space and adequate information permits the analysis of only some of these.[4]

Resource constraints

As explained, the taking of essential biographical and financial informa-tion consumes the bulk of interview time, so little remains for even a cursory examination of a claimant's circumstances and/or a full expla-nation of the scheme. However, since this predicament is more acute at fresh-claims stage than at subsequent interviews insufficient time can-not be an adequate explanation for policy shift.[5]

Lack of time is linked to work loads and manning levels. Because of the rapid rise in unemployment since 1979 these two issues have been a constant source of dissatisfaction among SSO staff, and they are quick to air their complaints. Front-counter clerks are not perfect and accord-ingly cannot be *au fait* with all the rules concerning benefit assessment and entitlement, especially as these rules change frequently. If time and trouble are taken to explain complications, other claimants have to wait longer, the workload on colleagues increases correspondingly, and clerical officers become flustered, tense, and abrupt.

Staff perceive many difficulties. The majority genuinely feel over-worked and under-staffed, and complain that the office manager cares more about the claimants than he does about his staff. Manning levels is a many-sided problem. Because work is heavy and the rewards low, staff wastage is high. This results in a high proportion of inexperienced trainees and temporary stand-ins, and a consequently heavier load on older, more experienced staff. Because of the complexity of the benefit schemes, clerks must be mindful of many procedural details, and the concentration needed for this, especially during a tense interview, can quickly lead to mental exhaustion.

Longer queues, an increase in tension, and more mistakes are the inevitable results of staff shortages and overwork. The correction of errors often involves the completion of extra forms, thus reducing the time available for new work, thereby increasing in turn the possibility of further mistakes. Claimants cannot be sent away on the excuse of work pressure until their cases have been dealt with. Additionally, because of the high case load for which each officer is responsible, only a short time can be spent examining any particular one, and most cases are more complicated than is generally thought. Informally, officers work a rationing system by attempting to foist case papers they do not want onto colleagues. Colleagues react by claiming that their work load is already too large. Sometimes the supervisor intervenes but usually it is this competitive negotiation which irons out inequitable work loads created by the supervisor. The result is that each officer tends to do about the same number of cases. If someone does too few, that officer is accused of slacking and extra case papers materialize on the desk. In this way most cases receive equal amounts of time, irrespective of how different they may be. Some cases are so confusing, however, that the supervisor gives a special dispensation for an officer to spend extra time on them. As the number of cases increases and staff levels remain much the same, staff either work faster, which they cannot realistically do, or backlogs become larger. This seems to have happened in several English offices, causing widespread chaos and dismay amongst claimants (Albeson and Smith, 1984).

Staff also complain that many claimants are unhelpful and unsympathetic, and that, with as much patience and tolerance as they can muster, they have to endure foul manners, foul language, and foul breath. They are on occasion, and as representatives of the Department, the victims of insults, aggression, and even violence; in the year prior to the research two officers were physically assaulted.

It is obvious, then, that the counter clerk has to be equipped with a rather startling array of qualities. However, benefit officers suffer from the same sort of failings as are to be found throughout the general population. Different officers can be judged in different ways, and the following is a list of criticisms collected during conversations. Counter staff may be abrupt, officious, condescending, too helpful, a soft touch, indiscreet, too self-opinionated, may see a situation as a personal encounter and hence conduct a vendetta, may allow personal attitudes and feelings to interfere with work, may become easily harassed, lack commonsense, jump too easily to inappropriate conclusions, etc. Those in the interior office may lack confidence, ability, or commonsense; perform sloppy work; be too slow, too indecisive, excessively pedantic; and so on. Indeed, the ideal officer is a rare breed of person. Given these perceived difficulties and their knowledge that their worth is not greatly appreciated by either management or claimants, it is not surprising that several officers manfully strove to disabuse me of the notion that they 'are a lot of lazy, tea-swilling bureaucrats'.

Insufficient space is a factor whose importance is difficult to determine. Nonetheless, few claimants enjoy waiting in cramped conditions, and on several occasions during the research queues stretched outside the main doors. The point is that officers rarely regard claimants as investing anything: they turn up merely to receive; but as Wadel clearly points out *'being a client takes time, planning and effort'* (1979: 377, his italics). Although in 1982 there was a fairly efficient appointments system for interviews, queueing arrangements for the query counter were non existent and often claimants had no idea whose turn it was.

A further factor concerns financial constraints. Although in theory the social security budget is unlimited, economizing takes place at various levels. Since the present Conservative government came to power it has abolished earnings-related supplements to insurance benefits, drawn some benefits into the tax net, and reduced the scope of single payments provisions. Additionally, the government now publishes figures on those on or under the 'poverty line' every two years, rather than annually as previously, and it has instructed the DHSS to discontinue publishing estimates of the extent of the underclaiming of means-tested benefits.

At the local level, in this office, some officers occasionally worry that the supervisor, who has to endorse all single-payment claims, will not pass a claim because it is too large. In fact, during the research he never did this. Nevertheless, on two occasions an officer pared down a claim before taking it to the supervisor. Moreover, officers' comments on the amounts of the claims were far more in evidence when the claims were large, and in these cases they ranged from well-worn jokes about Rolls Royce cars, through resignation to occasional sarcasm and resentment. Comments such as 'all we do is shell out money for anybody who wants it', 'its crazy, you get money for anything', 'you hear the same old sob stories over and over again, you just get used to 'em', were frequent, and the size of single-payment claims, rather than indicating the enormous extent of claimants' needs, was more often interpreted as an indication of the ease with which the Department could be conned into parting with its money.

Fraud and abuse

The emphasis on the prevention and detection of fraud and abuse has been a constant feature of arrangements for poor relief (M. Hill, 1969; D. Fraser, 1973; Deacon, 1976). Whatever the actual level of fraud, figures for detected fraud have remained low (Field, 1977: 56; 1979: 755); they have remained insignificant compared to other forms of fraud (Field et al., 1977); and individual cases of fraud have attracted excessive and exaggerated publicity (Golding and Middleton, 1982).[6] Moreover, while many of those receiving welfare benefits feel a sense of stigma, those obtaining fiscal and occupational benefits are generally not thought to be receiving welfare payments at all (cf. chapter 4).

With the regularly recurring promises to stamp on social security scroungers, and the ever-increasing number of fraud investigators allegedly using harsher and harsher methods,[7] it is not surprising that the level of fraud awareness in SSOs is high, and the office in question is no exception. The day before my stint of research began, a senior officer warned me: 'Everyone's doing it, it gets into your head everyone's doing it.' There is a general consensus that fraud and abuse are rife among certain categories of claimant, with unemployed tradesmen and single parents being the groups most often mentioned. Consequently, some staff are acutely aware of dirty hands, muddy boots, and greasy clothes, and of the difficulties of establishing the veracity of the circumstances of single parents. Many of the comments of staff after completing interviews concerned either the 'excessive' size of the claim, the possibility that it might be fraudulent, or the likelihood that the claimant was telling lies ('a bit dodgy that one'; 'that was a good story'; 'did you see the paint under his finger nails?'; 'what did you think of him then?'; 'bet she's got a man somewhere').

The local office codes, a monument to the complexity of the system, instruct officers not only to be aware of the physical appearance of the claimant, but also his demeanour, and if this suggests that he is working the supervisor should be notified. Concerning fraud, the principal manual at present is the Fraud Investigator's Guide (FIG), which expounds the view that fraud detection is an integral part of the administrative work of all grades of staff, and the following excerpts endorse this:

A powerful aid in the prevention of fraud is to ensure your colleagues' involvement and to reinforce their corporate responsibility for fraud prevention and detection. For example, if someone's suspicions eventually result in a successful prosecution, make sure that that person knows it! (para. 820)

A fraud officer is the Manager's *most valuable* resource and the Manager's *first priority* should be to do everything possible to help him become fully effective. (para. 905; my italics).

[Earlier sections] drew attention to the importance of creating and maintaining an awareness of social-security fraud risks. This is a continuing task overtaken by the day-to-day pressures in a SSO. It is suggested that management should regularly review the state of fraud awareness, both in the training of newcomers and to ensure that more experienced staff understand the reasons for procedural safeguards. (para. 936)

As these extracts emphasize, awareness of the possibility of fraud and abuse is inculcated in officers. This may not be a process of indoctrination, but the fact that the code asserts that a manager's first priority is to assist the fraud officers in the prosecution of their duties, rather than to promote his claimants' welfare, as the legislation stipulates, does indicate how significant the former aspect is (Foster, 1983: 125–6).

It is very important to note here how staff categorize claimants, irrespective of whether they think fraud might be involved. At the beginning of the chapter it was remarked that some claimants are thought to exploit or 'work' the system in an effort to get as much out of it as possible. Evidence suggests that staff classify claimants not so much in respect of their 'objective' needs, but rather in terms of their benefit status (unemployed, sick, single parent, pensioner, with variations within each category) and also in terms of their demeanour during interviews. Taking benefit status first, pensioners are generally considered 'deserving'. This is because officers attribute to them a long working history: they have paid their dues, are considered to be committed to the work ethic and to uphold notions of individual responsibility and self-reliance, and conform to expected patterns of family organization. That is, they are seen to adhere to a set of traditional

English moral values which office culture endorses and seeks to defend (see Flett, 1979: 143, for a similar argument concerning public housing allocation). Being proud and imbued with a sense of independence, however, pensioners are thought to dislike claiming benefit and to feel ashamed. But claiming is necessary because the retirement pension is considered inadequate. Thus pensioners should be treated with sympathy. In other words both staff and pensioners are part of the same moral community around which a boundary is drawn, this boundary being defined by a set of normatively supported moral criteria.

Other categories of claimant are open to suspicion. Single parents do not conform to ideal expectations of the 'normal' family system. Some of these may attempt to exploit loopholes in the benefit schemes: husband and wife may separate as a ploy to obtain higher total benefits; or the woman may be secretly supported by a working man. The unemployed and the sick may be malingering. Therefore it requires a vigilant and well-trained eye to discriminate between the genuine and the scrounger. In the terms of this perspective the 'undeserving' are those who deviate from the values of the moral community to which pension-ers and benefit staff conform. Here, then, despite the fact that official policy dictates that claimants should be treated equally, irrespective of their circumstances, office culture erects a symbolic boundary between those who are presumed to conform to these 'traditional' values and those who are presumed to deviate from them in some way.

However, the situation is rather more complex than this because a further, very important criterion comes into play within each of these major sub-divisions of the claimant population. Those claimants, irres-pective of their benefit status, who ask many questions, argue, appear self-confident, lodge large claims, are persistent, etc., are described as 'aggressive', 'grasping', 'ungrateful', 'greedy', 'shameless', and so forth. In contrast, what might be called the 'ideal' claimant is someone who merely answers questions, produces all the required documents, is subservient and deferential, and who does not mention complicating matters. Such passive and acquiescent people are described as 'nice', 'easy', 'poor', 'grateful', 'polite', and so on (cf. Kelvin and Jarrett, 1985: 86–7; Prottas, 1979: 38).

Behind these divergent classifications there is a strong conflict of interest. As already mentioned, officers are in their own estimation heavily overworked; at the end of most days they are cynical, tired, and irritable. Moreover, some claimants are very difficult; some do come in drunk; some do physically and verbally assault staff; some ramble on incoherently; others come in to lodge very unspecific claims because their weekly money does not stretch to a week's expenditure. In the eyes of staff, some claimants are perversely persistent, some are aggressively assertive, and some demand simple answers to complex questions. All of this merely adds work and stress to what is already a difficult and unrewarding job, and it is little wonder that staff prefer passive, self-effacing claimants.

Staff are not only concerned with fraud and abuse but with overpayments in general, since, while underpayments can easily be rectified, overpayments are, in many circumstances, not recoverable at all. Moreover, the discovery of overpayments entails much more paperwork, written reports if they are large, and possibly a reprimand. Claimants, on the other hand, are far more worried about underpayments which, if large, can plunge a family into desperate circumstances (Howe, 1983a; and next chapter).

From the perspective of staff, then, there is a need to reduce fraud, restrain the appetites of the 'greedy', identify the feckless and the malingerer, minimize overpayments, and contain workloads to manageable proportions. Many claimants, of course, have diametrically opposed interests. They are concerned about late giros, debts, hire purchase payments, high fuel bills, children's shoes, and, in general, ends that don't meet (Evason, 1980). The problems of SSO staff are the very least of their worries. Indeed, for many claimants it is precisely staff practice which creates the difficulties the former have.

It must be stressed that staff are no more ill-disposed to claimants than are other sections of society, nor is it being argued that all the problems are created by work procedures and resource constraints. Such frameworks ignore the facts that benefits are low (for the long-term unemployed particularly), that there is much genuine poverty and hardship, and that benefit claims have to be lodged in an atmosphere made the more hostile by unsympathetic public attitudes (see Holman, 1978: 146–83).

In summary, whereas in official DHSS policy priority is given to the promotion of welfare, in the local office this is to some extent reversed and there is a significant increase in the practical concern over fraud, abuse, and overpayments. It may be added that similar conclusions have been reached by Laurence (quoted in Douglas, 1980: 52), by Townsend (1979: 847–8) and by Stevenson (1973: 189–90).

It is necessary to add, however, that attitudes of staff concerning fraud and abuse do not often translate directly into action. Many occasions arise when an officer suspects fraud of some kind but refrains from initiating any action. Nevertheless, this does not mean that these attitudes have no repercussions on staff practice, as the following section should make plain.

Provision of information

It has already been mentioned that official policy demands that officers supply information about the scheme, and that they have a duty to promote welfare by inquiring into the possible existence of needs. Of the seventy-five interviews, the full range of information was never once supplied. In some interviews some information was given. In more than half the cases no information at all was supplied voluntarily. When information was provided it was often general and unspecific in character, e.g. 'you know about the exemptions from prescriptions and things like that?'; 'no, the scale rates include a sum for your electric'; and so on. In many cases when information was supplied it was in answer to claimants' questions and typically the response contained only the minimum necessary. For example, in reply to questions such as: 'can I get money for the new baby?', answers were of the kind: 'you might be entitled to some essential items'. Of the twenty-three single-payment cases, listings of some items were volunteered on only four occasions. These data, then, indicate just how sparingly information is allocated to claimants.

There are only two methods for the transmission of information: written and oral. It is supposedly because of the pervasive ignorance which surrounds the SB scheme that the DHSS prints numerous leaflets providing explanations and descriptions of its various aspects, and such leaflets are often well designed and easy to understand. However, the only leaflet regularly to cross the counter was the one containing the least information. Another, which even I had difficulty obtaining, was rarely handed out and never asked for. Finally, one leaflet, dealing specifically with single payments and considered 'essential' and 'vital' to claimants was rarely provided voluntarily.[8]

There is a variety of reasons why such leaflets are used so economically. First, there is simply no pressure on interviewing officers from their supervisors to supply claimants with leaflets. Second, officers note, truthfully, that many claimants discard leaflets very quickly and rarely read them. Third, officers assume that knowledge of the scheme is more extensive than appears actually to be the case, and therefore feel no pressing need to provide leaflets. When asked why little or no information was given during interviews, officers regularly excused themselves by remarking that claimants already knew the score, and that if they had a need they would not be slow in disclosing it. Thus, many officers reject the assertion that take-up rates for these benefits are low. Finally, and not altogether consistently, officers seem acutely conscious that an undisciplined supply of information would result in the office being inundated with a torrent of mostly bogus and manufactured claims (Berthoud, 1984: H11–H12). Such an argument not only indicates just how pervasive is the notion that fraud and abuse are rife among claimants, but it also supports the claim that for many officers a major difficulty revolves around the need to restrain claimants' appetites for benefits. Accordingly, the average claimant is not perceived as a pawn manipulated by an oppressive and complex bureaucracy but as someone who actively and cunningly exploits it; he is therefore someone who requires restraint rather than encouragement. Incidentally, this explains why staff are suspicious about the motives of social workers, since it is widely believed that they are naive and that they prime claimants on what to request.

Turning now to oral information, a further set of reasons can be examined. First, officers complain that there is no time to explain even a minimum about the system (though it takes but a moment to pass a leaflet over the counter). Second, if staff take too long over one claimant, colleagues accuse them of not pulling their weight. Third, officers note that it is embarrassing to go into great detail about what claimants might need, and it is also assumed, with good reason, that many claimants dislike the close questioning that can be entailed in such claims. In single-payment claims, the list of claimable items can be very large and a fully researched claim requires time, energy, patience, and a sincere willingness to make sure the claimant receives everything the law allows. It not only involves detailing what can be claimed, but also determining what is already possessed. Once a claim has been taken, it would need to be assessed and costed, taking into account whether items should be purchased new or secondhand, how many of each to award, what quality to award if different pricings are available, and so forth. Such research should entail repeated consultation of the S-manual and relevant circulars as well as reference to the legislation. However, the legislation is not available in the public office, and officers tend to rely on advice from colleagues, as regular perusal of the codes and manuals is denigrated as 'code bashing' (Berthoud, 1984: B28). In each case of fresh claims there are many different types of AR to look into, as well as earnings' disregards and allowable job expenses, and for many of these some form of documentational proof is required.

Fourth, just as officers assert that the provision of information can lead to numerous bogus claims, so they are also loath to itemize what can be claimed, because it is generally thought that leading questions and the provision of detailed lists serves merely 'to put ideas into their heads'.

Discussion

Given such a position, staff in this local office are more concerned to prevent abuse than to detect it. The problem is, however, that whilst detection depends on evidence, prevention depends on suspicion, and while the former acts selectively, the latter tends to be applied universally; that is, the large majority are denied information on the grounds that some may use it to abuse the service. I should note here that no discernible patterns of allocation to different categories of claimant (pensioner, unemployed, single parent, etc.) were detected. However, this may be due to the comparative smallness of the sample of interviews witnessed, and the fact that it contained very few pensioners, these being dealt with mostly by home visits. Moreover, those claimants who did receive unsolicited information and a somewhat superior service than was usual were invariably described in favourable terms.

Local practice then, rather than being unambiguously devoted to the promotion of claimants' welfare, instead withholds information, gives practical priority to the prevention (and occasionally) detection of fraud and abuse, and generally impugns, by implication, the motives of most claimants. Severe resource constraints, typical working arrangements, and the endorsement of wider social values and attitudes concerning poor relief underpin this local model.

It is obvious that many aspects of official policy cannot be put into practice because of resource constraints, but the data on fraud and abuse, and on the retention of information, indicate that the failure to implement such policy is also due to the various decisions taken by local office staff, influenced both by their defence of a particular moral outlook and by their desire to reduce work loads.

There seem to be two overlapping and inter-connected consequences of this local practice for claimants. The first is social and the second is financial. Socially, it would appear, from what many claimants have to say, that such practices aggravate the feelings of shame and stigma that they evidently feel. A large majority of the unemployed SB claimants in the core samples from both Eastlough and Mallon Park complain of (amongst other things) the lack of information given, and many register their dislike of claiming with remarks such as the following:

Nobody told me anything: there's an awful lot we don't know.

They don't tell you what you're entitled to; you have to ask.

If you don't know anything and you're not told anything, how can you know to ask?

It's like trying to get blood out of a stone.

You'd think the money was coming out of their own pocket the way they act.

They treat you like an animal. Their attitude is 'you're bloody rubbish – you're dirt'.

They give the impression you're there to rob them and they're there to stop you.

Those people at the desk, I see their job, they're just buffers to put you off.

If you want to get anything you just have to keep on at them; don't give in.

Everything I know I've had to find out myself.

Push them for all you can get and if they turn you down, well and good; but how many people are going to do that?

I think you have to throw yourself on their mercy and see what they can . . .

I don't like asking for anything down there; it makes me feel inferior, it makes me feel like a beggar.

You just accept what they tell you, you take it for granted that the clerk is right, you're not allowed to question her. This is what our attitude was.

Not everything claimants have to say is so critical. They do, for example, often acknowledge how difficult the job is, that some officials are very helpful, and that they have to endure a good deal of gratuitous abuse. However, the critical comments far outnumbered the complimentary ones.

Financially, the conclusion that many (just how big a proportion is difficult to compute) claimants do not, *and cannot*, get what they are theoretically entitled to under the provisions of the SB Order seems inescapable.

The 'deserving' and the 'undeserving'

It remains to analyse the manner in which the distinction between the 'deserving' and the 'undeserving' accords with what has been said. This contrast, in fact, is rarely used to classify individual claimants. As already mentioned, irrespective of benefit status claimants are labelled in many ways, though generally speaking these can be divided into two broad categories: those who are seen as 'greedy', 'grasping', 'difficult', 'ungrateful', etc., and those who are 'nice', 'polite', 'poor', 'grateful', 'easy', etc. That the latter group is more numerous is indicated by the fact that most interviews are conducted without any visible sign of animosity on either side. Conversation here is limited to the officer's questions, the claimant's replies and general topics not connected with the claim in any specific way. These encounters are also characterized by a relation of power which is almost tangible: claimants are deferential, they come as supplicants, usually they speak when spoken to, if they initiate a topic they do so anxiously and with trepidation (Berthoud, 1984: H6–H7).

The distinction occurs in conversations with staff concerning claimants as a totality. In such contexts they are divided into the 'truly eligible', that is, those who have genuine claims and deserve what they get, and the less eligible. These latter submit claims which are not necessarily fraudulent, but which are seen as either bogus (because the claimant is taking advantage of a loophole, or claiming items not because of 'need' but because they are there to be claimed, or because the claimant is malingering and could make private provision for himself but prefers dependence on the state benefit system), or excessive (the existence of a need is accepted but the claimant is asking for too much). In all such cases claimants are not considered as deserving either what they claim or what they receive. In addition there are cases in which, despite the fact that entitlement to a claim is disputed by officers, the claimant insists on pursuing it. In general all such claimants are thought to take advantage of a system which, on the whole, is considered to be quite generous. Viewed from this perspective, officials tend to assert that most claimants (the 'deserving') get what they are (morally) entitled to, but some obtain too much, this latter group then being designated as the 'undeserving'. From the evidence adduced here it can be argued that many claimants get less than they could under the law, whilst only some receive their full legal entitlement. It must be emphasized that whereas DHSS policy is now firmly rooted in a legal framework (staff are enjoined to treat claimants equally irrespective of their manner or circumstances; claims should be dealt with in accordance with legal entitlement; and all reference to such notions as 'deserving' and 'undeserving' are eschewed), local practice exhibits a significant moralistic complexion.

While staff assert that one of their primary goals is to promote the welfare of the truly eligible, they also acknowledge that a related objective is to restrain the 'undeserving'. The point here is that by impeding the undeserving (the moral deviant, the feckless, the malingerer, and the aggressive claimant) it is alleged that a better service is provided for the truly eligible, since the latter will feel less stigmatized by association with the former. With the stress on prevention rather than detection, this dual objective is thought to be accomplished by the transference of responsibility for welfare promotion onto the claimant, the pervasive practice of withholding information, the reluctance to supply even partial lists of claimable items, and the sometimes unsympathetic treatment of single-payment claims in which not all items are awarded or mentioned, or costings are provided at lowest prices. Though staff insist that these two aims dovetail, that a good service can only be offered if the truly deserving can be identified and therefore targeted, the evidence suggests that in fact these two objectives are mutually exclusive. Action designed to restrain the 'undeserving' actually impedes the welfare promotion of most claimants.

Furthermore, lack of time, staff, and space, the complexity of both the scheme and claimants' circumstances, general economy measures and prevailing social attitudes concerning welfare, all tend to militate against a close and sympathetic scrutiny of a claimant's needs. Thus both in terms of what officers choose to do and also in terms of the way in which they are constrained to act, local practice effectively penalizes most claimants, either by creating circumstances in which it is unlikely that needs will be exposed or, if they are expressed, by not examining them in sufficient detail.

Additionally, the judging and labelling of claimants can rarely be carried out on the basis of accurate information regarding the existence or not of unmet needs, for the simple reason that in many cases such evidence is not available, either because the interviewer makes little attempt to elicit it, or because the claimant does not mention it. Labelling and stereotyping are therefore determined by what is known about the claimant: status, appearance, demeanour, income and savings, and, in the case of home visits, visible material possessions, etc.; that is to say, characteristics only some of which have any bearing on present welfare. In sum, then, the cumulative and systematic effect of all these practices and resource constraints is not one which victimizes a particular set of claimants (the 'undeserving') as is intended; on the contrary, it can be argued that, to one degree or another, the majority of claimants reap the consequences.

If this is the overall effect on claimants, it remains to describe what their response is. The tactics adopted by claimants differ considerably. At one extreme, claimants simply accept unquestioningly the assessment of their needs and the amount of their weekly benefit by DHSS staff (Howe, 1983a: 69). Because of embarrassment, reticence, or stigma, some may refrain from claiming (Lister, 1974; Townsend, 1976; Supplementary Benefits Commission, 1978; next chapter); because of ignorance some may not realize that they are entitled to a benefit or that the assessment is incorrect; because of 'red tape' or difficulties associated with prior claims, some may refrain from lodging further claims (Howe, 1983a: 64, 66). At the other extreme (not counting those who knowingly attempt to commit fraud) are claimants with a greater knowledge of the scheme and a greater willingness to claim, even if this means pursuing claims relentlessly and despite any opposition encountered. My own data (see next chapter) include several cases in which people have fought tooth and nail to secure payments initially denied them, on occasion reduced to tears of frustration by their seeming impotence and the numbing intransigence of SSO staff. Other such episodes have been documented by M. Hill (1969), Colin (1974), Gould and Kenyon (1972), and Marsden (1982). No lesser an authority than Peter Townsend (1979: 848) has concluded that 'the payment of additional grants or allowances will more often be the result of intense pressure than of any anticipatory action' (cf. Collman, 1981, and his analysis of 'client resistance' and the process of becoming a client).

In order to obtain various benefits, it is claimants who have to initiate action: demand information; inform the officer that they have this or that need; itemize the things they require or feel entitled to; assert that their benefit has been incorrectly assessed; and so forth (P. Moore, 1980). In order to receive benefits they feel, or know, they are entitled to, claimants are placed in an invidious situation where they must needs be assertive, demanding, and aggressive. This is not to say, of course, that claimants having recourse to such tactics are inevitably in the right, since often they are not; but given the make-up of the system, such claimants can find that this is the only way to obtain what they feel they have a right to. Moreover, while many pressure tactics are available to claimants: requests to see superior officers; repeated visits and phone calls; lodging of appeals; verbal abuse; use of outside pressure groups; use of children as an emotional weapon; etc. (M. Hill, 1969; Weightman, 1978), these entail severe social, psychological and financial costs. Officials can retaliate by refusing to talk to claimants, by asserting that there is no entitlement, by refusing to divulge names, by ignoring demands to see the supervisor or manager, by threatening or actually calling the police, etc.

Since a prominent feature of the moral system espoused by the office culture is that claimants should be deferential, thankful, and docile, and think themselves lucky, those claimants who are grateful, un-demanding, compliant, and know their place are, by extension con-sidered to conform to all the other aspects of this system (i.e. those ideas concerning the work ethic, self-reliance, thrift, family life, etc.). Those claimants who, on the other hand, adopt combative tactics are just those who are characterized as morally deviant and thus described as 'grasping', 'pushy', and 'greedy', (the truly deserving claimant would not resort to such a brazen and shameless course of action). However, so long as their claims are within the law, they must be processed and, in many cases, awarded, and it is this which generates the notion, often heard, that 'those who shout loudest get the most'. Furthermore, in the eyes of officers, it is claimants such as these who exploit the system for their own ends thereby demeaning it for more 'deserving' claimants, and who therefore, at a more general level, are designated the 'undeserving'. As a consequence of this, officers cynically note that the 'undeserving' get more than the 'deserving', a belief which appears to be widely shared by the general public (Schlackman, quoted in Golding and Middleton, 1982: 170–1). However, it can now be seen that the practices which are thought to deter and militate against the 'undeserving' are just those which spur some claimants into adopting tactics which then result in their being characterized under this pejorative label. In short, it is only because local-level practice is constituted in the way described that some claimants feel compelled to resort to a course of action which, while it might secure them a benefit they would not otherwise have received (Prottas, 1979: 41), serves also unintentionally to reinforce the validity of those distinctions officers use to classify claimants. Thus the very processes which are supposed to vitiate the distinction between the 'deserving' and the 'undeserving' in fact work in such a way as to perpetuate and reproduce it.

Conclusion

Benefit-office culture divides claimants into two categories, the 'deserving' and the 'undeserving', which cut across the major benefit classes (unemployed, sick, single parent, pensioner). At the most general level, pensioners are considered more 'deserving' than, for instance, the unemployed, for the joblessness of the latter and therefore their conformity to a widely held set of moral values is always open to suspicion. However, this cultural distinction also operates within each class so that, for example, some unemployed are deemed more 'deserving' than others. Here again one of the principal criteria for deciding on inclusion in or exclusion from the moral 'community' is the degree of presumed adherence to shared ideas of individual responsibility, self-reliance and the necessity for work.

Various types of claimant are branded as deviant, as scroungers, or as malingerers, either because of their apparent circumstances (unemployed tradesmen who, it is assumed, should be able to get a job; people who get married and have children while on benefit – they should not start a family until they can stand on their own feet; and so forth) or because they are people who take advantage of loopholes in the rules to claim things they have no 'real' entitlement to, or because it is considered that they make excessive and too frequent claims. In cases such as these, the contrast between the 'deserving' and the 'undeserving' is continually reproduced by the regular appearance, as claimants, of people who are assumed to fit these characteristics.

Additionally, other criteria have a bearing on how a boundary is drawn between the 'deserving' and the 'undeserving'. Deservingness partly depends on conformity to the set of values which staff are concerned to defend. These values entail that claimants should be grateful, polite, and deferential. Those claimants who are unwilling to be subservient and instead are assertive, knowledgeable, and persistent are, by definition, 'undeserving', and are considered to adhere to a set of values (distaste for work, preference for state support, rejection of the virtue of self-reliance, etc.) contrary to those espoused by staff and the wider community. However, some claimants adopt aggressive tactics as a response to what they see as routine obstruction and hindrance perpetrated by staff. But recourse to such practices merely confirms officers' cultural categorization of claimants into 'deserving' and 'undeserving'.

Claimants who are persistent, demanding, and troublesome, and who increase the work load of staff, have interests which are in direct conflict with those of the latter (Prottas, 1979: 115), hence the occasional bitter exchanges between staff and claimants. Other claimants who may have similar needs but who do not introduce difficulties, who do not request information or express needs, and who in general acquiesce in officers' decisions, may also not share common interests with officers. However, because of the course of action they follow, or feel themselves forced into, such potential conflicts as may exist do not come to the surface, and hence such claimants are viewed more sympathetically.

It is argued, then, that the distinction between the 'deserving' and the 'undeserving' as used by SSO staff does not classify 'objective' differences between claimants in terms of the extent to which they are or are not deserving of assistance, though this is the discourse within which staff establish the authority, validity, and dominance of their schemes of social classification and cultural categorization. The evidence adduced in this chapter indicates that it is more appropriate, analytically, to understand the contrast as emerging out of social actions based on and shaped by, not only a particular set of moral and evaluative criteria endorsed by benefit officers acting as representatives and guardians of the wider moral community, but also by manifest conflicts of interest between officers and those more knowledgeable claimants who prosecute their claims with persistence and aggression.

A major issue remains to be discussed, and it is this: why is it that some claimants respond to benefit-staff practice in a meek and reluctant manner, while others resort to combative and assertive tactics? This is one of the questions to be addressed in the following two chapters.

Chapter 6

Claimants and the claiming process: the reluctant claimant

Introduction

Since the war there has been political and academic debate about the respective merits of creative as opposed to proportional justice within means-tested benefit schemes. Creative justice 'is concerned with the uniqueness and therefore the differential need of individuals'; while proportional justice is concerned with 'fairness as between individuals in society' (Stevenson, 1973: 25–6). When National Assistance was re-structured and renamed as Supplementary Benefit in 1966, a principle of 'entitlement' was introduced which carried the implication 'of a "right" rather than a "need", thus shifting somewhat the formal power relation between the official and the claimant' (Stevenson, 1973: 26).[1]

However, with the massive increase in the numbers of people claiming means-tested benefits, creative justice is no longer a practical option, everyone now being treated in categorical terms. In such conditions, individuals with different biographies, circumstances, and needs are, in their encounters with the bureaucracy, transformed into 'claimants', 'identifiably located in a very small number of categories, treated as if, and treating themselves as if, they fit standardized definitions of units consigned to specific bureaucratic slots' (Lipsky, 1981: 59). In short, people are processed into claimants, and this is characterized by the complementary process, in which they begin to conform to the classifications and behaviour patterns imposed upon them.

These two interrelated processes work themselves out in a variety of contexts: in the SSO; in the home; and in the wider social environment. This chapter and the next deal mostly with the way people learn to become claimants within the context of the SB system, whilst chapter 8 discusses some other arenas in which being a claimant is important. Whereas the predominant concern of the previous chapter was the beliefs and practices of SSO staff, this and the following chapter focus mostly on the attitudes and activities of claimants. What marks all these situations, however, is the disagreement and conflict in the nature of the social reality being construed, imposed, asserted, and accepted.[2] This is because, as Lipsky (1981: 60) remarks, there is conflict between the parties involved over the objectives aimed for; and because there is a significant imbalance, in favour of the bureaucrats and those in work over claimants and the unemployed, of power and access to resources. The previous chapter dealt more specifically with the role of SSO staff in the social reproduction of the characterization of claimants as deserving and undeserving. These two chapters explore the processes of acquiring the claimant role, and the different routes which lead to different people becoming different types of claimant.

Becoming a claimant

Many factors conspire in the social construction of a claimant. Quite literally people are processed (Prottas, 1979), from one building to another, one office to another, one desk to another, and one official to another. For many it is a bewildering experience (Rayner Report, 1981).[3] Claiming benefit entails waiting, queueing, being interviewed and means-tested, depersonalization as a consequence of the routine processing of large numbers of people, the imposition of a new and little-valued status, the adoption of new forms of behaviour often of a dependent and supplicatory kind, and the possibility of stigma by association.

Registration for unemployment benefit requires orderly queueing. In turn each applicant is summoned to an officer to answer a variety of questions, one of which is whether the individual wishes to make a claim for SB. If that is the case, as it mostly is for married men, the claimant is directed to another station where an appointment is arranged. A day or so later a second interview is conducted, in which the claimant is means-tested. After this, a weekly or fortnightly giro cheque should issue through the letter-box (dependent on the claimant 'signing-on' at the appointed time each week or fortnight, when he declares he has done no work but is available for work) to be encashed at a designated post office. In general, very few claimants have at this stage gained much of an idea of the intricacies of the scheme or how their benefit is calculated. Nevertheless, they have begun to learn how to be claimants.

The first thing that impresses itself on new claimants is that waiting is inevitable: 'I waited two hours till it closed and the ol' doll gave me a slip of paper and told me to come back in the morning' (Tom Haslett); 'first time I ever was in the bru, it was bunged. Nobody knew where to go, you waited all day for to be seen' (Gerry Murray). Many claimants have stories to relate in which waiting is a major but often taken-for-granted element: 'I had an interview at 10 but your man didn't see fit to see me til 11.30.' Waiting makes explicit the fact that while an officer's time is precious and full, a claimant's is empty and cheap, and that therefore for the latter there is little cost in the expenditure of it. Most claimants, however, resent this wasted time, and it often has a psychological cost, as is sometimes discovered when a hitherto quiescent claimant suddenly erupts in anger. Additionally, waiting is an obvious token of a claimant's dependence, impotence, and subordination (Prottas, 1979: 24–5; Swartz, 1974: 856). Moreover, while waiting can induce friendly relations between co-claimants, it can also unleash hostility, as when queueing arrangements are such as to provide opportunities for queue-jumping, or when one claimant, to the dismay of others, takes up an inordinate amount of an officer's time. Finally, waiting and long delays can be used as an informal method of rationing services, since some claimants for a variety of reasons may have to leave before their cases have been dealt with. Such a rationing system does not effectively sort the more from the less needy (Page, 1984: 141).

A second aspect of the claimant role is that of interrogatee. Most claimants in the samples described their experience as one of providing information to specific questions, without the reciprocal opportunity of being allowed to ask questions. There are very few social contexts, if any, in which the interrogator is subordinate to the interrogatee, and to obtain knowledge about another is to acquire power and control over that person (Prottas, 1979: 29). This is one of the reasons why SSO staff generally refuse to divulge names to claimants, especially as about the only time claimants demand them is when they wish to make a complaint. The reluctance to disclose names is also fostered by the impersonal ethos of all bureaucratic agencies, since in the ideal case officials are supposed to act in identical fashion when confronted with the same circumstances, in which case it is irrelevant which officer one deals with.

It is not simply that the situation presents few opportunities for reverse questioning; claimants articulate the view that they feel inhibited, blocked, and subordinated by the interviewer: 'you just don't feel you have the right to ask' (Hugh McGregor); and, 'I had a list of things I wanted to know, but . . . it's funny, he was so quick and jumpy I didn't like to push it' (Dave Irvine). Billy Stewart provides a vivid and funny account of the first time he signed on:

My first impression was it was like a cattle market; I went down the [SSO] with a lot of questions to ask for advice and it just . . . maybe I wasn't pushy enough but they just gave me the impression that they didn't have any time, I mean, my name, address, insurance number, wife's name, kids, rent, other basics . . . filled it in; sign this – I signed it; handed me two forms, that form's for [other SSO], that form's for here, fill them in and send them in; there's your white card for attending, there's your yellow card for something else; and then he was gone. I mean I was outside and I realized, Christ I wanted to ask this and . . .

IOs do not explicitly refuse to answer questions, but the numerous and diffuse cues claimants receive tend to have an inhibiting influence.

Since many claimants soon learn to feel reticent about asking for information, it is clear why the role of claimant is characterized by ignorance of the very scheme which creates the role in the first place. Many claimants mention their unease when making fresh (new) claims, and that this makes them unwilling to ask too many questions, either out of a fear of displaying their ignorance or out of a desire to remove themselves quickly from a situation they find disturbing (Cooper, n.d.: C46). When Pat McVeigh returned home after making his claim his wife asked him what he had found out: 'Aw, they said they'd sort it out. You know, I just wanted out, couldn't stand the place.'

The waiting and questioning are only part of the initial shock. Particularly for first-time claimants (and especially those of middle age) the experience can be disarming. The public waiting areas of SB offices are often filled with a motley crowd of society's underclass, most of them poor, some extremely shabby, occasionally a drunk providing by turns either distraction or revulsion, women with crying children, and so on. The atmosphere is often depressing, sometimes tense and nervous, rarely pleasant. Stigma by association (Goffman, 1968; Ritchie and Wilson, 1979: 7; Stevenson, 1973: 16) is not pervasive among claimants, but even if it is not present the first step along the road to this new and demeaning status can be a hateful episode. As Ray Carlile put it; 'There's all kinds down there, I get in and out as quick as I can'; and 'Going down there, unemployment, poverty, you know, it just brings it home to you, you're living in poverty' (Joe McCartney); and again: 'I was sitting between a fella and a girl, and they were girnin' [complaining] away, "this bloody place – I hate it"; you know, everybody must feel the same' (Joe McHale).

A major consequence of the waiting, queueing, questioning, and general mass processing is the very typical feeling of depersonalization so often noted in surveys of claimants. Repeatedly, both men and women chorus: you're just a pawn; just a number; just a lump of meat; just a name on a form. Of course, given the resource constraints within which staff work it is small wonder that claimants are treated in this fashion. Claimants are not normally perceived as persons with unique problems but as members of categories, and their demands are treated not as individualized needs but as aspects of a category profile: expectant mothers get a cot and a pram; unemployed tradesmen are worthy of suspicion; knowledgeable claimants have been primed by advice workers; smartly dressed people do not really need what they claim. What claimants often perceive to be complex and manifold difficulties can only be handled by the bureaucracy if these are fragmented (inappropriately most of the time) into simple and single issues which the agency can cope with. Conversely, many claimants understand that they cannot be treated in any other way; they acknowledge it and see it as inevitable: 'Sure down at [the SSO] every time you go it's packed. So if they were to start taking time to tell you everything they'd need a lot more offices. I mean I can see their point of view as well – they get fed up people cheeking them' (Ray McGrath). But none of this assuages a claimant when he is on the receiving end of a long wait, or a brusque officer, or when the benefit cheque does not come at the appointed time. Understanding why officers do not do a better job does not make the process of claiming any easier.

Evidently the basic social situation within which SSO staff and claimants interact is a role relationship, not a personal relationship (Kelvin and Jarrett, 1985: 84). Claimants are constrained to adopt this role so as to achieve their aim of obtaining benefits. The role that most claimants adopt, or adapt to, includes ideas and practices of deference, subordination, acquiescence, and humility (Blau, 1964: 22; Prottas, 1979). Such dispositions conform most closely to the way benefit officers expect and wish the role to be played and so those who do so conform are conceived of as the 'ideal' kind of claimant. However, even though there are various expectations associated with this role, and a considerable degree of pressure to act accordingly, it is clearly not the case that all claimants accept it in the same way or to the same extent. Claimants with different prior attitudes to unemployment and social security, different present circumstances, and different orientations to their new status may attempt to negotiate the role relationship in ways which confer individualistic advantages, and in this book I call these 'assertive' claimants. Generally speaking, such claimants become sensitized to the fact that their relationship to the SSO and its staff is not predetermined but can be manipulated. When, or if, this happens, these claimants begin to perceive the situation in a new light, and become aware that, *within limits*, it is possible to play a more active and ambitious role. Before analysing, in the next chapter, the factors which predispose some individuals to become assertive claimants, it is necessary to present some detailed ethnography concerning 'reluctant' claimants.

The reluctant claimant

Introduction

A crucial aspect of the SB scheme (and IS) is that it is non voluntary (see Lipsky, 1981: 54–6). It is a last-resort, safety-net system of poor relief, originally designed to catch those who fell through the holes in the contributory schemes (Kincaid, 1973: 27–42; and see chapter 2). Lipsky (1981: 56) argues that the non-voluntary nature of such public services has significant implications for claimants. Basically, they cannot withdraw from the service should the costs become too high, for they have no other recourse. Trapped in this way, claimants must sustain the relationship with the SSO even if the costs become very high. Because most claimants can be forced to accept high costs (of time, patience, forbearance, psychological well-being, etc.) officers can extend further their control over them. As the numbers of claimants rise, officers do not fret if claimants stay away, restrain themselves from phoning the SSO, or resist the temptation to register claims. On the contrary, there is accumulating evidence that at some offices in England phone callers are deliberately cut off, the switchboard is periodically left unmanned, and claimants are left waiting inordinately long times (P. Moore, 1980; Berthoud, 1984). Furthermore, Cooper (n.d.: 74, 83) has documented how some officers 'nil' single-payment claims (i.e. refuse them) if they suspect the claimant of 'chancing his arm'. Such officers assume that if the claim is genuine the claimant will return. If the individual does not renew the claim or appeal against the decision this serves to justify the officer's original judgement, validate his categorization of claimants as deserving and undeserving, and verify his ability to distinguish between the two types accurately. However, the evidence available suggests rather that claimants so rebuffed often do not appeal or renew claims despite feeling that they have a legitimate entitlement. This is the old, yet still substantial, problem of the low take-up of means-tested benefit, the basic underlying cause being the high costs of claiming.

The take-up of benefits has been a persistent problem in the history of poor relief. In the eighteenth and nineteenth centuries, the administrators of the Poor Laws were concerned to discourage take-up, fearing the assumed catastrophic consequences of too many dependent paupers (Jordan, 1974). In the 1920s, the 'genuinely seeking work' test was enforced very strictly in an effort to keep the National Insurance Fund out of the red (Deacon, 1976) whilst in the 1930s the Public Assistance Committees, using their wide discretionary powers, dismissed claims with alarming regularity (cf. Max Cohen, 1945, for a harrowing personal testimony). After the war and the passing of the National Assistance Act in 1948, many hoped that the state would be able to inaugurate a de-stigmatized service. By the 1950s many believed this had been accom-plished, and that take-up no longer constituted a serious obstacle. However, it is now recognized that such an assessment was based on inadequate and misleading evidence (Atkinson and Trinder, 1981; Deacon, 1981).

Studies of poverty in the 1960s (Abel-Smith and Townsend, 1965; Marsden, 1969; Coates and Silburn, 1970) demonstrated that National Assistance, far from diminishing in importance, was in fact playing an ever greater role. This prompted the setting up of the Supplementary Benefits Commission (SBC) in 1966, in yet another attempt to remove stigma from means-tested benefit. Atkinson (1969: 75) demonstrated why the new SB scheme was not the resounding success some claimed it to be.

Ever since, studies of take-up rates have appeared at relatively frequent intervals. In 1972 Lister estimated the rates for all means-tested benefits and found, for example, that 380,000 households were eligible for SB but were not claiming it. She concluded that it was not state benefits in themselves that were the problem, since universal benefits, such as Family Allowance, had near-universal take-up; rather it was the means-tested, individual-selective benefits that had the lowest rates of take-up (Lister, 1974).

In 1976 the National Consumer Council (NCC) published its own findings, and these supported most of Lister's arguments. The amount of SB left unclaimed during 1975/6 was estimated at between £200 million and £450 million, the lower figure being that of the SBC itself (National Consumer Council, 1976: 34–5). Two years later the SBC provided some new estimates which, while lower than previous studies, were of the same order of magnitude (SBC, 1978). More recently Bradshaw (1985), using both survey material and government figures, has estimated that in 1983 the take-up rate of SB was 72 per cent (1.64 million eligible but not claiming) and the estimated amount of unclaimed benefit was £1,161 million. As far as Northern Ireland is concerned, the take-up rate for SB is higher (at around 90 per cent) than in Great Britain, partly perhaps because the province is considerably more dependent on it. The rates for single-payment grants however remain at stubbornly low levels (Evason, 1980: 50–1).

Notwithstanding that there are very severe difficulties in arriving at realistic estimates of take-up rates, it appears incontestable that the differences between universal and selective benefits, and between insurance and means-tested benefits, are considerable. Most of the studies mentioned agree that low take-up rates are due to factors such as ignorance, pride and stigmatization, technical and administrative complexity, and the inefficiency and unfriendly attitudes of staff at SSOs (see Townsend, 1976; Golding and Middleton, 1982).

Workers and beggars

The present study did not set out to investigate the reasons why people apparently eligible for basic SB do not claim it. However, the research did gather substantial data on the claiming (or not) of extra benefits such as single payments and additional requirements, and it is reasonable to assume that the reasons people give for not claiming, or for failing to pursue claims for, these benefits are likely to be similar to those preventing the universal take-up of basic SB.

The most obvious cause of low take-up is simply that claimants lack sufficient knowledge of what is available. Since this was discussed in detail in the previous chapter, little more will be said here. It is important, though, always to keep that analysis in mind, as it is an integral part of many of the processes to be explored in this and the next chapter.

More serious analytical problems arise with claimants who are aware that such benefits exist, that they might be eligible for one or another, but nevertheless refrain from registering a claim. Actually, few unemployed people fall into the category of the claimant who draws basic benefit and consciously decides to make no other demands (those doing a double often make such a choice but for quite different, and fairly obvious, reasons). One such however is Fred Beattie, who has experienced several lengthy spells of unemployment. At our first meeting, his wife mentioned that she had recently bought bed linen at considerable cost. When asked why she had not claimed a single-payment grant from their local SSO, she replied:

WIFE: Well I've never tried to ask . . .
FRED: I wouldn't try them, I wouldn't beg off them for anything.
Q.: Is that how you see it?
FRED: That's the way I see it. If I went down there and asked them for things like that and they turned me down, I'd lose the bap [temper] because I know . . . for a fact there's a lot of people getting stuff off them and they don't need it, and they just walk in and they get it handed to them. And then, people who do need it, genuinely, go down, and ask for it, they get shot down . . . it would just make me lose my head . . .
Q.: Do you feel the same way about it?

WIFE: I would go down and ask, he's against it.

FRED: I wouldn't let her go near them, I wouldn't let her ask them for anything.

Q.: Why would you not?

FRED: Well . . . it makes me feel that I'm begging off people. I wouldn't stoop to nobody. If I can't work for what I'm getting, I'll do without it.

Another extreme case is Kevin Hurley. Married with three children and on the dole for eight months (at first meeting), he expressed a strong feeling of degradation at having to claim SB, to the extent that he now forbids his wife to make further single-payment claims. The next time we met, he told me that his wife had gone behind his back and put in a claim. She forged his signature and managed to cash the giro without his knowing. He found out only when he questioned her about the money she was spending on the kids' clothing. He was so enraged that he kicked a hole in a bedroom door ('better the door than the wife').

KEVIN: You feel like a beggar. You're running to somebody for a favour, to ask them for charity. We have claimed some things, but that's enough. I hate to go to people 'I need money; I want this'; its begging.

Q.: But why is it begging?

KEVIN: It's just the way they come into your house. Just an air about them. They make you feel that you're claiming for things that you already have, and you're hiding them, or you're doing the dirty on them, or trying to bluff them. That's the way they make me feel. Its bad enough being out of work without them'uns comin' in lordin' it over you. I'd just rather be out working and paying me own way, even if it's on the double.

The two cases described above illustrate two important themes. The first, discussed in chapter 4, concerns the evident domination of husband over wife in relation to the control of crucial decisions. The second concerns the general sense of shame and stigma attached both to prolonged unemployment and to the claiming of benefits. In most cases such shame is not serious enough to prevent the claiming of basic benefit, without which the families forming the focus of this research could not subsist at all. But it may be sufficient to stop or curtail the claiming of extra grants.

There is considerable overlap between those who feel a sense of personal shame at being without work and those who find the experience of means-testing humiliating. What this indicates is that loss of work is a separate burden to that of claiming benefits or, put another way, to the injury of unemployment is added the insult produced by the process of claiming poor relief (see Schlozman and Verba, 1979). Moreover, more claimants from Eastlough than from Mallon Park express feelings of private shame, as is made evident by the fact that most of the reluctant claimants mentioned in this chapter live in the former estate, a point to which I return in the next chapter.

A major component of such shame is the inability to provide for the needs of the family by the sweat of one's brow. The lack of a job deprives the adult male of what he conceives as his most basic role, so it is unsurprising that many men feel useless, impotent, and rejected. However, when discussing shame it is necessary to specify the contexts in which it is experienced. Some admit to a diffuse feeling of degradation which pervades most aspects of their daily lives, even to the extent of avoiding all unnecessary social contact. Others do not feel ashamed at becoming unemployed if they had no control over their dismissal. But they may well be embarrassed in situations where they cannot pay their way. Some feel stigmatized when in the company of workers as they cannot contribute to discussions of routine topics (pay, work, holidays, purchases, etc.). Whilst different people may feel debased, stigmatized, or unworthy in different ways or in different contexts, these are associated. What relates them is the loss of the basic role of worker and wage-earner, and the consequent substitute role of claimant and benefit-receiver; but both, as far as reluctant claimants are concerned, are interpreted by reference to notions of deservingness and individualism.

As argued in chapter 4, family life in Western industrial societies is underpinned by complementary economic roles for men and women. Because these are separated into the distinct spheres of factory and home, and by divergent evaluative ideologies which do not commodify domestic female labour, the long-term unemployment of the man can have serious consequences for the perception of various role relationships.[4] The most significant point is that the role of worker, and the status of being in a job, is what might be termed an *integrating* role/status combination (in much the same way as Epstein characterizes ethnic identity as a fundamental and integrating identity; see chapter 2) in that such a combination conditions many other statuses (and their related roles), and hence not only a person's apperception of his own identity, but also the way he sees others and the way he thinks others see him (Kelvin and Jarrett, 1985: 42–50). Whilst in employment the basic integrating function that the work role plays is not clearly evident; being widely shared, it is taken for granted. When unemployment strikes, however, the tacit nature of this supporting role framework is disclosed in stark relief. The long-term unemployed man has not only lost the status of being a plumber, a ship-yard worker, a welder, or whatever (that is, his occupational status), he has also lost the status of worker altogether:

What follows from the loss of status of being a working person is a threat to the integrity of the person's self-image. Implicit in this notion . . . is the view of the individual at the centre of his or her conceptual world in which it is the individual who decides and chooses how he or she is going to be seen by others and ultimately by his- or herself. Of course, these decisions are made within the structures laid down by the particular social system in which the individual exists, but the norms of the work ethic are so powerfully embedded within this structure that it is for most people an unquestioned facet of their existence.

Thus what we have is the individual's personal identity being developed, managed, and affirmed through the status of working person. When this status is removed, it is not simply a question of the individual who loses the status of working person, but more importantly he or she loses the means by which the integrity of the self-image is maintained. It is in this sense, then, that the individual loses some of the control over how he or she is seen. (Hayes and Nutman 1981: 86)

Being a fundamental loss, prolonged unemployment entails that many related statuses (father, husband, neighbour, friend, football-team member, etc.) can no longer be taken for granted, and the unemployed person begins to see these as conditional. The realization that such social roles are sustained by the working role means that the unemployed individual is faced with the problem of how to maintain the former when he is prevented from performing the latter. Becoming conscious of the fragility of this very significant role set also induces acute awareness of the necessity to re-negotiate and manage his status within the new limits imposed by unemployment. This requires, for some at least, a continuous effort at impression management (Goffman, 1971), that is, a conscious attempt to act roles in ways which, it is hoped, will influence others to view the person in the manner desired. As we saw in chapter 4, a prominent difficulty faced by the unemployed individual in negotiating his status is the partial undermining of his authority within the family consequent on his inability to provide, through work and wages, for the financing of the household.

Moreover, losing a job, for the vast majority, requires becoming a claimant. Instead of earning a living through paid work, a claimant receives a subsistence benefit without apparently having to do any work. Whilst the relationship between work and wages is seen as one of (reasonably) balanced reciprocity (Turner et al., 1985), that between claiming and benefit is widely judged to be non reciprocal:

Welfare status has the unique quality in that the state accepts obligation for the individual only because of his inability to hold any other status from which he can claim rights . . .

The welfare person, by social definition, is an individual whose status is not defined by reciprocity. There is nothing that the welfare person does, by virtue of his status that matches the responsibility assumed by the state . . . There is nothing that the welfare client can do within the context of his dependent position that merits respect. (Stone and Schlamp, 1971: 241)

Although they may not hold themselves in any way responsible for their own unemployment, it is reluctant claimants who are the ones most likely to evaluate benefit as charity, hand-out, or gift. Some assert that they have paid taxes and contributions and are thus entitled, as of right, to the benefits they obtain. But the process of claiming, the perception that the benefit is administered in a mean-minded way, the awareness that poor relief is considered shaming and the fact that contributions do not cover, actuarially, the benefits received is sufficient to override this, and the longer the spell lasts the greater is the perceived disparity between benefit as entitlement and as charity.

Wadel (1979) has argued that people in this position in fact do a good deal of work, and there is no doubt that for some at least being a claimant is a very hard job. While this view of claiming can be read into the depressing accounts given by many claimants of the time and effort they have had to devote to this activity, this is not a reading shared by most of the employed (including SSO staff). On the contrary, the unemployed assume that those in work believe it is a relatively simple matter to claim benefit, and there is evidence to support them: 'Signing your name once a week is not what I call hard work' (Mick Givens). The socially imposed definition of the act of claiming as non reciprocal and devoid of work and effort is translated into ordinary experience for many of the unemployed as the 'beggar' syndrome and for many of the employed as the 'scrounger' syndrome, and related to this is claimants' felt powerlessness to do anything to change either the dependent role that they perceive they are forced into or the balance of goods and services that flow, one-way, across the counter.

Clearly, claimants are not seen as more deserving on the basis of the effort and energy they put into the business of claiming; as has been shown, it is rather the reverse: the more claimants 'work' at being claimants, the more they are likely to be stigmatized as scroungers and parasites. Additionally, because the effort of claiming is not socially perceived to be a return for the benefit, the relationship of authority and power between benefit officer and claimant is constant and irreversible. Although some claimants dispute the validity of this definition, they are not in a strong position to impose their own version of it. Again, it is the reluctant claimers who more readily accept their socially defined status as dependent supplicants and who thus tend to act within this frame of reference. More assertive claimants act in ways which reject these limits.

We're not scroungers

A very general theme, already alluded to, is that some people ration their own demands on the service so as both to promote an image of being deserving, and to combat the possibility of being labelled a scrounger. So, while virtually all the unemployed claimants assert their own poverty and acknowledge they might be eligible for one grant or another, it is often those who are reticent to claim who make disparaging comments about other unemployed claimants, describing them as forever running to the dole to put in claims. Just as SSO staff argue that those making excessive claims on the scheme demean it for the truly deserving, so some claimants argue likewise, indicating that bureaucrats' categorization of claimants is adopted by the claimants to describe themselves and others. (Of course such categories pervade our society, but they are most clearly seen in action in these particular contexts.) Thus it is, by virtue of the power they hold over claimants and by the fact that their categories and classifications mirror those of the wider society, that the bureaucrats' version of social reality becomes the version to which some claimants conform, and they therefore view the activities and beliefs of themselves and others in these terms. Dave Irving had been unemployed only a few months when the following conversation took place:

WIFE: All them have suites bought for them . . . it's not that me and him's never been, . . . we don't like going down [to the SSO], we're not beggars, we're not asking for money. I wouldn't go in and ask for half of the things.
Q.: Why do you think they claim these things?
WIFE: I don't know why they do – they've got the brass neck, so they have. I mean why claim things when you don't need them.
DAVE: See, all this stuff, the suite, TV, tables and chairs, the fridge-freezer, it's ours, we paid for it out of my wages when I was working.
Q.: Would you not claim these things?
WIFE: Well I would; if you really need it and can't get it anywhere else.
DAVE: She would, I wouldn't.
WIFE: He wouldn't, cos it's hard enough to get him to go to the bru in the first place.

Mervyn Lawrence and his wife display similar reasoning. When they had their second child they put in a claim for a cot, and this was all they received. When asked why they had not claimed for various other items (baby bath, pram, feeding bottles, nappies, baby clothes, etc.) they asserted they didn't know these could be claimed (they had a pram, anyway). However, even had Sandra Lawrence known, she would not have claimed:

SANDRA: I wouldn't have asked for that there. It seems wrong, it's degrading to ask for all them bits and pieces. You make do with what you've got . . . We're not like that. There is them up the road, your man [ ], his wife is always getting the woman [VO] out. She was telling me 'you're not wise; look I got this, and I got that', I got, I got.

A similar case in this respect is that of Roy and Eileen Price. In the two years Roy has been unemployed, they have claimed only for two mattresses and bed linen, and this was because the girl next door had explained to them what to do:

EILEEN: She got a cot and all, and then she got money for a fireguard and a pram and different things. They allowed her money for clothes because she put on weight, and then she got another grant for losing weight, and she got money for to buy the baby clothes. I think its all wrong.
ROY: We had clothes stolen off the line. Its bad luck simple as that. Never even reported it. She [next door] lost kiddies' clothes off the line . . . She put in a claim and got it.
Q.: Why do you think it's wrong?
EILEEN: I think an awful lot of people abuse it. They expect too much.
ROY: What she means is . . . you try your best to scrape things together, to get some money, so you can say to yourself 'I paid for that', without these people [VOs] comin' up. The lowest thing in the world is these people comin' up and saying 'oh you need this, and you need that'.
EILEEN: See the man across the street in them flats. They moved from one flat to another . . . they stayed in one flat for a couple of months and moved, and got a grant for the same things all over again. It shouldn't be allowed but they done it. Now see, if I went down and said I need money . . . I wouldn't get it. A husband will be living up here and a wife living in that flat, and both of 'em claiming; and they're hiding beds and hiding this and hiding that. I don't like abusing. I think people should get what they need, but you should never abuse it. There's an awful lot of people do up here.
Q.: Would you not claim these things yourself?
ROY: Well that cooker's about done. I know I can put in for that.
EILEEN: See when I go down there [SSO] I'm afraid to open my mouth. Sometimes it's an awful wrong thing.

Before moving on to the next section, some further general data on how reluctant claimants perceive the SB system are in order. Few claimants in the two samples have more than a very vague understanding of how the basis on which decisions are made had changed as a result of the 1980 reforms. This is strikingly evident in the language that many claimants, particularly the reluctant ones, use in discussing single-payment awards. Repeatedly, claimants talk about success or failure in receiving such grants in terms of whether the officer involved is helpful ('oh she's nice, very helpful') or not ('she's nasty, she won't give you'); or whether the officer is in a good or bad mood: 'It's on the individual visitor, like that's what you call them, just what their heart's like. They either give you or they don't' (Janet Reid); or whether the officer takes present possessions into account: 'the likes of the ornaments and all the stuff and the wee table and that, and when she came out and seen my living room – I think that's why I didn't get as much, because she looked round my living room' (George Lynn's wife). How much one receives for a claimed item is thought to depend as much on the generosity or meanness of an officer as on any general pricing rule. Claimants sometimes compare what they get in grants for various items and they report frequent discrepancies: 'Next door got £98 for paper and paint, like we only got £72, and it's friggin' well the same house' (Eddie McCann); and, 'My sister, up in [ ] got nearly twice as much as me for her kiddie – I don't know what way they work it out, I don't understand it, maybe he didn't like my face' (Brenda McGrath). One of the major differences between the reluctant claimants and those who are more assertive is that the latter usually justify their disposition to claim anything and everything in terms of their entitlement, and that therefore the moralistic stance of SSO staff is a bogus one which has to be circumvented.

A lethal combination

Obviously the dispositions which characterize the reluctant claimant are not found in isolation but are generally combined. Some combinations; however, seem to produce very debilitating outcomes. The following extracts from two cases do not in any way reveal the complexities involved, the tensions in the households, nor the depths of depression encountered. I provide these extracts from interview material merely to illuminate how the themes so far discussed feed off each other. In both cases, lack of systematic information, stigmatization, and a reluctance to appeal decisions combine in the view of the claiming process that Bill Green and Ray Carlile have learnt during their present unemployment spells (the first for Bill and the second for Ray).

Q.: Would you put in a claim for those sheets?
BILL: You see, the point is, you claim these things now and you're turned down, you just say 'what's the sense?'
BARBARA: They come round and take a look round the living room and the

working kitchen and say, 'you're well enough provided for, you don't need anything'.

BILL: Tell you the truth, the time I put a claim in [for a bed for a daughter], see the TV and the stereo [not especially grand] I shifted it out before even I went and claimed. This is the thing, they just have to come along and say you're well enough provided for and that's the end of it, we accept that.

Q.: Would you not appeal if you were turned down?

BILL: Well, if I knew yes, if I was well enough educated, was able to quote, you know, certainly I would appeal; but as I say if they give me an answer which I don't understand, to me that's me defeated; I can't challenge it because I don't have the information to work on. I don't understand the system.

Q.: You don't seem to like the idea of claiming.

BILL: Don't like it at all. There's no doubt about it, I'm disgraced at it. It makes me ashamed to have to say I can't even afford to buy coats for the girls.

Q.: Would that stop you from claiming?

BILL: No, I think that the situation is bad enough, so if I could help that I would. But as I say if I seek help and I was given an answer that I didn't understand, I wouldn't challenge it, I would accept it that I hadn't got it.

Q.: You've been unemployed over a year now. Why don't you know more about it. Have the bru ever told you about these things?

BILL: They tell you nothing . . .

BARBARA: Do you remember when youse come out of work, we had the suite and something else on the HP and you asked if you could get help with that. First they said no and you said you knew somebody was getting help. So this woman comes up and says, by rights you're not supposed to get this [in fact, there is provision for HP payments for essential furniture under certain circumstances, and the Greens fulfilled the conditions] so 'don't be telling anybody about this' says she 'because it could open the flood gates'.

Ray and Rosemary Carlile, from Mallon Park, are the Greens' *alter egos*. The same age, same number of children, same length of time unemployed, and very similar orientations to jobs, work, and benefits. Ray, chronically depressed, feels profoundly ashamed at his situation, and the whole process of living on SB and claiming grants aggravates it. Ray, like Bill Green, has a fragmentary understanding of the scheme, picked up mostly from friends and neighbours, and indeed from his local SSO. As a family with four school-aged children, they are probably in the worst situation of all the claimants. One of their financial problems is that two of the children are long-time bed-wetters. They have been to the doctor on several occasions and have various gadgets designed to help the children, but to little effect. Before I met them, Ray had made a claim for mattresses and sheets as those they had were quickly destroyed by the urine. They explained the situation to a VO and were given money to get two new mattresses and sheets. But of course the problems continued. When I saw them, I suggested they should claim a laundry addition, which is a weekly sum of money to meet the costs of extra laundry bills. They did claim this and were awarded £3.40 a week extra benefit. By rights this should have been awarded at the time of the first claim, but it was not. Neither Ray nor Rosemary are willing to go back and ask for the new award to be back-dated. More recently they had a claim for clothing refused on the grounds that their need was not due to any medical condition but to mere wear and tear. However, there are provisions in the regulations which stipulate that if basic benefit money is spent on items which can be obtained on a single-payment or additional-requirement grant, then a single-payment grant can be awarded to meet the cost of items which the basic benefit covers. In other words, by not having the laundry addition the Carliles had spent excessive amounts of money on laundry costs, and so could not afford clothes; therefore they are eligible for a single-payment grant for clothes to the value of the amount they had overspent on the laundry. It would appear that they have forgone a considerable amount of money, as they did not receive the additional-requirement grant for the laundry until Ray had been unemployed for eighteen months. Nevertheless, Ray is quite unwilling to complain or lodge an appeal, partly because he feels it so degrading to have to claim grants to get his sheets clean.

Thank God for the means-test man

Another characteristic of the reluctant claimant is brought out by the ambiguity in the word 'claim'. As Kelvin and Jarrett (1985: 89) point out, this word has two connotations:

there is 'claim' in the sense of 'due', 'right', 'title to' or 'to demand'; and there is claim in the sense of 'allegation' or 'to allege', with the quite strong implication of possible falsehood . . . consider, for example, the under-lying mismatch in communication if the dominant connotation of the word 'claim' is 'entitlement' to an unemployed individual, while to a Benefit Officer it is 'allegation-to-be-sustained'!

The point is, however, as has already been made clear, that for many claimants there is in fact little mismatch, for they themselves accept the officers' version of the meaning of 'claim', and hence are worried about whether they can sustain their allegations in a 'legitimate', 'deserving' way. As was argued in the previous chapter, claimants such as these may not have interests in common with SSO staff, but this does not prevent them adopting the latter's global distinctions of claimants as deserving or undeserving. If people do construe aspects of social reality in terms of these contrasts, they are far more likely to remain reluctant claimants than if they can escape the basis of such a dualism. In this regard, it is especially important to notice that because the scheme is a non-voluntary one, and survival depends on its benefits, claimants have a tremendous psychological involvement with the agency, for better or worse, and this further exacerbates their feelings of dependency and powerlessness. It is not surprising, therefore, if some claimants, accepting or persevering with the categories bureaucrats use, see themselves as undeserving and hence as 'lucky to get anything at all' (Lipsky, 1981: 66).

It is not very difficult to provide evidence of claimants who, despite asserting their need for various houshold items, nevertheless admit that they do not deserve them or at least have ambivalent feelings about their right to them. The following short extracts reveal this facet of the process. Basically, some reluctant claimants do not claim often, or do not appeal, because they feel thankful for what they get and are worried about pushing their luck too far.

Billy Reid and his wife Janet have been on SB for several years, yet they know little about the technical details and still have a model of the claiming process which woud be more appropriate to the Public Assistance Committees of the 1930s (or, perhaps, the scheme has not changed so much since then). On one occasion Billy explained that whereas he was only allowed £30 for a cooker, his cousin had been given £85 (from a different SSO):

Q.: Is that right, are you sure about that?

BILLY: Quite positive. But I think why they gave us £30 was because we were claiming so much off them at once. The cousin said if you claim things separately you get more.

Q.: Did you not complain?

BILLY: Ach no, what's the point; I was just glad for what we did get. Because if they hadn't give me anything we were beat.

Q.: Do you see it as them giving it to you?

BILLY: Yes. I don't like taking it but I've no choice . . . I don't like them'uns at the bru and I don't like begging, but we have had a lot of stuff – too much sometimes – so you see like, I am grateful so I am.

During Billy's considerable time on the dole he has become increasingly embarrassed by the fact that his home is furnished almost entirely with the help of SB grants. Yet he has had to pay a price for this. After one year's unemployment they moved to their present home, and since they had no furniture of their own (they had been living in rented, furnished accommodation), Billy phoned his local SSO to see what he could get. He got more than he bargained for.

BILLY: It was the way I said it, it must have sounded funny. I just said I needed this and need that; it sounds funny to me. But like her turning round to her mates on the other end of the phone, laughing, saying, 'he's nothing here, he wants everything'. It did sound funny, but at the time it wasn't funny, we had nothing. Saying to her mates over the phone, 'Jesus, he wants everything' and the next minute I hear all this laughing, and I just said, 'away and fuck yourself', and just put the phone down.

JANET: Yea, to them like it was just a big joke, they think we're . . . just like, sort of way, stupid,

Hugh McGregor and his wife have a similar outlook in being grateful for what they receive. They put in a claim once for household furniture on moving into Eastlough (another relatively young couple moving into their first home with few possessions of their own to furnish it with; and a group regularly singled out by other unemployed and by many of the employed as examples of how soft the 'supplementary' is with some claimants). They were so pleased, on getting the giro, that they did not dare tempt fate by asking why they had not been allowed for a table and set of chairs which they had requested, but which did not appear on the list they received with the cheque. Almost certainly this was a simple error of omission which could quite easily have been rectified, but they never even considered querying it, let alone lodging an appeal.

A similar sort of timidity is evident in the thinking of Joe Robinson. He tends to see the claiming process as one which involves tentative probing, apparently based on his belief that grants have to be fished and landed rather than claimed as of right:

JOE: So when I get the landing painted and get the bathroom done I'm going to take a chance of going to supplementary and saying, 'any chance of getting paper?' Depending what they say, I'll say, 'what about carpet?' I'll say, 'we need new carpet', and 'what about pots and pans?' because ours are done. And I never knew nothing I could claim for till the welfare lady [social worker] told us.

This inclination to feel grateful for what is received is quite widespread and again points to the fact that despite the various changes in legislation and the incorporation of the notion of entitlement, a large proportion of claimants still represent the scheme as one riddled with discretion, and thus as founded on Poor Law principles of eligibility, genuineness, and deservingness.

Practical problems

Even though people are prepared to make claims and even lodge appeals if turned down, various practical difficulties often prevent the

successful execution of this course of action. For some, appealing is just a
'waste of time', mainly because it is assumed it will end in failure; it is
therefore wiser to cut one's losses by not getting involved in the lengthy
appeal process. For some, the practical problems are inherent in the
system (see next section); for others, they are also generated by other
features of unemployment and working-class life. This can be demonstrated by Matt Davis' wife's attempt to claim a maternity single-payment
grant. When Matt took voluntary redundancy, he used the £1,000 to pay
off debts accrued whilst he had been working for very low wages. At the
time his wife was some four weeks off having their third child.

MATT: Everybody was saying, 'sure claim off the bru, claim this, claim that'. I
     didn't know anything about it; I'd been in work these long years and missed
     out. Anyway the wife filled in the form for the bru saying she needed a pram
     and clothes, which is what we were told [by a neighbour] we could claim.
     Well the money didn't come, so she phoned your man and he was very
     cheeky, told her we had £1,000 in the bank and so you're not entitled till it.
     She explained it had all been paid off in debts. He said, 'Well, you are bound
     to know you were expecting', and, 'Do you not think your child is more
     important?' The wife said, 'It's silly coming home from hospital, when you'll
     probably get thrown out of your home for not paying the rent' [their largest
     debt was for rent arrears]. You see all the money had gone, we hadn't a penny
     left. That £1,000 didn't even go in the bank book, because I went round
     doors paying it back [they have several relatives in Mallon Park to whom
     they owed money].
Q.: Couldn't you have appealed?
MATT: Well the attitude I took was, well let it go at that because they're not
     worth bothering with.
Q.: So you didn't think it was worth following up?
MATT: They just didn't want to give it, they weren't giving it.
Q.: Didn't the bru say you could appeal?
MATT: No, he just told her she wasn't entitled if you've money in the bank,
     over £300 he said. She kept telling him there was no money in the bank.
       I did go and see [an advice worker], and he said you've to get receipts for to
     show how you spent the money. Well, sure enough I can get one from the
     [Housing] Executive, but how can you ask your mother for a receipt, or the
     wife's brother [especially when he is on the bru himself and doing a double].

A much more complicated case, which cannot be fully described
here, is that of Ray and Brenda McGrath. At the same time as the
Housing Executive informed them they could move out of their condemned flat into a new house in Mallon Park (which on entry they
found to be unfinished and in a terrible mess), Ray signed on as
unemployed. The following two weeks, during which they received no
benefits and became poverty stricken, were characterized by a series of

almost farcical encounters with various statutory agencies, including the SSO, the Housing Executive and the Northern Ireland Electricity Board. In striving to sort out their numerous difficulties they came up against a host of practical problems (vandalized telephone boxes, erratic bus services, long waits in depressing public buidlings, referrals to other officials and agencies, and so forth) that would deter even the most persistent, and all this at a time when money had to be borrowed from impecunious relatives merely to buy food. Experiences such as these are not uncommon for that large section of the population that has become impoverished through unemployment, sickness, and old age.

I can't take this carry-on

Two further cases demonstrate how people become both too physically and emotionally exhausted to pursue claims beyond a certain point, indicating again that while many are willing to pay high psychological costs for essential benefits, there is a limit. Pete Turner (a Protestant, not in the core sample) had to leave his last job on health grounds; he registered as unemployed and claimed SB the Monday following, when he was told that since he had left with a week's wages he was not eligible for SB for one week. He signed on on the Friday and was told he would get something on the next Tuesday. Tuesday came but the cheque did not, neither did it come on any of the next fifteen days. During this time they had to borrow money from various relatives to keep body and soul together. Pete went to the office on two occasions and phoned up on several others. Each time he was assured his money was on the way. Finally, Pete, his wife Brenda, and their child, walked the two miles to their local SSO. Again he was assured the money was in the post and if they had not got it it was the fault of the post office. Brenda would not accept this and started to cry. She dumped her child on the counter and pleaded, 'my child is not going to get anything to eat to-night', to which, according to Pete, the officer replied, 'Ach, there's no such thing in this day and age as a starving child.' At this, Brenda became hysterical and rushed out of the office. Pete, unflappable to the last, remained long enough to grab the now-crying child and to hear once again that the money must be in the post. In fact a cheque for £127, two weeks' benefit, arrived two days later, and Pete attests that the post-mark was for the day before, that is the day after their visit to the office. Moreover they did not get another cheque for eleven days. Since SB is paid wholly in advance, it is difficult not to conclude that the family 'lost' two weeks' money. Once the money arrived they cashed it and began repaying debts. The whole affair so exhausted them and gave them such little confidence in the system that they could not bear the thought of further complaints, further repetitions of the same sorry episode, and more bored expressions from uninterested bureaucrats.

When Jim Kelly (a Catholic not in the core sample) was laid off, he claimed unemployment benefit and supplementary benefit. Because his wife was receiving £19 a week invalidity benefit, and because they were paying a very small rent, their income was slightly above the SB assessment of their needs, and so they were ineligible. Some two months later Jim informed the clerk, when he signed on, that his wife's invalidity benefit had finished. According to him, she said she would take care of it. By this he assumed she meant she would arrange for him to get supplementary benefit. He continued however to receive the same amount of money. A couple of further inquiries and two weeks later his benefit was still the same. They were so desperate by this time that Jim went to their SSO to 'sort it out'. It was finally explained to him that if he wanted to claim SB he would have to fill out form B1, which he had never done, before he could proceed to claim. He completed all the formalities and was assured things would now run smoothly. But they refused to pay him the arrears. When he got home and told his wife nothing could be done, she packed him off back to try again. 'But sure, everytime you go down there you see a different person and have to tell the whole story over again.' When he was told he was not entitled to the arrears he got angry and asked to see someone higher up. He was ushered into a cubicle, and another officer took a statement from him, and asked him to phone up the next day. This Jim did, and found himself having to explain it all over again to yet another person. He was told to hold on, and got cut off. He phoned again, explained, was told he was not entitled, asked for the supervisor, and was cut off. When he phoned a third time the clerk was heard to say, 'Oh, it's him again.' At this point Jim completely lost his temper and demanded the man's name, which he would not give; Jim again asked for the supervisor, and the phone was put down. He waited a long time and finally himself hung up. By this time Jim was prepared to leave it: 'What'll I do, I couldn't go through this here, this carry on. I'd rather scrub the money.' His wife persuaded him to give it one last go. Eventually he managed to speak to a supervisor and had to explain everything once more. According to him, this was the first person who listened to him sympathetically and reasonably, and seemed to understand what the problems were like. She told him she was not sure whether they could help him, but asked him to call in half an hour. His mother, from whose house he was phoning, advised Jim to let it rest, she would see them through it (they had already borrowed from her). He did not ring back, he was prepared to let the matter drop: 'Ach, to hell with 'em.' Two days later a giro for £57 arrived, which seems to have been the arrears for three weeks.

JIM: Now it may be only two or three people down there, but my attitude could never be right. There was a couple of weeks but for my mother and her mother, we couldn't have got through it. You know foodwise and all, you'd think you'd never get as bad as . . . you know, no food there, but I seen us sitting there . . . nothing, you know, no money, maybe half a packet of cornflakes; I'm saying, 'my God'.

I hope to God I never have to go through that again. You see the set up of those people out on the desk. I just see their job, they're just buffers, to put you off. I know why they have that thick glass on them windows. I never thought I would be in that position.

I've seen that man I talked to on the phone. I was sitting face to face with him before. If I'd a been there instead of on the phone, I'd a hit him. When you hear him talking funny to somebody else and you're not there, I just . . . hate him. He near brought me to tears. I'm just disgusted; it makes you feel so small; you can't seem to get through the barriers.

WIFE: You know you sort of take it for granted that the clerk is right, you're not allowed to question her. This is what our attitude was. If she says to you you weren't due anything, well we just took it for granted we weren't, until my benefit ran out and then we *knew* we were entitled. Next time I'm going to try and get everything out of them.

Conclusion

This case evidence reveals a decided reluctance on the part of many claimants to attempt to meet SSO staff on equal terms. Reluctant claimants are much more likely to accept without dissent decisions made concerning them rather than to challenge such decisions, and to limit the demands they make on the scheme. This is because they endorse the officers' authority and status and hence the adjudications they reach; because most claimants have neither the technical nor legal knowledge to dispute a case; because, to one degree or another, they feel stigmatized and thus will not bear the costs of pursuing a claim; and because, espousing the distinction between the deserving and the undeserving, they fear being branded as 'scroungers'.

Since SB is an involuntary scheme, the context of interaction is defined by the bureaucracy. Reluctant claimants wish to preserve an image of themselves as deserving, genuine, and reasonable. They thus adopt the role of 'ideal' claimant and ration their own demands on the system by the various means described. This does not always lead to success, however, because the system distributes its diswelfares in a rather random fashion, and so even 'ideal' claimants can experience severe problems (late benefit cheques, lost case papers, very long waits, rude officers, etc.). Moreover, whilst they follow these reticent and timid paths, the particular labelling decisions of staff cannot be guaranteed to conform to those made by claimants. Thus such claimants also make strenuous efforts to manage their status and identity within other role relationships by, for example, designating other claimants as scroungers, distancing themselves from claimants they deem lazy or satisfied with life on the dole, insisting that they themselves do not abuse the service, and by accepting, to one degree or another, that their situation is a subordinate and discreditable one.

Chapter 7

Claimants and the claiming process: the assertive claimant

Introduction

The characteristics of reluctant claimants have been described in some detail, yet a major issue remains to be addressed. This concerns why it is that some unemployed individuals become ideal or reluctant claimants, while others become persistent and assertive. Generally speaking, there is a variety of factors implicated in this process. One is the way the SB system works. It was argued in chapter 5 that the routine practices of SB staff, despite officers' protestations to the contrary, tend to victimize the majority of unemployed claimants rather than some particular group of them. However, the fact that only some claimants emerge as assertive in response to these practices indicates that staff action has only an indirect or partial impact, rather than a determining one, on the production of such claimants.

A second factor concerns the change from wage-earner to benefit-receiver. Again, though, this change, being common to all the unemployed, does not allow us to draw a distinction between the two types of claimant. While it is clear that the typical practices of SB staff, the resource constraints of the SB system and the move from wage-earner to benefit-receiver are all necessary elements in the explanation, none of these factors, either by themselves or in combination, can sufficiently account for the creation of a *distinction* between reluctant and assertive claimants.

In addition to these general aspects of the process, there are several other factors which have an effect on the claiming dispositions of particular people. Thus the sympathetic and moderating influence of close kin and friends may ameliorate the stigma and isolation that some unemployed experience, making it more likely that they will become assertive claimants. This is certainly the case, for example, with Gerry Daly, who not only has very good relationships with his parents, who live close by, but he also has several brothers and brothers-in-law in a situation similar to his own, and who all support each other in a positive and tangible manner. On the other hand, some unemployed, particularly in Eastlough, have strained and bitter relationships with some of their close kin, which they attribute to the latters' (imputed) belief that the unemployed are scroungers. This tends to exacerbate feelings of inadequacy and stigma. Related to this is the availability of people who are willing to support, in a material sense, their unemployed kin and friends, though this is a mixed blessing, as most of those who have generous relatives dislike the fact they are unable to reciprocate; unidirectional transfers ease financial problems, but they may also reinforce the dependent role of the recipient and induce self-loathing.

There are still further factors which shape the process whereby claimants become either reluctant or assertive. The existence of opportunities for doing the double, the extent of local unemployment, and the perceived state of the labour market, all intrude at some point and render it impossible to predict the outcome, in particular individual cases, of the many processes involved.

For example, an important mediating factor is the state of the Belfast labour market for working-class jobs. The sheer lack of jobs allows the unemployed to be more successful in arguing that the causes of unemployment are large-scale economic forces rather than personal deficiencies. But because massive unemployment has been much more chronic in west Belfast than in east Belfast, structural explanations of unemployment are more in evidence in Mallon Park than in Eastlough, in which latter estate the causes for continuing unemployment are frequently attributed to lack of motivation and effort. What this may indicate is that the worse the unemployment situation, the more likely it is that the views of both those in work and those unemployed will tend to converge, and also that that they will converge towards a macro-structural rather than a personal explanation of the precipitating conditions.

I do not want to argue, however, that as the level of unemployment rises joblessness automatically becomes easier to tolerate. This may be true for some people who find safety in numbers; but for others a large jobless total simply means increased competition for jobs and hence reduced chances of success. I am also not arguing that when the views of those in work become more sympathetic this necessarily ameliorates all the difficulties of being without work. There are three reasons, at least, why such relatively compassionate attitudes have only a partial effect. The first is that they have little or no impact on the material constraints of unemployment; second, they leave untouched the social and psychological problems and conflicts between the spouses; and third, despite the fact that the employed appear more genuinely sympathetic in areas of very high unemployment (and I tend to think the unemployed have to be in a majority for this to occur, and also for there to be good, obvious reasons for such a level of unemployment, which is the case in Mallon Park), since there is not a great deal of conversation between the two groups about unemployment, some unemployed may still think that those in work have disparaging views of the jobless. The point I wish to stress is that more generally sympathetic dispositions towards the unemployed can reduce the effects of stigmatization and thus promote the emergence of more assertively oriented claimants.

Yet another feature of the situation is the difference in the amounts of knowledge about the SB scheme that people have. Evason (1980: 49–50) found that the claimant population of the two Belfast Protestant areas she and her team studied were far less knowledgeable about single-payment grants than were those of the two Belfast Catholic areas surveyed. Since one of the most important means of acquiring information about the scheme is through kin, friends, and neighbours, it is possible that because more unemployed east Belfast residents live in a fragmented and isolated social environment, created in part by the conception that people are deserving or undeserving, they have not been as able or as willing to build up information networks through which to swap experiences and knowledge as have Catholics living in west Belfast. On the other hand since the rate of unemployment in Eastlough is only half that in Mallon Park, unemployed Catholics are much more likely to be in close contact with other unemployed people than is the case for unemployed Protestants in Eastlough. In other words, the sheer social density of unemployment, over a long period of time, can shape cultural notions concerning the interpretation of that unemployment. Where the density is much less, as in Eastlough, unemployment is more likely to be conceptualized in the individualized terms of deservingness.

Given that there is such a variety of inputs, and that people differ widely in their personal circumstances, it could be argued that reluctant and assertive claimants are the particular outcomes of some specific combination of these various factors. But this formulation treats people on analogy with physical objects, whose movements are the product of a variety of forces acting on the object in simple and reproducible ways. However, the theoretical framework that has been used through-out this work is one which treats these factors, not as determinants of action, but as the context of action. They are the real historical, social, and economic conditions within which people have to make some-thing of their lives. But these are not encountered directly; they are apprehended, conceptualized, and interpreted in terms of the knowledge, interests, and goals that people have. This is not to deny, of course, that people's ideas and beliefs are unaffected by these material conditions; that would be entirely untrue. It has to be recognized, further, that perceiving and acting in terms of the cultural frameworks people possess inevitably entails that the cumulative effect of this action has a real impact on material conditions, so that they are shaped in patterned ways, as the discussions in chapters 3 and 5 attempted to demonstrate. These patterned outcomes then take on the appearance of 'objective' structures of advantage and disadvantage. In order to understand how claimants become reluctant or assertive, it is necessary to inquire into claimants' conceptualizations of the factors of constraint and opportunity.

Orientations prior to becoming unemployed

There is a difference between claimants who are assertive and persistent when forced by material circumstances to be so, and claimants who actively attempt to negotiate a different and less-subordinate role relationship with SSO staff. The cases of Pete Turner and Jim Kelly, described in the previous chapter, fall into the former category. These men had to become persistent and even mildly aggressive because of their catastrophic financial situation, precipitated, as they saw it, by uncaring and inefficient benefit officers. By and large, however, their typical dispositions had been acquiescent and moderate. Moreover, after the events recounted, Pete Turner and his wife resumed their previous disposition, and while it is possible Jim Kelly might have become genuinely assertive, he was fortunate to obtain a job. The assertive' claimant, on the other hand, is characterized by a more positive orientation to what he believes is his rightful entitlement.

Such claimants do not necessarily begin unemployment in a persistent and abrasive mood. Rather, they learn to be assertive, just as others learn to adopt the role of the reluctant claimant. However, I should add a note of caution here. While I argue in terms of 'reluctant' and 'assertive' claimants, the empirical situation is such that the behaviour of many claimants resists neat classification. What I am suggesting is that claimants' dispositions and orientations fall along a continuum, that this can be divided into two broad analytical categories; that these categories have fuzzy edges; that claimants may move from one to the other either more or less permanently or as context demands; and that individual personality and situational factors must play an important role. Categorizing claimants as either reluctant or assertive facilitates the exposition of the data and the argument, but it also over-simplifies the real situation. In short, my intention in the use of these terms is to present them as Weberian 'ideal-types' (Weber, 1964: 12–13).

Generally, this learning process has received no analytical attention in the relevant literature. The available material on SB claimants contains very little in the way of descriptive contrasts, in terms of practice, between different types of claimant. When the claimant population is disaggregated, it is usually in terms of benefit status (pensioner, single parent, unemployed, etc.) or in terms of demographic criteria (age, sex, ethnic group, and so forth). Surveys which employ these parameters tend to reproduce the typologies they started with. What is required for present purposes is an analysis which highlights the dynamic and dialectical nature of the processes involved.

Erving Goffman's (1968) theory of the moral career of stigmatized people is relevant in this context. Goffman isolates four separate patterns of socialization into a stigmatized identity. Two of these, involving inborn and congenital stigmas, and another which involves socialization in an alien community, do not concern us. The pattern which does parallel, to some extent, the moral career of the SB claimant, is that in which an individual becomes stigmatized late in life, and has therefore learnt all about the normal and the stigmatized long before he sees himself as deficient. What is interesting about this process is that the individual has to negotiate a new identity and a new set of relationships, both with those he had known previously and those with whom he will come into contact as a result of the stigma; and some remarks concerning this process were made in the previous chapter. Most of Goffman's examples tend to employ physical and irreversible stigmas. What is important in the context of the present study is the fact that the stigma involved is not physically identifiable, is conceived to be temporary, and is usually reversible. This means that the unemployed man has powerful motives to prevent his old identity and old relationships from being completely and irrevocably altered, since these will need to be re-established once he regains work and ceases claiming. It is for these reasons that the unemployed man so often emphasizes the fact that his unemployment is an interruption of normal life (less so with the Catholics of Mallon Park, though). For the same reasons, he talks a great deal about his past work experiences, stressing how he still could work if only he was given an opportunity (Wadel, 1973; Bakke, 1933) and, while attempting to manage the impressions others have of him, implicitly plays down the need to modify his self-image, claiming that whatever adjustments are required are imposed on him from outside. Thus he pleads that he cannot help being unemployed; others may be layabouts content to live on the dole, but his unemployment is not his fault, and he is just the same person he always was, merely temporarily without work. The tensions, ambiguities, and paradoxes (Kelvin and Jarrett, 1985: 43) inherent in such a fraught situation make analysis of it very complicated, and what follows must be seen as an exploratory argument. Broadly, the contention is that those who are able to reject, in some measure, the legitimacy of the distinction between the deserving and the undeserving, are the most successful in sustaining a positive identity and image of self, and are the ones most likely to become assertive claimants. A crucial point is that the felt pressures on unemployed people, deriving internally from their own previous self-image and view of the world, and externally from the beliefs and practices (and imputed beliefs and practices) of significant others, are different for different individuals.

Reluctant claimants, then, are typified by several characteristics. Feelings of personal shame and stigma encourage the adoption of a subordinate and acquiescent role in relation to the SB system, and these beliefs and actions are also associated with a definite tendency to locate other unemployed people in a moral hierarchy defined by ideas of deservingness.

Moreover, there is a strong correlation between those who feel stigmatized and those who were prone to stigmatize others when they were themselves in work. Thus, some of the presently unemployed feel others think of them as scroungers or layabouts, because that is how they thought of the unemployed when they were in jobs (see Goffman, 1968: 48). For example, Alan Martin (a Protestant) had been a lorry driver for many years until he was made redundant in 1980. He was unemployed for four months before he finally took a job as a bank messenger. He describes his period out of work as one of the worst of his life, bored, depressed, and ashamed. He hated going to sign-on, would not cash his benefit cheque himself (or would wait until the post office was empty), and thought that other people considered him lazy and content to live on the dole. However, he admitted that when he had been in work this was how he had always thought of the jobless himself; he had always felt that there were jobs for those who really wanted them. Moreover, this was partly how he still felt, that is, he considered other unemployed (he knew very few personally) to be indolent and uninterested in finding work. He was able to distance himself from these by claiming that at his age (49) it was very hard to get a job as a lorry driver, and by noting that since he had been working for the past thirty years he deserved a bit of a break. Getting the job as a bank messenger after only four months, which he considered a comparatively short time, in fact served to sustain these views, for after his unemployment he continued to think of the unemployed as 'lazy buggers'.

Generally speaking, those who, when in work, conceived of unemployment, or at least its continuation in individual cases, in terms of personal factors of effort and motivation, when unemployed themselves often persist with this particular representation of the moral universe. But because they are themselves now out of a job, it becomes necessary to distance themselves from other unemployed so as to try to convince the employed that they are on the right side of the moral divide. It is clear, then, why unemployment can be such a fragmenting and isolating experience for many people. Such a view of the world, tightly structured by these all-embracing conceptions, is perhaps reassuring when the consequences of the labelling process are not felt personally, but it is debilitating when its repercussions come home to roost. Such unemployed people feel much more insecure about their status both within and outside the home, a greater pressure to manage the impressions of others, and a more pressing need to invest time and energy shoring up their self-image. Having adopted a view of reality which has an easy tendency to blame the victim (Ryan, 1976), it becomes a problematic task, on becoming unemployed, to deflect the feeling that not only is one partly responsible for one's own predicament but that others too are likely to distribute blame in a similar fashion. Remarks which to some unemployed people appear as innocuous, trivial, guileless, or inadvertent may to others, and particularly those who themselves use ideas and expressions of individualism and deservingness, seem offensive, premeditated, and tendentious, and to carry threatening implications for one's own personal situation.

What makes some people prone to become reluctant claimants therefore is, firstly, a personal conceptualization of the world in terms of the distinction between the deserving and the undeserving *prior to becoming unemployed*. Once out of work, such individuals often continue to use this cultural apparatus to interpret their experience and this has unforeseen and unpleasant consequences. Second, individuals are prone to become reluctant claimants because they feel themselves powerless to repudiate the authority and validity of the divisive model which many of the employed use to conceptualize reality. These people have a continuing interest in maintaining such a distinction because, remaining in work, it provides them with powerful evidence that they are the elect.

In short, it is the manner in which both the SB system and the process of moving from wage-earner to benefit-receiver are interpreted and conceptualized within the framework of ideologies of individualism and deservingness which generates claimants who are reluctant, timid, and reticent. Assertive claimants, on the other hand, emerge out of those who are less enmeshed by these ideas and values. Such unemployed people tend to view SB as a right rather than a hand-out; they do not readily accept a subordinate role *vis-à-vis* SSO staff; and they do not easily succumb to feelings of shame or stigma on becoming unemployed. Of course, various events, such as a sudden financial disaster or a particularly bitter experience with the SB scheme, can make even reluctant claimants assertive and aggressive for a time, or even more permanently. Conversely, the impact of the practices of SB staff and the feeling of oppressive hostility, real or imaginary, emanating from those around one, might be so profound as to render reluctant a claimant otherwise disposed to become assertive.

The reason that there are more reluctant claimants than assertive ones is that whilst holding the contrast between the deserving and the undeserving reinforces and compounds the impact of SB staff practice and the stigmatizing effects of becoming unemployed, rejection of it does not necessarily act as a successful countervailing force to these other factors. In short, other things being equal, there is a greater likelihood that people predisposed to being assertive actually succumb to the pressures experienced from a variety of sources and thereby become reluctant, than there is of the reverse process occurring. But other things are not equal. Catholic west Belfast has, and always has had, a much higher rate of unemployment than east Belfast. Additionally, while Protestants in Eastlough are better placed to obtain legitimate jobs in the formal economy, the Catholics of Mallon Park are in a better position to obtain work on the side. The kinds of orientation these social and economic conditions have engendered, described in earlier chapters, have a feed-back effect in shaping people's ideas and dispositions towards claiming and the claiming process. Evidence will be provided to show that more Eastlough than Mallon Park employed people endorse the distinction between the deserving and the undeserving. Because Eastlough unemployed are still largely committed to looking for jobs in the formal economy and because, numerically, the unemployed are in a minority, such ideas are more likely to be sustained and reproduced, and this is why there is a large proportion of reluctant claimants in this estate. In Mallon Park, on the other hand, the unemployed are less orientated to the formal economy, more involved in doing the double, treat benefits as a subsistence base on which to build, and live in a social environment where not only do the unemployed outnumber those in work, but the proportion of working-class people living on one kind of benefit or another (invalidity benefit, sickness benefit, SB for single parents, and so on) exceeds 75 per cent of the adult population.

A final factor in all this is that Protestants wish to distance themselves culturally from Catholics. According to the former, it is Catholics who know all about SB, know what and how to claim, know all the dodges and loopholes and can exploit the system to their advantage, and who claim everything they can whether or not they need it. This itself adds to the pressures on Protestants to be circumspect about how they make use of the SB scheme. It is interesting to note here what happened on an occasion when a renowned Democratic Unionist Party (DUP) politician addressed a gathering in Eastlough. After the robust speech, which was only indirectly concerned with jobs and unemployment, an unemployed man asked a question about something connected with the SB scheme. The politician retorted very quickly and with some annoyance that Protestants should concern themselves with getting jobs rather than devoting themselves to claiming every benefit notionally available. That might be the way Catholics do it, but Protestants want jobs, not benefits. I have heard this view expressed quite frequently in Eastlough. The implication surely is that Protestants who know the system too well and claim too often and too much are in danger of negating their Protestant identity. Or, Protestant identity (when contrasted to Catholic identity), is in part predicated on being reluctant in regard to means-tested benefits.

Mallon Park

In Mallon Park, only eight of the employed sample provide evidence that they think of unemployment in terms of deservingness. They attribute blame for continuing unemployment to personal factors, as well as structural ones; they argue that many of the unemployed do not want to work; that many claim more than they actually need and hence abuse the system; that benefits are generous and indeed too easy to obtain; etc. Moreover, some of these eight do not like to utter such views in public because of the trouble it sometimes causes. The rest of the employed, to varying degrees, say very little about unemployed people that is obviously hostile. Indeed many express a great deal of sympathy; they argue that it is stupid to feel ashamed; note that the vast majority want to work but that there are no jobs; and acknowledge that living on benefit is difficult.

Of the Mallon Park unemployed, there is evidence that when in work only six expressed hard-hearted views of the jobless, and only three still do so (Pat McVeigh, Ray Carlile, and Kevin Hurley). Of the other three,

Connolly and Davis have been too busy doing the double to be over-concerned with what other claimants do, and Tony Madden is too difficult to categorize. It is true that some others of the unemployed make disparaging remarks about their fellow sufferers, for example, that they are not prepared to take low-paid jobs ('I would'), that unemployment does not seem to bother them ('it depresses me'), that they seem to manage very well on the bru ('I can't make ends meet'). However, they usually attribute these defects to the 'system', which has created a situation in which even though there are some jobs it pays people to remain out of work, and are generally circumspect about attributing blame to factors of personal motivation. It is also true that some of the unemployed excoriate particular individuals, but these are usually seen as exceptions ('you'll always get the odd one or two') to the general rule that the vast majority of unemployed would work if they had decent jobs to go to.

It is this group of six unemployed that provides three reluctant claimants (McVeigh, Hurley, Carlile), and it seems quite clear that their reticence appears to stem from holding the contrast between the deserving and the undeserving. All three feel strongly that SB is a handout which they are forced into accepting; they intensely dislike making claims even though they can see the material advantages of doing so; they all think that others see them as scroungers; and they all have a tendency to label others in these terms (that is, they estimate that many of the unemployed do not want to work, that they claim for things they do not need, etc.). What is interesting, however, is that Pat McVeigh, after some eight months of unemployment, has begun to change his mind. Seeing so many of his friends and neighbours unemployed, discovering that they do not feel ashamed, and that they make claims, he has begun to argue with his wife that perhaps they too should jump on the band wagon and start to take advantage of the scheme.

For Mallon Park, it would appear that rates of unemployment of over 50 per cent make it difficult for both the unemployed and those in work to sustain the view that unemployment is due to the personal characteristics and wishes of particular people. With so many unemployed, and with virtually no ready examples of people finding work (hardly any member of either Mallon Park sample knew anyone who had recently obtained a job; most comments on this subject were of the kind: 'no, all I see is people being paid off'), there is a tendency to reject explanations based on individualism and deservingness and instead to attribute unemployment mostly to structural factors such as the recession, government policy, the Troubles, rapacious big business, Loyalist discrimination and so forth. I would suggest, then, that while there is a sizeable minority of workers who subscribe to ideas of deservingness, the proportion is smaller amongst the presently unemployed, and there is some evidence that prolonged spells out of work in an environment of very high unemployment are likely to erode their grip further.

Claimants predisposed to become assertive emerge out of those who are less enmeshed by the distinction between the deserving and the undeserving, and who therefore tend to view SB as a right rather than a handout, who do not readily fall into a subordinate role *vis à vis* SSO staff, and who do not usually experience feelings of shame or stigma on becoming unemployed. On this basis, fourteen of the Mallon Park unemployed sample can be classed as potential assertive claimants since, to one extent or another, they all meet the above criteria.

Whether or not they had suffered previous spells out of work prior to becoming unemployed on this occasion, these individuals attest, again in varying degrees, that they did not think of the unemployed in a derogatory fashion. Of course, very great caution has to be placed on evidence of this kind, since it is clearly possible that some people may be trying to present a caring and compassionate image of themselves. However, it is not an improbable finding, for three reasons. The first is that twelve of the employed group have very similar views and this statement is based on much sounder contemporary evidence. Second, many Eastlough unemployed people are not at all shy in voicing their derogatory opinions of other unemployed people, and many admit that this is how they have always thought of the unemployed. Third, if the Mallon Park unemployed are representing themselves as holding more sympathetic attitudes than once they did, this is itself significant, for it indicates that intolerant views of the unemployed are now generally less acceptable.

If these fourteen thought about unemployment at all, and about distinctions among the unemployed, it was in terms of education, luck, the availability of jobs, being in the right place at the right time, having good contacts, possessing the appropriate skills; and in structural terms: the recession, the Troubles, discrimination, etc. In general they tended to argue that most of the unemployed would work if there were jobs to be had at reasonable wages. As already mentioned, this set of explanations is also characteristic of a majority of the employed sample, and in my experience of many of those I met in Mallon Park. Having become unemployed, they have continued to endorse these same views.

Not subscribing to the contrast between the deserving and the undeserving, they seem to feel no pressing need to distance themselves from other unemployed because these are not, by and large, conceived as morally deficient persons. Because many of their friends, kin, and neighbours, whom they see regularly, are unemployed there is no necessity to manage others' impressions as everybody is 'in the same boat', 'there's no difference, we're all the same way off'; and the situation is considered to be beyond their control. To these people, unemployment is a phenomenon of the wider economy and the practices of a discriminatory Protestant state. In such conditions they see no sense in erecting barriers amongst themselves by creating invidious distinctions. They are, of course, fully aware that some others, both in work and out, have different views from their own, but what is characteristic of them is their apparent indifference to those who might label them as scroungers or, if doing the double, avaricious. If individuals in this group do feel a need to manage impressions, it is less those of other unemployed, and not very frequently those of workers; rather it is more likely to occur with very close kin and particularly with wives who, experiencing the material hardship of life on benefit and unable to do anything about it themselves, find it difficult to resist the temptation to blame their husbands for not getting work.

However, of these fourteen only four (Morgan, Chapman, Hardy, and Stewart) have emerged as genuinely assertive, in the sense that they show a positive willingness to claim regularly, to claim items not really needed as a route to obtaining money for other purchases, to claim items fraudulently by hiding present possessions, to collude with others by hiding others' possessions to enable the latter to claim fraudulently, to appeal decisions, to seek information actively, to be aggressive with SSO staff if the need arises, to refuse to be fobbed off with excuses, and so forth. Of these four, Mick Morgan has engaged in most of the above activities, and seems to have transformed claiming into a vocation. When his wife had their second child, he hid all the baby paraphernalia left over from the first, in the loft, and put in a single-payment claim for everything he could think of. He received a grant for £113, most of which went on a new fridge. On another occasion he intentionally fire-damaged the living-room carpet and successfully claimed for new floor covering. He kept the old carpet, put the sofa over the damaged part and spent the £48 on a night out and some records. He is constantly thinking of schemes to extract money from the system. Mick confided all this quite soon after I had met him, and subsequently I found he was very free with his advice and encouragement to friends and neighbours to follow his example.

Danny Chapman is not quite so ambitious or imaginative, but has hidden things of his own and for a neighbour so as to claim grants they otherwise would not have been able to obtain. In the two years Danny has been unemployed he has claimed successfully on five separate occasions and appealed against two decisions rejecting his claims, both of which he lost. In default of getting a job or a double, he takes the view that the only way he can increase his income, and thereby put money in his own pocket, is to claim for items he already has. Despite being assertive in this fashion, Danny is usually very bored and deeply depressed. This makes him lethargic and he spends most of this time gazing out of the window, reading cheap novels, or watching films on a neighbour's video. All of this makes his wife angry and she harangues him for not getting off his backside to look for work. He defends himself stoically by a ritual recitation of many of the companies that have closed down during the last five years: 'But she takes no notice. See her, she's always got every job she ever went for, so she can't see why I can't get one. That really bugs me.'

The other two of this group of four claim items they know they are eligible for, even if they do not feel they need them, and will appeal against decisions if they think they are in the right. Pat Hardy is loath to claim fraudulently but Billy Stewart would if his wife would co-operate, and Billy has hidden things for a neighbour. As far as the Stewarts are concerned, claiming grants is a way to get things they could not afford while Billy was working, and of course this is a major source of aggravation to some of those in low-paid jobs (see next chapter). Additionally, Betty and Billy Stewart swap experiences and information with their neighbours:

BETTY: Well one tells the other. If you're on the bru, they'll tell what they get so that if you need it you can get it too.
BILLY: We have good neighbours, there's a lot of coming and going.
BETTY: I mean they wouldn't keep it to themselves if they got something.
BILLY: Its not even a case of that, if they get something they're dying to have a wee gossip.
BETTY: Its like one-upmanship; I got this, did you get it? So therefore they wouldn't tell you if they were knocked back on it, that's the impression I get.

Whereas in Mallon Park the attitudes to claiming evinced in the above extract are quite frequently encountered, and could even be described as an incipient system of prestige based on the success or failure in the claiming of grants, very few of the Eastlough sample spoke in such effusive terms about the relation between claiming and neighbouring. Although Eastlough claimants do occasionally mention that others urge them to claim ('I got this, why don't you get it?'), this is almost always in the context of the claimant, who has received the advice, attempting to distance him or herself from such actions by labelling them as wilful abuse. Thus while Mallon Park claimants may sometimes be jealous of what their neighbours and friends obtain, they are not unduly critical of the claiming process, the way it distributes its rewards (or if this is criticized it is in terms of others getting more, rather than, as in Eastlough, others getting too much and thus abusing the system), or those who claim often. In Mallon Park the discovery that a neighbour or friend has made a successful claim is more likely to spur others into doing the same than it is to inhibit them: 'it was Theresa [Hurley]. She told Marie that she got sheets and mattress and says why don't we claim. Well, rightly, we did need a new bed; so I put in the claim and we got it, no problem; Marie thinks its great' (Pat Hardy). This can be contrasted to the way Eastlough claimants disassociate themselves from others by criticizing what they do as wrong and not to be copied: 'She told me she got carpet and curtains and I don't know what else; and she says to me, wise up, youse claim. But like, we only claim what we need, she does it for to go out at night' (George Lynn's wife). This is not to say that the Lynns do not themselves lodge claims; the point is that they construe what others tell them in a quite different manner to the way many Mallon Park residents do who are given similar advice. Finally, on those occasions when I was privy to a discussion between neighbours or friends in Eastlough, in which one admitted to having made a successful claim, the other would sometimes interpret this later as a shameless boast.

Of the other ten in this category of potential assertive claimants from Mallon Park, one was not eligible for SB and is back in work, and another is ineligible for single-payment grants due to large savings. A third, Joe McCartney, who has two disabled children, is visited regularly by a social worker, who gives him advice about benefits and assists him in claiming. He therefore has no need to be assertive or aggressive. A further six (Carlin, Daly, McGrath, O'Neil, Cavanagh, and McCann) are all involved in doing the double to one degree or another, and while they do make claims, they tend to do so mostly when not working, and even then try not to draw attention to themselves by being noticeably assertive. The final member of this group is Jimmy Nolan. He and his wife live very frugally; they neither smoke nor drink and rarely go out except to visit relatives. They are one of the very few families which seems to be able to subsist on basic benefit without any outside assistance.

The evidence outlined thus far, while not perhaps conclusive, very clearly suggests that reluctant claimants are precisely those who, prior to becoming unemployed, explain unemployment and the anomalies of the benefit system in terms of personal factors and the distinction between the deserving and the undeserving. Those who become assertive, knowledgeable, and regular claimants of single-payment grants are a sub-group of those who give few reasons to think that they endorse such explanations or distinctions. Those who are not reluctant but nevertheless keep a low profile are most likely to be working the double.

Eastlough

A majority (twelve out of twenty) of the Eastlough employed sample conceptualizes the continued unemployment of the workless largely in terms of their personal characteristics and dispositions, and criticizes the benefit system for its largess. For Colin Jackson, there are jobs but the unemployed are lazy ('too bone idle to get out of their beds; they won't get up off their arses'), and the whole situation has been 'blown up by the media'. Not only this but: 'they've all videos and tumble dryers. They're up to their eyes in tick [loans], it's the way they do it. How they get it, how they get the tick, I don't know.' David Cordell, while arguing that some are genuine cases, says: 'there's plenty who are just content to live on the dole; they've got so used to it they don't know any better . . . they don't even try anymore'. Their standard of living 'can't be bad. I see them walking down to the bar every night. I don't know how they do it. It surprises me, they're better geared [dressed] than I am.' Many of these employed explain the purported extravagant life-style of people they assume to be unemployed as due to the non-payment of bills (rent, electricity, etc.); in John Fraser's words: 'Something must be going to the wall, somebody is not getting paid. I know guys in the [bar] changing tenners and twenties and all; there must be something wrong, must owe rent, know what I mean; you can't do that.' Frank Hill knows very few unemployed personally but: 'there is one at the back here, he's off these four years, he's on invalidity. He says it's his back, I think it's "workitis" is wrong with him.' For Frank the attitude today is still 'bugger you Jack, I'm alright', and anyway he considers the unemployed well cossetted: 'See them new houses up there, we call that Supplementary Row. The only people can afford to pay the rents is the unemployed, cos they *don't* pay them, and they get the bru to put all the furniture in them. I haven't half the things they can get for free.' Harry Kerr has two unemployed brothers doing the double in Derry, and he tends to extrapolate from them to the unemployed in general: 'I don't honestly know anybody that's unemployed that's breaking his heart to get a job'; and his wife echoes this: 'I don't know anyone sitting in the house saying, "this is terrible, I'm cracking up; I want a job".' Alan Martin, described earlier, says: 'The unemployed don't seem to want to work; they don't try. I was looking in last night's paper and there was a whole stack of jobs. If they only tried that wee bit more.' While all these quotations are extracts from conversations and interviews conducted in private, it must be stressed that similar sentiments were expressed on more informal and public occasions.

Views such as these are representative of the employed in Eastlough. While doing the survey of employment in the estate I had many conversations with people still in work, and the purported indolence of the unemployed and the ease of access to, and the assumed generosity of, the benefit system were topics people spoke about in a passionate and angry way. Because the presently unemployed know full well that these views are prevalent ('when I was in work you'd hear it all the time, the unemployed are work-shy'), both what they do and say is in fact shaped by the mere imputation of such beliefs to others. That is, many of the unemployed perceive adverse implications for themselves in what others say, despite the possibility that such readings are quite unwarranted. This means that these ideas have a sociological significance even when not explicitly invoked in contemporary social encounters. When these ideas are indeed used in specific interactions this is not only very disconcerting for those on the receiving end, but it also reinforces the tendency to detect and sense hidden meanings even when not intended.

Those in the employed sample (eight out of twenty) who repudiate such views, are disposed to consider the unemployed as victims of economic and political forces beyond their control. They point out, for example, that there are very few jobs worth applying for, that good jobs attract huge numbers of applicants, that wages are very low, providing little incentive to work:

It's ridiculous some of the wages. If I was unemployed I wouldn't take jobs like that, so I can understand why the unemployed don't bother. It stands to reason, if they get more on the bru than in a job they're not going to take that job. As I say, I wouldn't do it, so I can hardly expect anyone else to do it . . . No, course its not the benefits. The unemployed I know [Bill Green being one] are barely scraping by, so how anyone can say benefits are too high I don't know. (William Long)

Because of the recession and the high numbers of unemployed, people soon lose heart and stop trying: 'they probably had that many rejections they just think what's the point, they can't even go to see the foreman for to ask for a start, it's all done by forms now' (Harry Lyons).

George Osborne, who has two unemployed children, thinks there are very few jobs, and those that are available are too poorly paid:

I think they're too low, I really do. I think some lorry-driving jobs, to my mind, are very low paid for the responsibilities they take on . . . You see some of those jobs [advertised] in the library, and they're very low paid. There was one I saw, I think it was £80 a week for driving a minibus for the Education Authority – it's ridiculous. When you take your insurance and tax out of it, you'd be lucky to come out with over £60; I think it's ludicrous.

It does surprise me, to a certain extent, how many jobs there are [in the newspapers], and how many times they are repeated, night after night, and some every week. Are the people not good enough to take the jobs, or are they holding out to get somebody to do it cheaper . . . you think about these things.

What this extract indicates is the implicit assumption that there is something 'fishy' about jobs that are not filled quickly. Rather than entertaining the possibility that unemployed people are not bothering to apply, George Osborne automatically thinks there must be something wrong with the jobs. In contrast to this, those who are less sympathetic to the unemployed often point to the many jobs they see advertised, and interpret this as a sign that the unemployed are uninterested in them and hence must be lazy.

It is necessary to add here that of those twelve who espouse antipathetic views of the unemployed, half have themselves experienced prolonged spells (six months or more) without work, though in several cases this was many years ago. Of those who are lenient in their opinions, three have never been unemployed for over six months. There is therefore very little relationship between attitudes towards the unemployed and personal experience of unemployment. This should occasion no surprise, since the evidence shows that those who espouse notions of the deserving and the undeserving are, when unemployed, those who are more likely to distance themselves from other unemployed, and to condemn some of these latter as undeserving in order to maintain an image of themselves as deserving and genuine.

Turning to the Eastlough unemployed there is evidence that, when they were in work, thirteen out of twenty explained unemployment in individualistic terms. This figure is similar to the proportion of Eastlough employed who endorse such explanations at present. Although no statistical evidence can be presented, on the basis of informal conversations with many others in the estate over a long period, I would suggest that this proportion is fairly representative.

Joe Robinson, for example, explains that when he was last in work so too were all his friends and family; he could see no reason why anyone who really wanted to work should have been idle. In those days, there were few good reasons to be unemployed and anyone who was must have been jobless from choice. Nowadays, he thinks, things have changed, and whilst there are still plenty of people unemployed from choice there is in addition a considerable number (including Joe) who are genuinely unemployed (involuntarily) and desperate to get back into work. One of the problems for Joe and others who interpret the situation in this way is how to distinguish themselves successfully from the undeserving cases.

Dave Irvine is a very good example of someone who has always subscribed to the distinction between the deserving and the undeserving. During his first spell of unemployment when eighteen years old and unmarried he even refused to sign-on: 'I was no beggar; I didn't think it was right for anybody not to have a job.' Ever since he has had very little sympathy for other unemployed people:

> D A V E: What I do know is . . . people just haven't got a will to work. They are happy living on the supplementary. I think anybody that has been unemployed, unless they live in a real bad area where there just is no jobs, they're just not trying to get work.

Another eight of this category (most of those discussed in the previous chapter) argue in similar ways. When in work they conceptualized the unemployed as undeserving. Now themselves out of work, one way to sustain a positive self-image is to erect a barrier between themselves and others who are labelled as scroungers, malingerers, and parasites. Since frequent claiming is constitutive of the definition of the undeserving, these unemployed can only retain an image of themselves as deserving by becoming reluctant claimants. Of course, it is not too surprising that many unemployed retain this distinction for the predominant ideology in Eastlough is predicated on it; it is not only the basis of the employed/unemployed division and the basis of divisions within the unemployed, it is also one of the criteria for the division between Protestants and Catholics since, as already mentioned, the latter are thought by many Protestants to know all about the SB scheme and to prefer to exploit it rather than to work.

This is not to say that some unemployed do not change their views. Three men (Hughes, Marshall, and McHale) used to think in terms of this contrast, but no longer do so to the same extent. The clearest and most extreme example of this change is Jim Hughes. When he was in regular work he used to think the unemployed were all lazy and that they did not look for work because the benefits were too good: 'my attitude was if you want a job you can get a job. I honestly believed if you wanted work you could get it.' Jim's experience of unemployment has been very complicated: many occasions when his benefit cheque did not arrive; appearances in court over debts; being employed in a job for four weeks that left him worse off in work than he had been on the dole; regular borrowing from generous relatives; a long spell doing the double which paradoxically did not alleviate his chronic financial position; etc. Through his period of two-and-a-half years' unemployment Jim, and to a lesser extent his wife, have gradually changed their view of economic reality. Jobs are not to be had simply because people want them; the unemployed are victims of forces beyond their personal control, not architects of their own destiny; claimants are not cossetted by a generous and efficient benefit system, rather they live on the edge of poverty harassed by mean-minded, hard-hearted bureaucrats. What he now believes is almost a mirror image of what he says he used to think. He now conceives of the SB system from a different perspective: it no longer merely presents obstacles, it also creates opportunities. With so many unemployed, how can they keep an eye on everyone; despite the fact that staff are miserly with information, there are other ways of obtaining knowledge (CAB, welfare-rights workers, etc), and armed with this Jim now makes claims not only for things he never knew were available, but also for items he already possesses. If a claim is rejected, he appeals; he tries not to get into arguments but nevertheless is persistent; and now he understands office jargon and uses it himself. In his own fashion, then, Jim no longer confronts SSO staff as a subordinate, but can present himself as an equal because he now possesses a fund of resources which he did not previously have. None of this should be taken to mean that Jim and his wife are content with their lot. Jim still looks for jobs and would prefer to be in work than in his present situation; he and his wife still argue over money and both get depressed and irritable, but at least Jim feels more in control of his life than he has for several years. Jim's present orientation is neatly encapsulated in the following, perhaps somewhat embellished, account of a claim he lodged for a steam iron:

Cath's iron went, so I went down to the bru. I waited a while and then I went up to the desk, and the fella said, 'Yes? can I help you?', and I said 'Yes. I would like to make a request for a home visitor to call out and see me. There's some stuff we need.' 'What is it you need?' says he. I said, 'We need an iron and a couple of pots and pans.' And he said, 'Are you and your wife in good health?' I said, 'Yes. What's that got to do with the iron?' He said, 'Well, if you're in good health you're not entitled to an iron.' I turned to the other people and I was laughing (I was in good form that day), and I says to him, 'Do you mean to say if you're in good health . . . in other words, you can run up and down your clothes and iron them with your feet?' . . . and I turned round to the people and gave them a big smile, and turned back in again and said, 'Wait till I tell you friend, I'm out of work nearly three years. I think I know what I'm entitled till and what I'm not entitled till, and I wasn't born yesterday. I'm going to appeal this decision.' He said, 'I haven't made a decision.' I said, 'You told me I'm not entitled to an iron', and I got him all hot and bothered that much he went away, probably to speak to a supervisor, and he came back and said, 'Right', and he took down the details. He said it was to the discretion of the home visitor.

Interestingly, Jim continued his tale by relating what happened to another caller who was dealt with while Jim was waiting.

There was somebody came in, and he was called to the desk, and your man [the officer] told him he wasn't entitled. Don't ask me what it was, but he told him he wasn't getting it, and the poor fella walked away and didn't argue.

Five of the Eastlough unemployed group did not subscribe to the distinction between the deserving and the undeserving prior to their present spell of unemployment. Norman Kincaid and Dave Martin typify these. Norman was sacked from his last job as a radio operator for falling asleep. His longest period of unemployment was one year when he was much younger. Whilst he felt some embarrassment at that time ('there was no call to be out of work in the sixties'), he does not suffer any feeling of shame to-day: 'It's totally different now; there's thousands like me.' While he does make distinctions between the unemployed: 'some people give up looking, but I don't think I will'; and 'the younger lads don't seem to try as hard as they might', these do not seem to be based on moralistic notions of the genuine and the scrounger ('it's the situation; there just is no jobs, people get into a rut, the rejections pile up and they get depressed'). The result of this demoralization is that those unemployed for very long periods adapt to it and no longer bother to look for work: 'but if you was to offer them decent jobs, 95 per cent would jump at it'. However, Norman cannot be classified as an assertive claimant for he is ineligible for SB: since his wife works full time he finds it worth his while to take the thirteen-week government training schemes, which give him a bit more than he would get on unemployment benefit; he also referees football matches at the weekends, from which he derives a modest income.

Dave Martin, before he got into work, argued as Norman Kincaid. He also could not be classed as assertive, because although he was eligible for and claimed SB, he and his wife had considerable savings to fall back on, and additionally Dave was able to do the double on three occasions during his spell of eleven months out of work. One revealing feature of Dave's attitude came up as we walked down to the dole together: 'I know ones that have been unemployed a long time, but whether it bothers them I don't know. Maybe they're not showing it. People just don't like to let on how they're really feeling, they put a brave face on it.' On the other hand, those who do try to establish a moral superiority over others usually take such superficial evidence of contentment as definite proof of it.

The remaining two members of the unemployed group, Bill Green and Tom Haslett, are worthy of extended description and comparison.

Both experienced their first major spell of unemployment after working many years, and both had quite similar views about unemployment before this. However, their unemployment 'careers' have turned out rather differently. While Bill has succumbed to the stigmatizing pressures he finds all around him, Tom has learnt the arts of assertiveness.

Bill Green, coach-builder by trade, and unemployed for over two years is one of those who, despite not morally categorizing other unemployed into the genuine and the discreditable, nevertheless feels very degraded being jobless and having to live on benefit. When he was in work he claims he never gave unemployment or the unemployed a thought because there were plenty of jobs and few out of work. But with so many unemployed now 'it's a whole different atmosphere'. He maintains that the vast majority 'of the people that's unemployed would dearly love a job, but they can't get one'. What frustrates and angers Bill are the unsympathetic opinions others (including his parents) take towards the unemployed.

The dilemma for Bill and those like him, is that he is virtually powerless to prevent others from classifying him in a derogatory fashion. He can only demonstrate that he is willing to work by actually being seen to look for work. But this poses numerous problems in itself. When first paid off, he went to the job centre, but he has never seen a job in his own trade advertised there. He has applied to numerous other places, and even tried for a job as a floor sweeper. He has not been interviewed for most of the jobs he applied for, and many firms no longer even acknowledge the receipt of applications, which is considered a contemptible practice by all the unemployed, not least because such acknowledgements can be used as tangible proof of a desire to work. He walked all over east Belfast and met continual rejections:

You begin to think there's something wrong with you; do I look as if I've got two heads or something? I've got to the stage where I feel so dejected that there's nothing to look forward to. I'm wasting my time going up and down to these job centres, there's never anything for me.

Having completely exhausted all the possibilities, he had little confidence of ever getting a job. Knowing from past experience that all he will encounter are rejections makes the prospect of looking for a job a desperately unpleasant burden. One can deflect the needling accusations of being work-shy only by laying oneself open to the equally debilitating effects of continual rejection from potential employers.

The other major factor in Bill's situation is his commitment to working for his living, and therefore his detestation of claiming benefits. Living on benefits would not be so bad were it not for the deplorable way in which it is administered (see chapter 5). Bill is reluctant to claim extra grants, to lodge appeals or even to expand his knowledge of the scheme, as in his eyes this would be a clear signal to others that he was a scrounger. In short, though Bill does not himself appear to use ideas of deservingness, he painfully realizes that others use it to categorize him. His feelings of shame, reluctance, and frustration stem largely from the fact that he considers his efforts to manage the impressions he thinks others have of him as continually failing, and that therefore being branded as work-shy is inescapable. Having been defeated by the big battalions, self-defeat is never very far away:

You get into a frame of mind, I haven't got the get-up-and-go; you feel dejected all the time. Nobody really wants bothering with the sad old story. There's nobody to talk to to get it off your chest, and it puts quite a pressure on me when you have all this building up and building up. And then I can't sleep and you get so tired and exhausted. You're lying in bed, turning it over in your mind, how're you going to solve this, pay for that. You always look on the glum side for some reason. When you start thinking of all these things there's times it makes you very suicidal, you are apt to think that way.

Given the way Bill understands work, unemployment, and the dole, and given his susceptibility to the views of others, he can only conceptualize the constraints on his life as all embracing. Pushing against one merely brings another into play. If he makes no demands on the SB system, he makes life financially more hazardous for his family, but if he does he risks being labelled a scrounger; if he doesn't look for jobs he cannot demonstrate his willingness to work, but if he does he faces the danger of having his self-esteem continually diminished by failure.

Tom Haslett's first spell of unemployment between 1980 and 1981 paralleled in many ways that of Bill Green. Unable to shake off depression and self-pity he sat around the house moping, much to the chagrin of his amiable wife. 'That eighteen months was really terrible. It was very degrading. I knew in my heart I was able to do jobs but nobody wanted me. The jobs I could get, they were no use to me. Just felt I was useless, that I was no good to anybody.' Fortunately, through a friend of a friend, Tom obtained a job putting in loft insulation. 'It felt fantastic to be in a job again, felt like a million dollars.' However, the job lasted less than a year. Tom has now been unemployed over three years. But during this spell out of work he had gradually, unlike Bill Green, become less defeatist and more aggressive in his dealings with social security staff: 'I used to be green, but I've wised up; I've learnt alot.' One event which seems to have helped in this change occurred late on in his first spell out of work:

The twins had just been born, so we kept the heating on. It was that terrible winter. Anyway I expected a big bill, but £180 was a shock. There was no way we could pay that. So I phoned the bru and they refused to give me an appointment. Said I was getting all I was entitled till. I didn't let it rest at that. I went down the next day. I saw this cheeky oul bastard: 'I'm sorry, you're getting nothing else. You can't get any more.'

After a loud argument someone else came out and told Tom to come back the following day. At this meeting he was told nothing further could be done because he was already receiving everything he was entitled to.

At this time I was really angry. If we couldn't pay this bill we'd get cut off and then what would happen? So I went to see [my MP]. He said he'd call the bru and see what could be done. A couple of days later I got a letter to go and see the manager at [SSO]. So I went back to the dole and explained everything, yet again, to this other eejit. He had all my details in front of him: 'Under the law we can't give you anything at all. I see your position, I would like to help.' And then he said, 'Look have you got adequate bedding, all this sort of thing? I said, 'Yes, everything's all right that way.' He said, 'I'll ask you again, but don't tell me that.' So he asked me again. Here's me: 'No, we need bedclothes, blah, blah, blah.' 'Right', he said, 'as far as you're concerned I have personally been to your house and you need bedclothes. You'll have your cheque out by Saturday.' And right enough we got a cheque for £99.95.

During his second period of unemployment, Tom and his wife began to learn more about the SB scheme from friends, relatives, and a local community worker (passionately committed to increasing the take-up of benefits), and they successfully claimed single-payment grants for several pieces of household furniture. With a few weeks' work on the double, now and again, Tom's family was managing to get by without going into debt. On one occasion, whilst doing some work on a building site he received a summons to go for an interview at the local SSO. According to Tom, he was interrogated by two men who asked him a stream of loaded questions: 'What do you think will happen to your wife and kids if you go to jail? What's going to happen to them? Don't you think it would be better if you signed off?' We're happy if you get some work, but you're supposed to come and tell us'; etc. He didn't sign off because he was sure they had no real evidence. But he decided that if they were going to try to frighten him with such threats, he was no longer going to react supinely. Since then Tom has been claiming grants whenever possible. He has claimed paint and wallpaper twice for the same room. He claimed gardening tools for a virtually non-existent garden. He doctored a gas cooker so that it looked worse than it really was, and then claimed a single-payment grant for a replacement. With the willing connivance of the assistant at the shop to which the cheque was made out, he bought instead the fridge they had always wanted, and then repaired the cooker with bits from an old one his mother had.

If you want to get anything out of the supplementary you have to do it yourself. It's no good giving up when they say you're not entitled, which is what I used to do. At first if they said 'no' I'd just come home and sit in a corner and mope. Also as I say it was degrading, you felt like you was begging, and you just wanted to get out. Well now my attitude's different, if they say 'no' I'll put in for an appeal straight away, or I'll demand to see the manager . . . Yes, course you still get angry, but I'm learning now to keep my head, just insist without losing the bap. That way they can't touch you, and eventually they might just give in.

Conclusion

What characterizes the encounter between SSO staff and assertive claimants is not simply a conflict of interests, which may reveal itself in diverse forms, although of course this is the material expression of the conflict. More fundamentally, the point is that the divergence is generated by and interpreted within two mutually antagonistic cultural frameworks. SSO staff do not merely use the distinction between the deserving and the undeserving (and the practices derived from it), but in seeking to control claimants they also, unintentionally perhaps, impose on them this version of social reality. By and large reluctant claimants, already espousing such a view, readily enough accept the subordinate and deferential position implied by this set of ideas. This is not so much because their interests are the same as those of staff since, as has been shown, this is not the case. It is rather because they wish to appear as genuine and deserving examples of the poor and they cannot achieve this if they are seen to press their interests too far, for it is such a course of action which leads to claimants being branded as undeserving. Assertive claimants repudiate the validity and legitimacy of the distinction and therefore its associated practices. That is to say, they reject the basic premises which underlie the way SSO staff see their relationship to claimants (they do not reject the authority of staff to administer the system, only the set of ideas they practically use to accomplish this task). In their own way, assertive claimants attempt to impose their version of how this relationship should be constituted. This can only be done by becoming knowledgeable, aggressive, persistent, and importunate. The irony of this is that the practices both staff and assertive claimants indulge in serve unintentionally to reinforce the schemes of classification each subscribes to, and therefore the antipathetic image each has of the other. Thus it cannot simply be a conflict about material interests, because claimants are unlikely to press these in a tenacious and combative manner unless they conceptualize their situation in a different way to that of benefit officers. The conflict is really generated then by a clash of cultural categories, and disputes over benefits and the way in which the system is administered are the most tangible manifestation of this.

Chapter 8

The employed and the unemployed: conflict, discourse, and ideology

Introduction

Under most circumstances, male employment in advanced industrial countries requires little explicit ideological justification. Whilst to many unemployment is a largely unacceptable status, employment is an unquestioned good; it is what everybody does, or should do: 'the work role tends towards a kind of moral imperative' (Wadel, 1973: 109; cf. chapter 1). Moreover, being in work signifies more than earning a financial return. A regular job authorizes and influences experience, values, life-styles, consumption patterns, and much else; and such intrinsic functions are largely taken for granted (Jahoda, 1979). Employment also entails a reciprocal relation between society and the individual which legitimates a whole panoply of routine practices. The values which underlie such a valorization of employment are very strongly held and deeply entrenched in the central institutions of the family, education, and the state. In short, the positive value of formal employment is a presupposition from which much else in modern society is derived.

Unemployment entails the loss of many of these benefits just as it reveals their implicit nature. It also destroys much of the basis of a person's relationship to his family, community, and wider society. Consequently, interaction between unemployed and employed people is made difficult and sensitive. The activities and values underpinning employment provide the dominant cultural and ideological framework within which people evaluate, criticize, denounce, or praise the unemployed for the way they speak and act.

Precisely because the intrinsic rewards of being in a job are largely concealed to the worker but disclosed to the jobless, unemployment appears much worse to the latter than it does to the former. Consequently, the two groups have rather different ideas about the nature, impact, and consequences of unemployment. The employed, in advancing their view of how to look for work, how to start a business, how to organize budgetary priorities, what the proper level of benefits should be, and so forth, do not feel the pressure of the constraints that the unemployed experience. Thus what to workers seems a rational course of action for the unemployed to follow can appear to the latter not merely naive but, more pertinently, a personal attack on their self-esteem. Conversely, what to the unemployed seems sensible given their situation can appear unnecessarily cautious, unreasonable, and counter-productive to the employed. Conditions such as these generate an 'argument' between those with and those without jobs, and amongst the latter themselves (Wadel, 1973: ix). But let me add quickly that not all the employed engage in this argument. As we have seen, many of those in jobs, especially in Mallon Park, are sympathetic to the unemployed. The conflict is rather between the unemployed and those in work who subscribe to the deserving/undeserving distinction.

Mostly, this argument is couched in a particular discourse concerning the behaviour, attitudes, and life-styles the employed expect of the jobless. Because it is the unemployed's commitment to the ideology of employment that becomes suspect, they find themselves in a subordinate position *vis-à-vis* those still in work, and so have little influence to shape the content of these expectations.

However, the argument is not entirely one-sided. At first glance it might be assumed that employed people feel little pressure to reinforce and validate the ideology underpinning the legitimacy of formal employment, but the situation is more complicated (Wadel, 1973: 112). In communities with large numbers of unemployed, of whom some argue that they will only take jobs which 'pay' them, some receive benefits apparently bigger than the employed receive in wages, some belligerently insist that welfare is an entitlement rather than a privilege, and where household goods are apparently obtained just by the asking, the employed begin to find that the ideology of work might itself be under threat. This is the reason why those in work are so interested in what the unemployed do and think. Thus 'Unemployed men are squeezed out of the public realm – but their retreat into the private realm becomes public business. As . . . they become welfare recipients, their private lives are open to public scrutiny' (McKee and Bell, 1986: 147). The employed's vigilance and the social and psychological pressure they impose on the unemployed is the concrete manifestation of their own need to buttress the ideology of employment and to counteract any deviations from it.

The employed might of course reason that long-term unemployment is a consequence of structural problems in the economy and is therefore involuntary, in which case the jobless would not pose a serious threat. But in communities like Eastlough such an explanation does not easily accommodate the complexities and compelling realities of an everyday life in which many people do not positively enjoy work, where work is low paid, where the acquisition of the material necessities of life is a hard business, where, in short, it demands moral strength to withstand the costs of working. It is a small step from here to arguing that many unemployed are content to be unemployed and that they conceal their indolence and fecklessness behind the assertion that there is no work. In this way the employed can explain joblessness by seeming to convert a section of the unemployed (the undeserving) into people espousing a divergent and inferior value system, and in a sense to treat them as culturally different. By so doing, they can distance themselves from putative scroungers and malingerers and maintain the pre-eminence of the ideology of employment, but at the cost of introducing into their midst a hostile and divisive force. Analytically, then, it appears that these employed erect a symbolic boundary (Anthony Cohen, 1986) between themselves and the deserving jobless on the one hand and the undeserving on the other.[1]

At first sight this seems strange, for the presently unemployed were once employed, and in many cases the reverse is true also, so objectively there appear to be no grounds on which cultural differences can be argued to exist. But unfortunately for the unemployed, things are not so simple. An important parameter here is present employment status. Even if previously unemployed, the presently employed argue that they have a job now because, having looked hard for one, they were successful. Even if previously employed, the values, practices, and motivations of the presently unemployed are open to doubt and criticism because they remain unemployed. They do not have a job because they do not look hard enough, and this is because they do not want to work, and in turn this is taken as evidence that they espouse different values about work, reciprocity, and individual and social responsibilities. Hence the value of prior working records is always debatable. No matter how good these may be, the employed can always allege that the presently unemployed never really liked working, or were not very good workers, and their contemporary unemployment is an indication of this. Nevertheless, employment histories are useful, for they supply the unemployed with some tangible evidence that they respect the value of work and of what it entails. But the longer the present spell lasts the less convincing is this recourse. Whatever the situation before, what really counts is who is in work now. Clearly, from this perspective all unemployment is to be considered voluntary unless it can be shown otherwise. But what constitutes evidence of involuntary unemployment? Basically, beyond actually obtaining a job, a great deal of what the unemployed do and say is taken into account in assessing deservingness and willingness to work. This line of argument implies that the focus of investigation should be on the boundary that defines one group as different to another, that is, on the socially relevant factors that are diagnostic for membership (Barth, 1969: 15).

The boundary in question conceptually distinguishes the employed and the deserving unemployed together in opposition to the undeserving unemployed. This creates the possibility of being incorporated into the deserving category while remaining unemployed, which in turn entails that a large range of criteria can be considered pertinent for reaching decisions on inclusion and exclusion. To be classed as deserving and genuine, the unemployed have to conform, or at least claim to conform, as much as possible to the expectations the employed have of them. The problem is, however, that the extent of such conformity and the application of criteria to particular cases, is essentially contestable and not a matter of objective measurement (what constitutes 'diligence' in looking for work? How is 'restraint' in claiming benefits measured?), but is shaped instead by contingent and situational factors often unrelated to the world of work (is the unemployed man a friend, relative, or neighbour? What kind of friend, relative, or neighbour is he? etc.). It is also influenced by subjective factors, so that judgements of conformity vary between persons. Relevant criteria are interpreted and applied according to context, and so who is deemed deserving and who undeserving is open to continual negotiation. Moreover, what is being negotiated is the acceptance and rejection of claims to deservingness. Such claims are perforce based on assertions that one is fulfilling the criteria for inclusion that society lays down as appropriate. But again such assertions are predicated on evidence that is intrinsically disputable; no matter what one does there are always possibilities not tried, avenues not completely researched, opportunities allowed to pass by. It is thus all a matter of claim and counter-claim, assertion and counter-assertion; but it is the employed who are responsible for the discourse in which this takes place and who have the greater resources with which to make their judgements count.

On the other hand, the existence of these broader categories and the criteria which define them supply an incentive for the unemployed to become involved in strategies of impression management by means of which they can obtain entry into a more creditable category. The cost paid for any psychological and social gain is that these tactics, because they necessitate the denigration of others, are inherently fragmenting and isolating in their consequences (McKee and Bell, 1986). Moreover, success in such a game is often an illusion: those who play it most seem to be haunted by what they consider others think of them; claimants who are most restrained can never be sure they are restrained enough to satisfy their anonymous judges; those who are most diligent in the search for work seem impelled to soldier on by the ruinous anxiety induced by what they imagine others will think should they stop. The striving of the unemployed to be recognized as deserving, by claiming to conform to appropriate life-styles and by denouncing others as undeserving, is reminiscent of Tawney's jibe that the ideas that people entertain about upward social mobility betray what he caustically describes as the 'tadpole philosophy' of life:

It is possible that intelligent tadpoles reconcile themselves to the inconveniences of their position, by reflecting that, though most of them will live and die as tadpoles and nothing more, the more fortunate of the species will one day shed their tails, distend their mouths and stomachs, hop nimbly on to dry land, and croak addresses to their former friends on the virtues by means of which tadpoles of character and capacity can rise to be frogs. (Tawney, 1964: 105)

The set of criteria contrasting the deserving, genuine, and respectable to the undeserving, ineligible, and disreputable consitute a cultural apparatus by which apparent material differences, or indeed the apparent absence of such differences, are interpreted. What I mean by this should be clear from the following. Those of the employed who endorse distinctions between the deserving and the undeserving invoke such contrasts to conjure up a moral difference between themselves and the unemployed precisely because they perceive an absence of material difference:[2] the unemployed seem content; they have money to drink and gamble; they're well dressed; they have videos and hi-fi; etc., that is, characteristics, possessions, and practices which are associated with being in work. The unemployed, they continue, can only achieve a style of life ideally appropriate to those who have jobs if one or a combination of things is happening: the benefit system is over-generous, which encourages rather than deters the scrounger; the unemployed are engaged in dubious or illegal activities; they give up looking for work far too easily, fall into a rut, do not have the moral fibre to pull themselves together, and hence prefer to remain jobless; and so on; and all of this is deemed reprehensible because it is in direct conflict with the cultural values of workers. In other words the unemployed gain many of the benefits associated with work but without paying the costs.

Many of the unemployed, realizing that those in jobs make such assessments of moral worth, perceive that they can only resist being labelled in a derogatory fashion by invoking the same distinctions. This is done not only to distance themselves from other unemployed by engaging (or at least claiming to engage) in practices which emphasize their own moral superiority, but also to reduce the moral gap between themselves and workers. This can only be accomplished by stressing the existence of material differences between the two groups and proclaiming their own undiminished commitment to the value of work. Whilst 'we' are desperate for work, never go out except to look for jobs, can hardly make ends meet, do not fritter money away on trivia (i.e. values and practices which it is supposed meet with the approval of workers), other unemployed seem well off, are always going out, buying things, wasting their money. The unemployed explain this state of affairs in much the same way as do the employed: it is done by abusing the dole, cheating, neglecting the family, ignoring bills, etc., and they condemn it as harshly as do the employed, once again claiming their solidarity with this latter group.

In the former case (some) employed people established a moral distinction to explain the presumed absence of material differences between themselves and the unemployed. This, then, constrains and *enables* the unemployed to erect a further moral boundary to explain the presumed presence of material differences between themselves and other jobless. There is a dilemma here. The unemployed can secure short-term gains by trying to get themselves classified as deserving. But in so doing they sustain the saliency of a discourse which in the long term is disadvantageous. In this way we see how the jobless are implicated in the reproduction of their own subordination.

In each of the cases just discussed, moral superiority is claimed by invoking distinctions which denigrate a whole category of others. Such claims to moral superiority are based on the notion that those deemed undeserving do not conform to moral standards widely accepted throughout society, but rather style their life in accordance with a different moral view of the world. Such people, it is thought, want something for nothing; they are parasites; their attitudes and behaviour drag others (notably wife and children) into the same quagmire, giving rise to 'problem families' (Jordan, 1974), the 'cycle of disadvantage' (Rutter and Madge, 1976), and the 'culture of poverty' (Lewis, 1966; Valentine, 1968; Hannerz, 1969).[3]

Two models of unemployment

Much of the discussion of previous chapters indicates that there are two distinct ways in which long-term unemployment is thought about. Though the terminology is clumsy, these may be called models (Holy and Stuchlik, 1981), though ideologies might do just as well. One model (the 'Deserving' or D model) is predicated on individualism and the distinction between the deserving and the undeserving; these are its fundamental presuppositions, from with other, more concrete, aspects are derived. Such a view (see chapter 1) tends to explain personal misfortune in terms of individual attributes and practices. The second model (the 'Structural' or S model) professes that the unemployed are unwitting victims of economic, social, and political forces beyond their personal control, and therefore cannot be blamed for their predicament. While the former reduces structural problems in the economy, the polity, and the benefit system to the level of the individual, the latter dissolves the individual into the wider context.[4]

However, the D model must of necessity include aspects of the S model in its make-up. The former, being premissed on a moral distinction, must provide an explanation for the deserving, and this can only be done by incorporating ideas which form part of the latter; there can only be deserving unemployed if these are presumed blameless, viewed as the innocent victims of implacable forces; and this notion is central to the S model.[5] Given these competing views it is to be expected that those employed not subscribing to distinctions between the deserving and the undeserving would have rather different ideas about whatever material differences they perceive between themselves and the unemployed. In general, if they acknowledge very little difference in consumption patterns, this is explained by the chronic problem of low wages rather than generous benefits. It is less a matter of the unemployed living an inappropriate life-style and more a case of the employed not being able to afford anything better, which generates the lack of difference.

Of course, individuals differ in the extent to which their ideas about a topic are developed, or in the degree of attention they are willing to give to it. Those with little interest have little to say; their understanding of unemployment is poorly elaborated. In such cases, ideas are badly articulated and inconsistent and seem to be little more than superficial clichés and stock phrases. Others show a greater interest, hold their views more tenaciously, and have a more integrated set of beliefs. Many of those, both employed and unemployed, who avoid ideas of the deserving and the undeserving, discuss unemployment in a highly consistent fashion, both at a general and a specific level. A significant finding of the research is that many people in this group have an active background in the trades-union movement and claim to be socialists. They claim to have thought, read, and argued about unemployment-related issues on many occasions; in Mills' terms they have something of the 'sociological imagination' (Mills, 1970).

There is, therefore, a social distribution of knowledge about unemployment. Those who construct reality by recourse to the S model focus on the influences of wider processes, the structure of the economy and the polity, for example, which are thought to relate to the nature and causes of unemployment. Such people are more prone to consider these aspects as relevant to their understanding and to bring them to bear on particular cases. On the other hand, those constrained by ideas of deservingness are more likely to ignore these wider considerations or to give them a more peripheral place in the explanation, and to base their views much more on local events, on scapegoats, and on the imputed personal characteristics of the people they see and know (Jenkins, 1978: 132). There are thus substantial differences in the content of conversations I had with people holding different models. Those endorsing structural explanations make far more reference, and give priority, to the role of government policy, to the implications of world events such as the recession and the oil crisis, to the significance of external organizations such as the European Economic Community (EEC); they also know and cite statistics on aspects of the local unemployment situation and on regional imbalances. Contrarily, those relying on individualistic interpretations make few such references, consider them as mostly irrelevant, or deem them all so much sophistry disingenuously invoked to hide the fact that people do not want to work; on this latter reading statistics are used as a device to cloud, confuse, and mislead, removing blame from the individual, where it should lie, and foisting it on to suspect 'environmental' forces.[6]

Benefits, jobs, and life-styles

In what follows, I discuss the main themes of the argument between the employed and the jobless in the three spheres in which it is most evident: benefits, job-hunting, and life-styles.

Let me underscore the point, however, that by no means all interaction between the employed and the unemployed is conflictual; much goes on that is free of hidden meaning and veiled implication; and this is more the case in Mallon Park than in Eastlough because, in the former estate, being unemployed and receiving benefit are less stigmatized than in the latter. On the other hand, many unemployed are so sensitive to the statements made by others that even well-intentioned remarks may be interpreted as hostile and evidence of malice.

Benefits

The issues which divide those in work from the jobless find a safe and amusing outlet in jokes. Many of these play on three themes, the indolence of the unemployed, doing the double, and the incredible largess of the state welfare system. But the jokes have their more serious counterparts.

People kind of think you're well off. [Down at the shops] I've heard women saying, 'oh look at them spongers claiming off the government, claiming for this, and get grants for that, and the rest of us have to struggle . . . They get their grants for bedclothes, and there's us has to scrimp and save and do without, and they just walk down and get a cheque over the counter.' Because I had actually claimed I was too ashamed to say [anything]. I actually agreed with the people. I'd say 'oh yes'. (Cath Hughes)

This brief but telling encounter shows how those whose husbands are in employment are effortlessly able to implement their favoured discourse and thus to enforce their view of the benefit system, and Cath Hughes is constrained to participate on their terms. To avoid an argument, and to convey an impression that she herself would not dream of doing such things, she meekly agrees to a disparaging assessment of the claimant population.

Many employed insist that benefits are too high, and that therefore the life-style of the unemployed is hardly any different to that of the employed. Harry Kerr and his wife are convinced the unemployed manage very well:

Sure they all get money to decorate their new houses, and a spade to dig their garden. [In the pub] the banter is 'I'm wasting my time working.' You see someone coming in, ordering a pint . . . dressed like a lord, and you walk in with your working clothes, or even in your best clothes, and you're still not as well dressed. And I look at myself and say, 'now Harry, you could do with a new suit'. I can't afford to go out and spend £120 or £150, and yet I see people dandering about here with their sports jackets and everything on. I say to my self there's something not right. There's a bit of resentment, because you go to the bar and they're standing there, maybe full, you're saying, 'how the heck do they do it?'

The Kerrs, as others, explain such extravagance by noting the difference in priorities between themselves and the unemployed. The latter think only of themselves and neglect their children who run around without shoes. When the unemployed have money they just 'spend, spend, spend . . . on the silliest of things'. This is all wrong; 'the home and the children should be looked after first, and then you can treat yourself'. Much of the Kerrs' disgruntlement about the unemployed stems from what they think of Bill Green and his wife, on whom much of this talk of priorities and snappy dressing is based. After two years' unemployment Bill had recently obtained a one-year temporary job, but the Kerrs felt he was none too pleased:

Yes, but all the stories is that he wants out of it. He doesn't want to work. He's looking for an excuse out. He says he's denying a contractor this work which is leading to more unemployment. He was a coach-builder, I think. [In his last job] they had a mutual agreement, if he left they wouldn't sack him. He's a bit of a hot-headed character. [When he was in that last job] he complained alot about his nerves. [After becoming unemployed] he was happier, and I never heard much talk about [his nerves] then. Although right enough now he's working again, he's getting sore throats.

These extracts demonstrate how the employed can field counter-arguments to those advanced by the unemployed. If benefits are seen as too high, then the unemployed have no financial incentive to work, and so do not want to work; if benefits are merely adequate then priorities are scrutinized and found wanting. Once the moral boundary is erected, other characteristics are enlisted to reinforce it: Bill does not have the right temperament for work, he is hot-headed; he was happier when unemployed, but now back in work he's complaining again and looking for excuses to leave.

It is interesting to compare this account of the Green family with what Bill himself has to say (see previous chapters). I may add here that as far I know Bill is teetotal and rarely goes to the pub; he has few clothes and no money in his pocket. It is also instructive to compare what different workers have to say about the same unemployed person. William Long, generally very sympathetic to the unemployed, is another neighbour of Bill's:

WILLIAM: Oh Bill's been unemployed for about two years, although I think now he's got a job. Oh sure, you'd see him alot. He loved working on that oul car. He couldn't sit, always had to be out working on it. He also played bowls. You'd see him going over to play bowls in the park. He got very depressed because I remember his wife saying he was on nerve tablets for depression.

Q.: Does he have a history of that?

WILLIAM: No. Great lad he was. Always full of life. When we had the street party . . . now he doesn't drink, but honestly he had this place in an uproar.

He's just so full of life. But he was unemployed for a quare while before he was on nerve tablets. He's alright now he's back in work, back to his old self. [About unemployment] I think there shouldn't be a stigma in it. I think it could happen to anybody. But there's an awful lot of people that are very good at hiding their feelings, especially up around here. A lot of people like Bill . . . outgoing, he's cool, calm, and collected, but inwardly he's just smouldering away because he hasn't got a job. He maybe doesn't impart these things to you. You know, when you're talking to people it just doesn't come through.

The point of this ethnography is less to search out the 'objective' facts of the case, than to see how different interpretive frameworks produce vividly different descriptions of the same man. Many more discrepant versions (from both estates) of how the unemployed are pictured could be adduced, but the point is made that there are major differences in how the employed characterize the jobless.

Some of the unemployed assent or mutely conform to unsympathetic cultural stereotypes, as did Cath Hughes. But when attacked directly, many unemployed adopt a different strategy. Some react with an attempt to justify themselves by explaining how hard life is on the dole but at the same time agreeing that there are other unemployed people who do deserve such accusations. One evening, at the Harding's house, Pearl Harding was very upset because she had run out of money and the benefit cheque was not due till the following morning. She had earlier been to her brother's to borrow some money but as he was not in she left a message. He came round later and as soon as he got through the door Pearl was pestering him for £5. Her brother was very clearly annoyed and made this obvious by impugning the way she managed her money: 'Sure you get enough on the bru; you're going out all the time and living it up.' Pearl, on the defensive, tried to disabuse him: 'We're not like that, Jim and me never go out, we just sit in here and rot.' She carried on almost incoherently that just because others are out boozing that was no reason to tar her with the same brush. When she started crying the brother pushed £5 at her and left.

In this case the unemployed again find themselves arguing within the terms of a discourse the employed impose upon them. By invoking the same derogatory contrasts that those in work use they are able to deflect condemnation on to anonymous others. In doing so they gain some comfort for themselves, but at the cost of unwittingly demonstrating the appropriateness of such a discourse and thus maintaining its relevance. The other alternative is to argue back more forcefully:

I had a row with my brother-in-law. It was the stag night of Bill's wedding. He'd had a few drinks and he ranted and raved about keeping the unemployed, looking down on me, and I lost the head. He was saying, 'A job at £1,000 a week and you wouldn't take it.' I lost the rag and said, 'Wait till I tell you something. If I want to stay on the dole for the next ten years I'll stay on the dole. I paid my stamps for ten years; I paid my income tax. You're not paying for me. I paid for me all these years, you're not doing it.' The two of us fell out and more or less don't say hello to each other. The best of it was the other brother-in-law was unemployed and he sat there and never said a dicky-bird. (Jim Hughes)

The other major dimension of the arguments over benefits concerns single-payment grants (see chapter 5). According to the employed, these act as a disincentive to look for work because once in a job it is necessary to pay for items one could previously get off the SB scheme:

MICK: If you got an honest census of people who are on the dole and asked them if they would take a job tomorrow, a good 90 per cent would say no . . . It's not worth their while because they're getting more off the dole, and their rent paid, free milk, bus fares. You take McCartney's over there. Joe is on top of the world with the money coming into that house.

Q.: He's got a lot of children, he has two invalids.

MICK: I know. They're not invalids, the kids are out playing. Right they're deformed, but you want to see the gear going into Joe's house, washing machines and everything else, where I was sitting with a £10 cooker till last year. Joe's getting all this. Decoration, a big squad of 'em came in and painted his house top to bottom. Taxis come to bring his kids to school, but my kids are walking down in the rain. And I'm working and my wife's working to pay for all that. (Mick Franklin)

Several others in Mallon Park and a majority of the employed in Eastlough are equally scathing in their condemnation of such grants. The following account is from Eddie Canavan (who was himself unemployed between 1977 and 1979) and his wife:

EDDIE: See when you're unemployed you've all the benefits, you get your grants. If you need clothing you get grants for clothing; you get your house re-decorated. So unemployed you're better off. They're getting £50 for gardening tools!

WIFE: I think there is jobs around, but there's an awful lot of people don't want them.

EDDIE: People are getting too much unemployment money. I honestly think that. People say to me, 'You're a mug working.' But I like to pay for what I have. I have to go out and buy paper and paint, yet people [on the dole] are getting more than me and are able to go in and pick their paper and the social security pay for it.

WIFE: And the best of paper and the best of paint.

EDDIE: And you don't actually have to do it yourself, people are employed to go in and paper the house for you.

Q.: Didn't you know all about these grants when you were unemployed?

EDDIE: These things are all new things.
Q.: They've been available for years.
WIFE: We only just found out about it.
EDDIE: Know about them or not . . . the point is getting them. There's people just seem to get everything. What they want they get.
WIFE: It's much easier now, it's all changed since when he was on the bru. See he never got any of these things. They [SSO officers] never told us about all these wee things you can claim. Now, all you do is walk in and you can get anything you want.

These complaints were made repeatedly by employed in both estates, but especially in Eastlough. Such accusations attribute very lax moral standards to the unemployed: they give up work to get the grants; will not take a job because they would lose lucrative benefits; even ridicule the employed for staying in work; and so forth. Consequently the unemployed are seen as shameless, aggressive, and greedy. Demonstrably they are different to 'us' who work for a living (even if the living is hard, and no better than being on the dole), and who have to withstand the debasement of 'our' moral standards.

Four themes structure these resentments. First, there is a strong tendency to exaggerate the size of any grant obtained. It is in fact impossible to get £50 for gardening implements. SB regulations stipulate a spade or fork and a pair of garden shears, and the norm, in my experience, is between £12 and £17. Far from getting the best paint and paper, the allowance actually only provides for very cheap brands. Moreover, 'the amount to be allowed by way of a single payment is normally the cost of second-hand items, if available, in the case of furniture or gardening tools and new items in other cases' (Lynes, 1981: 143).

The second feature is a strong inclination to exaggerate the range of items available. People mention that TVs, fridges, washing machines, vacuum cleaners, etc., are indiscriminately available. Whereas a TV is quite unobtainable, the other items are available only under certain restrictive conditions: a fridge if a member of the household for medical reasons needs a special diet for which foods must be kept at refrigerated temperatures; a vacuum cleaner where a member of the assessment unit is allergic to house dust; etc. The reason Joe McCartney acquires more than others is that he and two of his children are disabled.

Third, the employed insist that these grants are too easy to get. Social security officers are naive, easily duped, suckers for a hard-luck story. They do not check up on details, and they give money to the husband (who is likely to squander it) rather than to his wife (who at least is more likely to spend it wisely). They give more to the greedy because these are brazen, chance their arm, complain, and use sob stories. This makes officers angry, and so those who really need help become too embarrassed to ask, for fear of being associated with scroungers and layabouts.

Finally, it is argued, especially by those who have experienced unemployment, that the system has greatly improved since the time they had to endure it. When 'I' was unemployed you never had all these things; there's much more available now than there was before; there's all kinds of people to tell you what you can get, and to help you to get it; they never told us anything when I was unemployed; its more generous than it used to be; in my day it was terrible, they gave you a real rough time, now it's a piece of cake; and so on. Conversely, many presently unemployed people argue that the system is worse than it used to be (fewer grants available, longer queues, officers ruder, more mistakes with benefit cheques, etc.).

It is not difficult to make sense of this. If, as argued in chapter 5, the claiming of single-payment grants is difficult and many do not receive their full entitlement, then obviously those who have been unemployed previously will remark on this; they are simply echoing the complaints made by the presently unemployed, reliving the experiences that many others are now going through. But, as has been shown, many presently unemployed allege that other jobless get more from SB than they do themselves. When back in work such people continue to be obsessed by the apparent ease with which the unemployed secure what appears to be a wide range of desirable benefits, only now it is the whole of the unemployed rather than some section of them that is assumed to be doing well.

Of course, strident press campaigns denouncing the welfare state and vilifying social security abuse, alongside the present Conservative government's attempts to inculcate 'Victorian' values of thrift, individual responsibility, and the work ethic, maintain local hostility to the benefit system, and this also partly accounts for the disapproving posture of those never unemployed. Amongst these latter there is a tendency for the low paid to complain more than the better off, but there are a significant number of poorly paid workers acknowledging that the unemployed find life on the dole a depressing financial burden.

One point worth mentioning is that those who bemoan the putative luxury life-styles of the unemployed often point to extreme cases, but deem these to be the norm. It is especially those advocating distinctions between the deserving and undeserving who argue like this. They explain what they see in terms of the assumptions that jobs are available, benefits are high, and the SB system is easy to dupe. Consequently most unemployed not only do not want to work but are also shameless enough not to be embarrassed about flaunting their ill-gotten gains. Since the behaviour and home life of the jobless are scrutinized, the arrival of goods into one home, which rarely passes unnoticed, not only corroborates these assumptions, it also triggers off other aspects of the representations of the 'scrounger' and 'malingerer'. Since evidence is selectively used and chosen in terms of its fit with presuppositions, misinterpretation occurs frequently. Mick Franklin's jibe about McCartney's washing machine is a case in point:

> Now that washing machine, came in to-day, and a couple of chaps going to work seen it and said, 'Joe, was that a washing machine going in? How the hell do you do it, and you on the dole?' They automatically think the welfare sent that up to me. Well that angers me, really needles me. They don't think about the proper reason, about the miscalculation. (Joe McCartney)

In fact the electricity board had been unintentionally, but systematically, over-charging for consumed electricity. When Joe's social worker discovered this, the board allowed Joe to choose goods from the showroom to the amount due.

The dichotomy between the deserving and the undeserving maintained by some is also used to expresss differences between Catholics and Protestants. For those in Eastlough, both in and out of work, Protestants, as opposed to Catholics, want work rather than the dole. In this context, all unemployed Protestants are lumped together and characterized as industrious and committed to the work ethic, in contrast to Catholics, who are seen as lazy, poorly motivated, and uninterested in being employed. Catholics, it is frequently stated, prefer either the dole or doing the double to legitimate work. Because so many have been unemployed for long periods they have become experts not only in what is available but also in the cunning arts of getting what they want (here the idea that the SB system is easy to negotiate is quietly dropped from the stereotype). According to Protestants if one needs to know anything about the SB system 'ask a Catholic', or still better 'ask a Catholic priest', because 'they're the experts on what to claim', the simple reason being 'it's bred into them'.

Jobs

At a general level the employed present the jobless with a set of priorities. The manner in which the latter are morally evaluated depends on how well they are perceived to conform to this. Pride of place at the top of this list is job-hunting. The greater the investment of time and energy in this activity the greater is the trust and confidence the employed place in the existence of an underlying willingness and desire to work on behalf of the jobless. So long as the employed are sure that the unemployed want to work and dislike being without it, they feel little need to defend the ideology which underpins it. There is therefore very little disgrace or stigma attached to short-term unemployment; because this is the period in which job-search activity is most pronounced, it is difficult to impugn an individual's motivation to work. Shock, anger, or bitter disappointment may be the reactions to job loss (Eisenberg and Lazarsfeld, 1938), but at this point few people feel that their adherence to the work ethic is under scrutiny. This spectre is raised at a later point when the problem has been transposed from that of losing a job to that of being and remaining unemployed. The difference is a conceptual one, but it has a real impact. Having just lost a job, the individual can still claim an occupational identity and that 'worker' is still a more appropriate status than 'unemployed'; and it is acceptable that the life-style and consumption pattern of the employed may be sustained by the jobless for a period. It is no surprise, for example, that a holiday is taken soon after becoming unemployed (Briar, 1977; J.M. Hill, 1977).

By the time the unemployed have been out of work for, say six months, the claim to worker status becomes progressively more disputable and contingent. After all, others have been successful in their search for work during this early period and success in job-hunting is the only incontestable sign of willingness to work. As Sean Donaghy once said to me, the reason some people obtain work quickly while others do not is simply a matter of having the right attitude: there are those with the right, positive attitude, and those with the wrong, negative attitude; those who metaphorically put coal on their fires and petrol in their engines. Those with this get-up-and-go will visit every factory until they obtain work. And indeed such people exist: a shining example is Brian McGonnell, who claims that he so persistently importuned the Council that, sick of the sight of him, they eventually gave him a job as a bin man. Having the right attitude, initiative, motivation, enthusiasm, is what sorts the genuine from the feckless, the real worker from the malingerer, 'us' from 'them'.

Socially, the difficulty for the long-term unemployed is how to persuade others that they are still looking for work when all avenues have been exhausted. Most continue to search for work, though sporadically, and while some methods, such as the use of the job centre, become neglected, others become more central. The possession of certificated skills is important in this context and generates some notable differences in job-search methods. A tradesman, as Kelvin and Jarrett note (1985: 33), has only to be identifiable in terms of his role, whilst the unskilled individual has to be credible as a person. This certainly receives support from the present research. Apprenticed tradesmen see themselves as 'painters', 'brickies', 'sparks' (electricians), 'joiners', etc., whilst the unskilled commonly describe themselves as 'good', 'honest', 'reliable', 'hard', workers. The skilled unemployed, therefore, write to, phone, or on occasion visit firms which are known to require their skills, and consequently their search is usually more focused. Many consider it essential to keep their telephones, because without them they may miss out on potential job offers. They also, of course, use the local newspapers and whatever personal contacts they may have. Bearing in mind the discussion in chapter 3, the unskilled tend to be less focused in their search and rely for the most part on the newspapers and personal networks.

Personal networks are valuable as information channels, but also for two other reasons. First, personal contacts, which require time to cultivate, can act as informal referees to vouch for the honesty and reliability of a job applicant, and this explains why it is so difficult for the unskilled unemployed to find jobs in areas where they are unknown (Kelvin and Jarrett, 1985: 30; Sinfield, 1981: 33–4). Second, asking friends and relatives for assistance ensures that these people at least are made aware of the individual's desire for work. This, though, can have unforeseen consequences, since the employed remark that their offers of help are frequently neglected or scorned. Many relate that, having informed an unemployed friend of a job opening, they find to their chagrin that the recipient of such seemingly good news appears less than interested; and such disdain is then viewed as one more piece of evidence of indolence, apathy, and dissimulation. The unemployed interpret it rather differently. They complain how such 'openings' are just rumours, or that the jobs are quite inappropriate, very badly paid, or too far away. It is one thing to give accurate information about a specific job, quite another to raise hopes falsely by casual remarks which lead to cruel disappointment and financial cost. Their guarded and defensive responses to such 'help' are conditioned by frustrated expectations in the past.

Moreover, employed individuals sometimes mention the possibility of a job being available merely as a means of avoiding other, more contentious, issues, and so as to appear sympathetic and helpful. Whilst the unemployed may be able to distinguish fact from fiction, the unemployed often have to endure a painful education before they too learn to be more discriminating. Going for a walk with Mervyn

Lawrence one morning we met an old friend of his who was on holiday. Inevitably Mervyn was asked where he was working. 'Och I'm on the dole.' After some remarks of commiseration, his friend volunteered that he thought there might be a job at his place of work; he would find out and let Mervyn know. As we parted Mervyn said, 'Sure I've heard that before; if I had a penny for every job like that I wouldn't need to work.' I witnessed encounters like this on many occasions, but particuarly in Eastlough.

By the time the unemployed (skilled and unskilled) have been out of work for several months, the vast majority have stopped using the job centre and ceased paying personal visits to places of employment. There are good financial and psychological reasons for this, as has been made clear, but it does have a deleterious effect on the way the employed assess the behaviour and values of the jobless. Time and again the employed, particularly in Eastlough, wonder why these methods are not used more frequently and conscientiously:

if you get up off your backside and go down into the factories and ask 'Any chance of a job?' OK, you might get turned down in ten places, but you might just go to one place and they'll say to themselves, 'This guy's willing to work. Yes, do you want a start?' Now that wouldn't have happened if you hadn't went in there. (Sean Donaghy)

While Sean claims this is what he would do if he was to become unemployed, it is not what he did when unemployed in 1980:

To be honest, I knew there was no work. I didn't see any point going round asking, for there was no work available.

Sean's views are further revealed in the following extract about himself and his employed neighbour, who seemed to exhibit a genuine concern when Sean was unemployed:

Me and Eddie used to talk about unemployment, and would talk about the guys who don't want to work; people who had no interest in work. I'd say, 'Well, I'd be out tomorrow if I could get the chance', and he'd say, 'That's right. I know you're the type.' He must have figured that 'he's not a lazy guy, he wants to work'.

The employed may consider it good practice for the unemployed to look for jobs by direct inquiry at places of work, but several workers described how, at their own places of employment, such casual visits by the jobless were seen as intrusive and unwelcome. Dave Irvine, for example, disclosed that many of his ex-colleagues, in his last job, thought the unemployed were 'skivers who just weren't trying to find work', but that if people turned up looking for work he had instructions from his boss 'to get rid of them'.

In relation to the neglect of the job centres, much the same sort of argument is adduced. The employed point to the numerous cards which, as far as they are concerned, cannot fail to impress as one walks past the window of the city job centre. Row after row of job specifications assail the eye: 'Surely there must be a job for someone'; 'Isn't it worth the bus fare if you get a job out of it'; 'Surely if they tried that wee bit harder, looked that wee bit more, surely they'd find one to suit.' This is sweet reason itself, until the job descriptions are inspected. To the unemployed married men of this study these cards read: male, aged 16 to 18; shop assistant, female wanted; part-time cleaner; refrigeration engineer, Saudi Arabia; insurance salesman, car essential; security guards, £1.25 per hour; garage assistant, nights only; etc., etc.

Crucially, these two methods of job seeking are highly visible, since the unemployed individual has to leave the house and walk about the streets. Indeed, it is quite common for some unemployed men, when met outside by the employed, to say they have been looking for work, even when in fact they have been engaged on some other business or simply passing the time. The employed like to see the jobless pursuing these obvious avenues because they best indicate willingness and motivation. Conversely, many unemployed complain that they feel forced into such unproductive and costly excursions because it seems to placate the animosity, and satisfy the expectations of, their working friends and neighbours.

The methods actually used by most of the unemployed (newspapers, personal contacts, telephone, letter writing) are all comparatively invisible. Because the negative effect of this on the employed is realized, records of applications made, stockpiles of letters of acknowledgement and clipped-together lists of rejection slips are kept, not so much to satisfy a latent bureaucratic inclination nor as a means of conducting their job search more efficiently, but rather as solid, tangible, irrefutable proof of industry, which can be brought out to impress inquisitive friends and researchers (I admit to being embarrassed every time an unemployed friend insisted on my sifting through his pile of job-search memorabilia).

Essential to both sides of the general argument is the fact that, in advanced industrial economies, the state of the labour market can never be known accurately, for it is in constant flux. Even in times of very high unemployment there is still a great deal of labour mobility: 'full' employment is variously estimated to entail frictional unemployment at levels between 3 per cent and 8 per cent of the labour force (Hawkins, 1979); the median duration of unemployment (the length of time it takes for 50 per cent of the unemployed to find a job) is historically very high, but still below six months (in the late 1960s and early 1970s it was less than one month). Because labour-market conditions can never be known with precision, they are open to continual dispute. Generally, those holding ideas of the deserving and the undeserving claim there are more jobs available than the unemployed are prepared to concede, and so the assertion that jobs are not there to be found is rarely an acceptable excuse for not finding one. In this way, structural problems in the economy are translated into personal ones of motivation and effort. The number of jobs available, then, appears to be the fundamental, but essentially contestable, premiss on which all else turns. By starting from different assumptions about the conditions of the labour market, the employed and the unemployed are set on a course which is bound to generate conflict.

In public the employed do not frequently voice critical opinions of the job-hunting behaviour of the unemployed, because of the arguments it can cause.[7] Several employed men of my acquaintance confessed that they try to steer clear of the subject because of unpleasant experiences. In such cases it is usually thought that the sometimes-violent reaction of the unemployed is ridiculously disproportionate to what the employed consider is little more than sound advice offered in a friendly spirit. But sometimes criticism is both gratuitous and malevolent. Bill Green, for example, was on the receiving end of some rather clumsy advice when he was using a local indoor bowling club:

there's one man in particular, a terrible arrogant wee man, saying, 'there's plenty of work about if you get off your backside and look for it'. And telling me what to do: have I been here, have I been there? Now that's wrong; he wants to be in the position where he's unemployed and then he'll see how he'll get a job.

Bill's extreme sensitivity to what others think and say is somewhat untypical, but a majority of the unemployed in Eastlough have had similar experiences: giving up hobbies and activities, even friendships, because of indirect allusions and explicit criticisms. The inability to pay one's way in social activities is a very common and major source of embarrassment in both Mallon Park and Eastlough, and few are insensate enough not to feel stigmatized by prolonged subsidy.

In chapter 4 it was noted how many unemployed with dependants claim they will not accept jobs which do not pay a premium above the dole. While some employed sympathize with this, others find it difficult to see the wisdom of such a perspective. To these any job (for the unemployed) is better than no job at all. They argue that should they become unemployed not only would they themselves look harder but they would also take any job rather than remain unemployed. Not only is having a job a reward in itself, but being in a job opens up new doors and provides further opportunities: overtime; possibilities of promotion; perks. Being in a job also makes it easier to get a better job, since prospective employers allegedly prefer to hire those already in work. Taking any job, even if inferior to ones previously held, demonstrates willingness to work, and such self-sacrifice and stoicism will eventually be recognized and rewarded. If you fall off the ladder, it is much better to get back on the bottom rung than to remain implanted on the ground:

If you're in a job, anything can happen, but if you sit on your arse all day, it'll just get sore . . . The banter is people won't take a job if it doesn't pay them. But what way they reckon it, I don't know. See when you're in a job you get overtime, you can claim rebates for your rent and there's that Family Income thing. (Mick Givens)

The unemployed's contention that presently available jobs do not in fact supply these incentives is rejected as special pleading by those in work. The clinching argument for the latter is that the failure to take any job is in reality a failure of will and initiative. That some unemployed (usually older workers with working wives or no dependant children) do accept low-paid jobs serves to reinforce the employed's view that those who reject such work do so because, behind the façade of righteous indignation and bombastic rhetoric about exploitation and slave wages, there lurks the scheming parasite who prefers to scrounge on the dole rather than work for a living.

Guys have told me umpteen times they wouldn't get out of their beds to take a job because they're getting more money on the bru. The fact that you got out of your bed and worked, it's doing something for you. 'Not at all, you're mad' [they say]. So these guys just sit around, get paid for doing nothing. They've no interest. See my father worked hard all his life and so I do. Maybe these other guys, their fathers were unemployed and the pattern would follow through. (Alan Matchett)

According to those in work, the unemployed are not only unrealistically ambitious in their desire for high wages, they are also too selective in the range of jobs that they will accept as appropriate. For the skilled unemployed, this particular criticism is more disconcerting than the one about wages. As William Beveridge noted pithily, 'The best carpenter in the world is unemployable as a compositor' (1931: 135). To a large extent the skilled tradesman is locked into his trade; he knows his job well, and has a wide knowledge of the state of the market for his skills.

Furthermore, to abandon a trade or profession is not only to lose an integral part of one's identity and status, but also to become 'unskilled' – and perhaps particularly unskilled in handling the situation of being 'unskilled', and in the tactics for finding unskilled work. (Kelvin and Jarrett, 1985: 37)

One may add that for a skilled man to look for unskilled work can, to a potential employer, look ominously like a case of failure. As far as most of the skilled unemployed in the present study are concerned, in contradistinction to the employed, trading down and looking for un-skilled work is not seen as a reasonable option. Their tenacity in clinging to their occupational niche does actually pay off: four out of fourteen obtained work in their own trades, while only three out of the twenty-six unskilled managed to secure jobs (see Daniel, 1974: 107; M. Hill et al., 1973: 61–5). It should not be forgotten, too, that, especially in Mallon Park, unemployed tradesmen are in the best position to find work in the informal economy. To some of the employed, holding out for a skilled job appears to be a species of arrogance:

To my mind the unemployed are too selective. They could maybe look for jobs they haven't tried before. If they don't get a start in their own trade, maybe they could try something else. I don't understand it, if you look in the [paper] there's a whole stack of jobs; are these jobs not good enough for them? Why should I pay their bru if they're too choosey to take a job that's going? (Dave Ross)

If the unemployed fail to find work, all is not lost, since the employed supply them with various fall-back positions. Most of these relate to how the unemployed should behave when not looking for work, and these are discussed in the next section. There remains one avenue of salvation, however, which relates to work, and this is the possibility of self-employment. It is in fact an unfulfilled ambition of many to be one's own boss, and since unemployment provides an unwelcome but perhaps adventitious break in a person's employment career, why should they not contemplate starting a business of their own? In this regard there is a scheme which is available to the jobless. If an unem-ployed person can demonstrate he has £1,000 in capital, the Enterprise Allowance Scheme entitles him to a payment of £40 per week for one year whilst his business (which is vetted) has a chance to get started.

There undoubtedly exist some unemployed who have the requisite finance and a good commercial idea for which a business can be started on so limited a capital base, but amongst the forty unemployed who make up the focus of this research not one was to be found. The only example I encountered was Mike Slattery (who is in the employed sample, but who lost his job during the research), who used his redundancy money to finance a small business, but on the double. As already reported, he has not yet been able to earn enough to enable him to sign off the register. Bluntly, the unemployed from both estates feel such schemes are pie in the sky, unless they can enlist free expert advice and constant help. To some extent such assistance did become available in Mallon Park in 1984, when the local community association helped to set up an economic development committee. By the time the research ended, four people had begun small businesses, but only one of these was an unemployed man (whom I did not know).

Generally, the financial and psychological constraints on the long-term unemployed are very hard to break through, and the ones who manage it are rather untypical: they need money, know-how, contacts, a good marketable idea, and immense energy, i.e. characteristics not noticeably present, at least *in toto*, in middle-aged, unskilled people with two or more years of unemployment behind them. Despite this, many employed argue strongly that the jobless should put their redundancy money to good effect. Unfortunately, of the forty unemployed, only thirteen obtained any redundancy payments; of these thirteen, only four received more than £1,000, and all of these were over forty years of age (Sinfield, 1981: 60–3). Nevertheless, several employed men in both samples maintained that there were good opportunities for the unemployed to start small-scale businesses:

I mentioned this time to one guy, you know, about starting up a little industry here, and he didn't seem interested. Very negative attitude . . . [The unemployed] can form committees. That would be a test for the people in the district; are they interested in setting up this? There'll be the few who'll just shrug their shoulders and say, 'Not for me, I've no interest in that.' Fair enough, forget about them, they've no interest in anything. But I'm talking about the people that want to work and want to create something . . . and sell the product, and people are going to buy it, and the products become a success. OK you'll have ups and downs, but still it's worth a try, I think. (Liam Hunter)

Liam is here reasoning much like an old-fashioned development economist who cannot understand why the peasants will not adopt new techniques to increase production, and rationalizes that it must be due to their being enmeshed in 'traditional' cultural attitudes which prevent them from realizing the advantages of new methods. Moreover, these are not just the private musings of Liam, for at one meeting of the economic development committee he aired these views in public and at some length, and was rather nonplussed by their poor reception. After the meeting, unemployed friends told me they were not so much against what Liam had said, but that he clearly had no idea of the practical problems involved, and the all-embracing constraints within which the mass of the unemployed lived. Incidentally it is worth adding that when Liam, who is a skilled tradesman, was himself unemployed for seventeen months in 1980–1, despite having substantial savings he himself did not attempt to do what he now preaches:

Yes, I could have thought about it but the thought of buying a van and taking the risk of going out looking for work, I didn't think it was really worth it because I hadn't really enough capital behind me to do it . . . If I had been a bit younger . . . at my age you're a wee bit more timorous at taking chances, and I just let it go. I didn't bother about it, and that was it.

Liam is by no means alone is his views, or in the significant discrepancies between how he states he did cope with and react to unemployment, how he would cope with and react to it if he were to become unemployed again, and how he thinks the presently unemployed manage their joblessness. In general, those employed who endorse notions of individualism and deservingness provide descriptions of their own past spells of unemployment (if they have had them) which are in many respects similar to those given by the presently unemployed. However, such accounts are strikingly at odds with the way these employed expect the presently unemployed to behave, and the way they stipulate they themselves would behave were they to become unemployed at some future date. There are two complementary explanations for this. First, the employed no longer feel the force of the social, psychological, and material limiting factors which so encumber and burden the unemployed, and so the exhortations to the unemployed about what to do, though apparently sensible and reasonable, take no account of these restrictions. Second, being employed, they are simply defending their own commitment to the ideology of work against the perceived threat emanating from putative shirkers who seemingly place little value in this (Howe, 1983b).

A life-style for the unemployed

Long-term unemployment clearly circumscribes what it is possible for the jobless to do. All the unemployed remark, to one degree or another, on the restrictions and constraints they have to endure: the perpetual lack of money; dwindling stocks of clothes and deteriorating homes; 'creeping shabbiness' (Kelvin and Jarrett, 1985: 37); the necessity of borrowing and the detestation of it; financial dependency on relatives who can ill afford it (the poor supporting the poor); aching boredom and intermittent depression; feelings of shame, stigma, and impotency; lack of choice in even trivial matters; collapsing social circles and lapsed friendships; eroding self-image and fractured personal identities; deep-seated feelings of being useless, unwanted, and incapable; and so on, and so on (Bakke, 1933; Marsden, 1982; Seabrook, 1982).

Despite the fact that the vast majority of studies concerning the social, psychological, and financial impact of unemployment paints a picture of misery and drudgery, many of the employed continue to be struck by how well the unemployed seem to cope. The perception that the unemployed are managing well (in certain cases, with consummate ease) not only irritates and offends them, but also stimulates a whole range of prescriptions and proscriptions about how the unemployed should behave, and which, ironically, if followed by the unemployed would produce behaviour patterns closely approximating those actually observed by researchers. The social processes involved in perpetuating this state of affairs are similar to those analysed in relation to the administration of SB. In chapter 5, it was explained how benefit officers contend that while most claimants get their full entitlement, some do even better. In contradistinction to this I argued that while some claimants receive their full entitlement, the majority obtain less than is their legal due. In the present case the employed argue that while most unemployed manage well, some cope very well indeed. The findings of academic research indicate that while some are able to cope in reasonable fashion, most find themselves in very difficult and precarious circumstances. The superficial explanation for this divergence is quite simple: the employed generalize from untypical cases to the mass of the jobless; they extrapolate from a few extreme examples and conclude all the unemployed are like these; they tend to exaggerate the level and range of benefits, while underestimating the force of constraints; in short, they transpose the exceptional behaviour of some unemployed men into the statistical norm and then deem the actions of these to be normatively inappropriate. The questions here are, what are the reasons which generate this image of the unemployed, and how is such a model of unemployment and the unemployed sustained and reproduced?

Clearly the answer to this complex issue lies in the kind of processes that have been the subject of analysis in earlier chapters. Thus we have seen, for example, that Catholics have always suffered greater unemployment than Protestants, and this is partly attributable to Protestant control of many employment opportunities. Catholics explain their unemployment quite naturally by reference to the economic and political structure of the Northern Ireland state, in which institutional discrimination is entrenched. Consequently, although individualistic explanations for unemployment are still found in Mallon Park, most unemployment is attributed to the political economy of a sectarian state within which Catholics occupy a subordinate position. In other words, structural explanations for Catholic unemployment are readily available, because they constitute an integral part of Catholic and nationalist hostility to the existence of the Northern Ireland state. As a result discrepancies between the way unemployment is conceptualized by the employed and the jobless are not so noticeable: low-paid work and unemployment are both ascribable to the policies of an antagonistic state apparatus. However, because Catholics share with Protestants a strong moral commitment to the reciprocal relation between work and rewards entailed in the work ethic, and because the immediate and compelling everyday experiences of the employed indicate that some people are better off on the dole than in work, individualistic explanations of unemployment will never be entirely absent.

By contrast, Protestants do not have such easy recourse to structural explanations of unemployment, since the state is supposed to protect their economic and political interests. While of course the rise in the numbers out of work since 1979 is often put down to the 'recession', this recession is less real to those still in work than it is to the jobless who are its victims. Moreover, there is some evidence (see chapter 3) that unemployment in east Belfast has always been seen more as a personal affair than as a problem of the economy. Since the employed consider that there are more jobs available than the jobless are willing to concede, and because it is the former who largely set the limits of the discourse within which unemployment is publicly interpreted, it is not surprising that individualistic explanations still predominate, and that a conflict between the employed and the jobless about the nature of unemployment is more prominent in Eastlough than in Mallon Park.

But the question of reproduction remains. To tackle this issue I need to add some further comments on the nature of the ideology, or model, of deservingness. It has been argued (Abercrombie, Hill, and Turner, 1980: 128–40) that the neo-Marxist concept of the 'dominant ideology' is not very useful because when attempts are made to specify its contents it is found that they lack coherence and even that some of the themes are contradictory. But it could be argued that an ideology does not need to be internally consistent to be useful. In fact, inconsistency, vagueness, and generality might be functionally advantageous.

One obvious fact to note is that ideologies do not exist in a vacuum, that is, they are not effective until they are invoked to justify, witness, or condemn particular practices. But when summoned up, it is rarely ever the whole of an ideology that is brought into play, but only some part of it that is deemed relevant. Moreover, when it is applied in practice it needs to take into account not only context, which is very important, but also historically variable factors which themselves cannot be part of the ideology, for their inclusion would render it cumbersome, complicated, and capricious. To be useful, ideologies need to be relatively simple and compact, and to have the appearance of being immutable and natural; in this way they come to appear as commonsensical explanatory frameworks. Analytically, therefore, an ideology should be conceived of in terms of specific historical relations between sets of ideas and types of practices and not, as is often the case, merely in terms of de-historicized relations between ideas (see Brook and Finn, 1978). If what is significant about ideas is the ways they are related to practices, then inconsistency between the themes which compose an ideology is a problem which is more apparent than real. The point is not so much whether the themes of an ideology are 'objectively' inconsistent, or even whether they are perceived to be so. The real issue is how useful they are in supporting a prevailing system of inequalities. The logical coherence of an ideology is not likely to be its most significant feature. More concretely, individualistic explanations couched in terms of deservingness tend to remain intact because they are capable of accommodating conflicting and anomalous information. Two examples should help to clarify these points.

One theme of the individualistic world view is that the benefit system is over-generous, simple to negotiate, and easy to hoodwink. This entails that the unemployed should be able to manage their finances quite well. A corollary of this is that the truly deserving are those with the moral fibre that makes working for a living preferable to scrounging, even if wages are little better than benefits. Despite the fact that the benefit system is seen as generous, nevertheless it is clear that some people face money problems. Rather than this being a threat to the belief system, such an eventuality can be explained by recourse to a whole battery of secondary elaborations and in this way deftly negotiated away. Thus debt and poverty are often interpreted as caused by excessive expenditure on inessentials, inability to budget, a husband who drinks and gambles and neglects family welfare. Others might say that such unemployed people do not take advantage of the benefit system, either because of pride (which converts them into the deserving anyway) or because they make no effort to find out what can be claimed.

The unemployed are in a difficult position here. If by whatever means (judicious budgeting, help from kin, loans, occasional work on the side) they are able to make ends meet and keep up appearances, this simply reinforces the employed's contention that the jobless are well cosseted. If the unemployed complain of insufficient benefits, they can be denounced as greedy and shameless. And if they look poverty stricken they can be accused of improvidence. Whatever they do, they seem powerless to refute the basic premisses from which the employed begin. Out of context, some of these explanations might seem contradictory, but because they are compartmentalized in their appropriate contexts little contradiction is acknowledged.

Let me give another example. Many employed argue, in the context of benefits, that over-generous benefits keep the unemployed out of jobs; but in the context of job-hunting, it is often asserted that the unemployed would be better off (with the help of low-income benefits) in *any* job than on the dole which, by implication, negates the notion that benefits are generous and therefore act as a disincentive. In either case, what separates those preferring jobs to benefits are different personal attitudes, values, and motivations. There is no recourse to 'structural' explanations, which see the unemployed as a heterogenous category in which different groups of unemployed are differentially placed not only in relation to the benefit system and the labour market, but also in terms of age, skill, and religion.

The various ideas within the ideologies of individualism and deservingness do not therefore form a logically coherent system, though they do provide a structured way of looking at the world (of unemployment). The point to note is that there is little interest or need to maintain logical consistency in the application of the model to particular events, but there is considerable pressure to protect long-standing values concerning the ideology of employment and the work ethic. Consequently, arguments are invoked tactically and piecemeal according to context, interests, and aims. On this reading, interpretation of what others do and say is not ruled by the iron hand of a compelling logic or system of rational argumentation, but instead by the need to defend the values and beliefs integral to a way of life (Bloor, 1976: 123–30; Barnes, 1982).

Moreover, generally speaking, people give priority to specific and concrete instances (of unemployment and social security in this case), rather than to general and abstract principles. These latter are taken for granted and are not open to negotiation except under rare circumstances (Evans-Pritchard, 1937). Since there are jobs, as the model explains, then the long-term jobless remain unemployed because they either do not look diligently enough for work, or are satisfied with the dole; the unemployed are content to live on benefits, both because these are conceived of as generous and because the unemployed are seen as deviating from other's stress on reciprocity and fair exchange, and hence they appear to be different sorts of people with quite different value systems. When presented with information which on the surface seems to deviate from the model, secondary arguments and *post hoc* rationalizations are enlisted to remove the discrepancies.

A prescription for how the unemployed should behave is implicit in many of the criticisms both the employed (and the unemployed) make, and it may be summed up in the idea: essentials first, luxuries when resources allow. The first essential is to look for work. When the unemployed are not occupied doing this, they should organize their life in fairly definite ways, deviation from which unleashes almost automatic condemnation. The unemployed need not be housebound, but only certain reasons, apart from looking for work, justify leaving the home. Venturing out for walks; shopping; visiting relatives; going to the library and sports centres; and so forth, are excursions that are culturally approved and demonstrate conformity to the values and insititutions of the wider society. Going to pubs, snooker halls, betting shops, and the like is liable to excite disapproval, particularly if done habitually. Occasional visits to the pub are permissible because 'everyone needs a pint now and again', and though it is something of a myth it is generally thought that job information can be garnered there.

Get-togethers with other unemployed outside designated community centres may be frowned upon because such associations can have repercussions on how the individual is perceived by workers. As Wadel notes (1973: 82):

The social worth of a welfare recipient . . . cannot be divorced from his position in the network of interpersonal relations . . . a non-recipient's reaction to the increase in interaction of a recipient friend with another recipient depends on the latter's position in relation to his own network.

Thus, visiting unemployed relatives and neighbours is usually acceptable, for this conforms to the values of neighbourliness and family solidarity. But frequent visiting with unemployed friends, even if in the same local community, may lead to stigma by association. One of the reasons why Bobby Marshall is considered a dubious case by some of the employed is because he is often seen in the house of another individual who has been unemployed for several years and has an unenviable reputation for being work-shy. Whilst virtually all the unemployed pay regular visits to nearby family relatives, very few maintain close friendships with other unemployed (although this is less true of Mallon Park, where quite strong friendships and frequent visiting have developed between some unemployed neighbours). Few unemployed give explicit reasons for this reticence, commenting usually that there is little point in such associations and that they feel uncomfortable in them. There is no doubt that the pressure to avoid such liaisons is quite strong in Eastlough. Dave Irvine, for example, was rebuked by his father and brother (both working) about a friendship he had struck up with an unemployed man in the same street, and because of this he stopped going to his house. Similarly Hugh MacGregor became pally with Joe McHale, until Hugh's wife told him that their next-door neighbour thought Joe a tear-away and a waster. Other unemployed, such as Bill Green, Joe Robinson, and Billy Reid, have virtually no unemployed friends that are not also relatives.

Slightly different taboos apply for the evening as apply during the day-time. The unemployed man may take his wife out for a social evening, so long as this is a celebration (anniversary of some kind), is not done frequently, expenditure is modest, and dress unostentatious. George Lynn's wife, for example, constantly attacks her unemployed neighbours for allegedly going out at night, dressed to the nines, and coming home 'full' in the small hours, and accordingly makes sure everyone knows she will have nothing to do with them. For men to be seen regularly going to bars is reprehensible because it implies access to greater resources than the employed command, neglect of family welfare, and lack of any feeling of shame that they are unemployed. Many of the employed in Eastlough point to this activity as definitive proof of malingering: 'Every night you see them going down to the [name of local]'; 'every time I go into the [local] there's [so-and-so] propping up the bar'. I have to say I visited this pub on several occasions and only rarely saw an unemployed man of my acquaintance from Eastlough taking a drink. As Joe Robinson said, 'I used to take a drink now and again but I'm afraid to show my face in there. The wife's friend told her it was full of dole scroungers.'

Stipulations about home life are made frequently, though phrased, as in other contexts, in negative terms. One stereotype often encountered depicts the daily lives of the unemployed thus: they lie on in bed till midday, get up and go to the pub, spend the afternoon in the bookies' and watch TV all evening; and it's enough for one aspect of this to be noticed for the rest of the representation to be invoked. Those employed who know few, or no, unemployed people are generally at a loss when asked what the latter do during the day. Not possessing concrete details, they either adduce an unflattering stereotype or pontificate about what they themselves would do if they were unemployed. This usually entails getting up at the 'usual' (early) time, helping the wife, looking for work, reading. It might include some comment on the advantages of joining an evening class ('to improve my mind and my prospects'), and implied criticisms ('I wouldn't waste my time, I can tell you that'). In general the unemployed man, if he has to spend a lot of time in the house, should do some housework, put his garden to good use, look after the children, and so on.

In regard to the allocation and expenditure of money, the employed insist that all benefit should be spent on the home and the family, for that is what its purpose is. It is not to be used to buy tobacco, alcohol, expensive clothes, or silly toys. Expenditure on these things is a sure sign of family neglect and a different (and largely unjustifiable) set of priorities.

In fighting against these criticisms, the unemployed complain in private (and sometimes in public) that they in fact conform to the majority of the prescriptions the employed impose on them, and that therefore the latter have little understanding of what it is really like to be unemployed: 'you can't tell anybody what unemployment is like, you have to go through it yourself to really understand' (Ray Carlile); 'if you've never been unemployed you have no idea what it's all about; them'uns with jobs, they live in a totally different world' (Roy Price). When there is a disjunction between what the employed prescribe and what the unemployed actually do, there are often sound reasons for the discrepancies. Thus while it is expected that the unemployed should get up early, the latter often complain that because they do not feel tired (i.e. work-tired, they may well feel lethargic) they stay up late at night, and even when in bed they sleep badly because worries assail them. Consequently, they feel exhausted in the morning and find difficulty in rising early. Similarly, some unemployed admit to feelings of guilt because, sitting around the house, they accomplish nothing, but explain that they cannot generate any enthusiasm or motivation to do something constructive and worthwhile. During the initial period without work many household jobs get done; however, procrastination creeps in and subsequently other jobs have a habit of being neglected. While evening classes may be free to the unemployed, the cost of travel and materials has still to be met, and benefits do not include an element for this. Moreover, the vast majority of unemployed had the minimum of formal education and do not like the idea of 'going back to school', and 'what's the point anyway, it won't get me a job'.

For the jobless, it is difficult to exaggerate just how pointless many activities become, and how they lose interest in things which, when in work, absorbed them. The reason for this is that employment is the activity which integrates, justifies, and gives meaning to many other relationships, interests, and pursuits. Once work is lost, the whole edifice seems to fragment. If employment forges links between the individual and society and provides a sense of purpose and productiveness, lack of it breaks such bonds and engenders isolation, indifference, and sloth (Hayes and Nutman, 1981; Kelvin, 1981).

A perennial complaint of those in jobs is 'why don't they *do* something?'. Well, despite what I have just said, many unemployed in fact do quite a lot, which is an unacknowledged testament to their fortitude. Some are active in community associations, some act as unpaid advice workers, some do charity work for the church and related associations, others help the retired in various ways, and so on. The 'something' that the employed want the jobless to do is often nebulous and unspecified. Whatever the unemployed do, it rarely seems to meet with the satisfaction and approval of those in work. In this way the unemployed find themselves fighting against constantly moving targets, and manoeuvring according to ground rules they do not clearly understand and which seem to shift perpetually. If they're involved in community work or stay indoors, why don't they instead use this time to look for work? If they're helping pensioners do their gardens, why don't they turn this into a business, as clearly there is work to be done? If they're outside they must have money to burn, so why don't they . . .? etc.

One final issue to be discussed concerns the nature of talk and topics of conversation between the employed and the unemployed, and amongst the latter themselves. Actual social interaction between these two groups is minimal in Eastlough when compared to the level existing amongst the employed. The obvious reason for this is that workers spend a good deal of every day in each other's company, in travelling to and being at work. This period affords tremendous opportunities for social intercourse of many kinds, which are of course not open to the unemployed. Outside of work it is very noticeable that the unemployed gradually lose touch with ex-colleagues and friends who live a distance away. Naturally, they still interact with employed relatives and neighbours, but there are few such encounters which do not impose some strain on the unemployed. Moreover, as has been made abundantly clear, it is not simply lack of opportunities which erects a barrier between worker and non-worker. Indeed the overriding reasons are, first, the suspicions each has of the other's intentions, interests, and opinions; second, the paucity of resources which incapacitates the social lives of the unemployed; and third, the lack of overlap between the experiences of each:

When I walk out of this estate I feel like I'm a hermit, I don't want to go away from my own house because I feel totally out of place in company. I've no job so I can't talk about this happening at work or that happening at work. Then they'll turn round and they'll talk about the wages they earned this week, and it hits me very hard, I haven't earned a wage this week; I just have to go and draw what the state are giving me. So you don't want to be going out mixing with people that's employed because you can't talk in the same language. People's talking about you, they're talking about you're lazy, don't want to work, you're too well paid – where they get all these notions from I don't know. (Roy Price)

Given that the unemployed are so concerned about what the employed think of them, and that the employed scrutinize what the unemployed say and do, it is little wonder that social encounters provide a particularly difficult terrain to negotiate.

There are very few topics of conversation between employed and unemployed which are clearly neutral and do not raise hackles. Talk about sport, what is on television, newspapers, gossip, and so forth, can be navigated without hitting too many rocks. But virtually all other subjects contain submerged obstacles. At a social occasion in Mallon Park I was chatting to Tony Madden, who was telling me he might get a couple of weeks' holiday in a friend's caravan, when Mick Franklin, who was also listening, asked where Tony would sign on. This quickly put a stop to the conversation and Tony looked fit to burst. The facts that an unemployed individual is allowed to miss one signing day so as to take a holiday, and that living rent-free in a caravan is as cheap as living at home, could not be explained there and then without making explicit what was a veiled and implicit attack. On an occasion in Eastlough Joe McHale got embroiled in an argument with an employed acquaintance of his, whom I did not know. Joe had been telling us, in graphic detail, the appalling state of his house when he had first moved in, when his friend commented that since the unemployed paid neither rent nor rates they had not much right to complain. After a few cross words Joe told his friend to fuck off. Let me describe one more incident. I was accompanying Hugh MacGregor to the dole one afternoon, and on the way we met an employed man I knew (but Hugh did not) who was on his way to work. Hugh mentioned a film that was to be shown on TV that evening and asked if we were going to watch it, whereupon the employed man remarked, I think jokingly, that 'some of us have to work for a living'. The atmosphere suddenly became strained after that and Hugh kept quiet until the other left us.

In talk about unemployment there are basically three types of context which stand out as significant. These are conversations with the researcher, conversations amongst the unemployed, and talk between workers and unemployed people. The mix of structural and individualistic accounts of the causes of continuing unemployment varies systematically from one context to another.

In conversation with me, seen as sympathetic, a large majority of the unemployed did not blame themselves for their continuing joblessness. Many pointed to their lack of the skills demanded in a quickly changing technological economy, but this was rarely considered to be a purely personal failing. Basically, blame was heaped on either economic forces (recession, oil crisis, competition from developing countries, etc.), or on the personal actions of powerful, distant others (Margaret Thatcher, business magnates, EEC bureaucrats, etc.). They tended to stress the employed's lack of understanding of the situation and to emphasize the efforts they had made to obtain work. Those using ideas of deservingness, particularly in Eastlough, often compared their situation to other unemployed who seemed unconcerned about looking for jobs. In short, they tended to use structural explanations to account for their own unemployment (and that of kin and friends) and to use individualistic explanations to account for the unemployment of others.

Talk between employed and unemployed, and amongst the latter themselves, reveals regularities which Wadel (1973) has discussed in his study of unemployed people in a rural area of Newfoundland. He notes that the unemployed individual has to handle encounters with employed and unemployed people carefully because he needs to say and do different things in the two types of situation. In order to maintain his own self-esteem and get others to think of him as a worthy member of the community, the unemployed man has to seek contact with those in work and persuade them that he is willing to work but cannot find any. He does this, for example, by invoking his past employment record or his present ill-health, or the fact that he has traipsed all over town looking for work. However, interaction with the employed is tense, for impression management has to be carried out continuously, and can be emotionally draining. This is a major reason why unemployed men also sometimes seek contact with other unemployed, for being in similar situations they are of equal status and can therefore talk freely about certain issues. Among these is welfare itself: the amounts of money received can be compared; different types of grant can be discussed; regulations mulled over; and information swapped. They can complain and commiserate with each other because they share very similar experiences and do not need to worry about being considered shameless should they moan about inadequate benefits. None of this can be done in the company of the employed, as it would appear to them that the unemployed attach more value to benefits than to work.

On the other hand, the unemployed must be careful about what they say to other unemployed. They cannot talk too easily about their own special, and to them unique, circumstances, because this can appear as a veiled criticism of the kind: this is my excuse for not working, what's yours? Conversely, it is precisely the unique circumstances of one's own unemployment which one needs to stress when speaking with the employed. In such encounters, the unemployed man can try to convince workers that he is himself a genuine and legitimate case because of his singular circumstances. By this device he is able both to disassociate himself from others who do not share these characteristics and who by implication are denigrated as undeserving, and to demonstrate conformity to the values held by the employed.

For example, an unemployed man from Eastlough (not in the core sample) used to go bowling on the local green. On one occasion when I was present, he was asked by an employed visitor where he worked. To answer this, he went through a series of verbal contortions, to make the point that while he was out of work there were several good reasons for this, and that anyhow he expected to be back in work again shortly. The irony of it was that when he had finished sounding off about the apathy and lack of initiative of other unemployed (of whom there were none present), the worker responded that in this day and age there was absolutely no disgrace in being unemployed.

It is clearly noticeable that in mixed company the unemployed hardly ever raise the topic of benefits unless they are sure of a sympathetic hearing. On occasions when the topic was raised and the employed reacted in a hostile manner, the unemployed responded in either of two ways. Sometimes they stood their ground and argued that benefits really are inadequate. In such cases, however, it is clear that the unemployed feel that they never really win such contests, because they are convinced that after the encounter the employed broadcast bad reports about them, which is something that the unemployed cannot counter. Alternatively, the unemployed quickly and rather meekly drop the subject, pick up another or, most likely, take their leave. Let me give a final example which neatly encapsulates these remarks. Ray Carlile and Billy Stewart are neighbours. When both were unemployed at the same time, they and their wives regularly aired complaints about benefits to each other and swapped information without embarrassment. They also talked a lot about the pointlessness of looking for work and supported each other's claims that there were no jobs. Quite frequently Ray also visits Sean Donaghy (who is also a close neighbour and in work) because they share an avid interest in gardening. However, Ray never mentions benefits in Sean's presence, but always manages at least one reference to his desire for and continuing search for work. This pays dividends, because Sean makes a point of excluding Ray when he disparages other unemployed as lazy and as having no interest in finding work.

Conclusion

Where there are significant differences in the way the employed and the jobless explain the nature, impact, and consequences of unemployment, the latter find themselves in an extremely delicate situation. This is because the jobless are involved in a double discourse with those in work. The first of these concerns the ideology of employment. In advanced industrial countries, formal employment is the principal means by which men achieve a status in relation to the family, the community, the economy, and the polity. Such statuses imply reciprocal relationships entailing a series of rights and duties. Employment further serves to justify and legitimate a host of routine, daily practices. Work and the social relations it creates and endorses is one of the most entrenched aspects of everyday life. And the 'reality of everyday life is taken for granted *as* reality. It does not require additional verification over and beyond its simple presence' (Berger and Luckmann, 1967: 37). In this way the need for work is self evident and compelling. Of course, individuals may dislike their particular occupations, criticize the structure of rewards, or muse about better ways to organize how work gets done, etc., but they rarely question the value of work itself.

The unemployed are just as strongly committed to this ideology as are the employed. Indeed, because to those in jobs many of the benefits of work are latent, the unemployed realize more fully and immediately just how irreplaceable employment is in the way it sustains and gives meaning and substance to the rest of social life, and in the way it bolsters a personal identity and self-image.

The second discourse, based on ideologies of individualism and deservingness, is related to the first, but is mostly concerned with the explanation of long-term unemployment. According to many of those in work, the jobless remain unemployed because they lack a commitment to the ideology of employment: it is assumed that many of the jobless are lazy, apathetic, and spineless, and do not like work; and it is argued that generous welfare benefits remove the economic incentive to work. When combined, these provide an image of the unemployed as parasitic moral deviants who accept little personal, familial, or social responsibility, and who reject the basis of the reciprocal relation between employment and rewards.

While the material constraints entrapping the unemployed are of the utmost significance, in order to grasp what being unemployed entails it is necessary to analyse people's conceptualizations of them. Material deprivation is a burden the unemployed have to endure, but it is a burden that is experienced by many within the terms of an ideological discourse that appears to magnify its impact.

Thus the major problem for the unemployed, aside from coping with financial hardship, is how to persuade the employed that they want to work. This is an exhaustingly difficult project, because, in whatever way the unemployed attempt to convince those in work that they are

committed to the ideology of employment, they find that their arguments are often interpreted within the terms of this second discourse.
To the twin assertions that there are no jobs and that benefits are
inadequate, there are numerous specific counter-arguments that the
employed can call upon. In this sense, even though a considerable
number of the jobless reject individualistic explanations of unemployment (their own and that of others), nonetheless representations of the
deserving and the undeserving affect people in profound ways and are
instrumental in sustaining the commitment of both employed and
unemployed to the ideology of employment and the work ethic.

However, while in a sense it is forced on them, it is often in the
interests of the unemployed to use this discourse, because by casting
aspersions on the motives and actions of others they can simultaneously
parry criticisms and imply positive claims about themselves. In the
short term this may result in individualistic advantages, but in the long
term such continual summoning up of notions of deservingness merely
serves to sustain the discourse as apparently appropriate. In this rather
perverse sense, the unemployed can be seen as implicated in their own
subordination through their role in the production and reproduction
of the practical power relations that exist between employed and
unemployed.

Another point of interest can be made in relation to the above. Some
unemployed people feel driven to use an individualistic discourse
because they find that accounting for their lack of work in 'structural'
and collective terms can be counter-productive. In practice, the use of
structural explanations ('there are no jobs', for example) to justify
continuing unemployment is often not very successful because many
employed people see this as a ruse to conceal an underlying unwillingness to work. The fielding of such structural explanations may serve
simply to get the unemployed classified as undeserving.

In these senses, the ideology of individualism and deservingness is a
dominant one, not because it is the only one available, but because it
pre-empts and incorporates other types of explanation, and this despite
the fact that some of both those in work and out of work find this form of
accounting anathema.

Out of a social context and set side by side the deserving model and
the structural model appear mutually exclusive. However, I have
already shown that the former actually includes aspects of the latter in
order to be able to supply an explanation for the deserving unemployed. In concrete social situations, therefore, individualistic explanations, so to speak, enlist structural ones but place them in a subordinate
position, so as to support and validate representations of the scrounger

and malingerer. So, for example, individualism includes ideas that obtaining jobs is partly dependent on factors such as age, skill, qualifications, contacts, etc. The point is, however, that if a person remains unemployed then whatever talents, skills, and contacts he may have, he has failed to make good use of them (see note 5). Thus, although the explanation of unemployment by reference to structural problems in the economy has a valuable social currency, in that it provides the unemployed with an argument that they are the innocent victims of large-scale forces, it often finds itself circumscribed and dominated by explanations founded on individualistic ideas of deservingness. Such an ideology, at least in Eastlough, constitutes a ruling or pre-eminent version of the way things are in the world. Mallon Park Catholics have been able, to some extent, to enforce a more collectivist interpretation of unemployment. Armed with a well-established and very widely distributed political and economic analysis of their position within the Northern Ireland state, Catholics can export collective blame for material deprivation and political oppression outside their own areas and away from their own people.

In its starkest form, my argument is that the employed are in a position of dominance *vis-à-vis* the jobless because their commitment to the ideology of employment is not in doubt, while the latter's is. This provides them with the social and cultural resources to impose upon the unemployed a particular discourse concerning the explanations of (long-term) unemployment. For three reasons the unemployed are largely powerless to dislodge this discourse. First, they lack the material and social resources to substitute an alternative vision of the nature of unemployment. Second, its use confers some personal but short-term advantages; many unemployed people endorse individualistic forms of accounting because it profits them to do so. And third, the discourse can accommodate conflicting and anomalous experiences, because the themes which compose it are used in a tactical and compartmentalized manner according to the contexts for which they are deemed pertinent by the user. Though they try to combat what they consider to be facile and simplistic statements, the unemployed meet with one counter-argument after another and the fact that these are often inconsistent, even contradictory, merely adds insult to injury. Moreover, should the unemployed become strident in the justification of their unemployment or explicitly condemn benefits as inadequate, the employed increasingly feel that their stake in life, their commitment to a moral orthodoxy is under threat, and consequently are inclined to double their efforts in keeping the jobless in their place.

Many of the unemployed, particularly in communities such as

Eastlough, experience considerable difficulty in resisting the labels and stereotypes that are imposed upon them. One major consequence of this is that the unemployed retreat into a private existence, shunning much contact with both employed and other unemployed. But this too has disadvantages: the loss of personal contacts which might otherwise be useful in terms of job information; inactivity, boredom, and depression; conflicts with other members of the family; imaginations which run riot, with the unemployed wondering what the employed think of them and the latter being suspicious of what the former are doing (or not doing) behind closed doors. It is a desperate, vicious circle. Everything conspires to fragment and isolate the lives of long-term unemployed married men, to break their links with the wider society and damage those within the family, to threaten their individual identities and personalities, and to divorce them from others in objectively similar positions. Is it any wonder that the unemployed, like the proverbial peasants, are just so many potatoes in a sack?

Chapter 9

Conclusion

Most of this book has been written in the present tense, which suggests that my description of unemployment in Belfast is as relevant now, in 1989, as when I first observed it between 1983 and 1985. But the question should be asked as to whether the situation has changed in the intervening period? England has experienced a fairly extended consumer boom and economic growth has been impressive. How has Northern Ireland fared, has it, too, benefited from this expansion? From a different perspective there has been much new legislation and various new initiatives, most of them supposedly designed to improve the position of the unemployed and the low-paid in the labour market. A new social security act, stricter rules concerning availability for work of the jobless, interviewing and counselling of the long-term unemployed to 'encourage' them to cast their nets wider and to help them find new jobs, new employment training programmes aimed specifically at the long-term unemployed to equip them to enter new occupations, are just some of the measures introduced recently. Have not these, to one degree or another and in one way or another, changed the conditions of life of unemployed people in Northern Ireland? Have not the new training schemes and tighter control of the unemployed reduced the rate of unemployment and constricted opportunities for doing the double?

Clearly, no easy or unequivocal answers can be given to any of these questions, as many of the recent changes are so new that it is still too early to tell what impact they have had and will have in the future, and to what extent they will have different consequences in different regions of the country. However, on the basis of what evidence I do have, it does not seem likely that my analysis of any of the major issues discussed in this work needs to be substantially modified.

Unemployment in Belfast, and Northern Ireland generally, has not improved much since 1985. Certainly no new major economic initiatives have occurred in west Belfast. Similarly the privatization of Short Bros. and the very precarious position of the Harland and Wolff ship yard

Table 17. *Total Northern Ireland unemployment (January figures, 1978–89) according to contemporary methods of counting (thousands)*

1978	1980	1982	1984	1986	1987	1988	1989
52.0	53.6	91.6	109.8	117.5	125.1	116.5	109.7

Source: Employment Gazette, April 1989 (Historical Supplement).

have not eased employment opportunities in east Belfast. But what about the more general unemployment situation in Northern Ireland?

Because the basis on which the number of unemployed is counted has changed many times, these changes usually eventuating in a reduction of the monthly count (see *Employment Gazette*, October 1986, p. 422, for a summary of the changes), it is not a simple matter to compare 1989 figures with those recorded in earlier years. Fortunately, however, the Department of Employment has now published a Historical Supplement to its April 1989 issue of the *Employment Gazette*, which provides new figures for previous years based on present-day methods of counting, thus allowing reasonably accurate comparisons to be made (see table 17).

From these figures it can be seen that unemployment in Northern Ireland did not peak until 1987, at 18 per cent of the labour force. United Kingdom unemployment peaked earlier – in spring 1986 – at 11.2 per cent. Since then, total UK unemployment has fallen to 7 per cent, whereas Northern Ireland unemployment has only come down to 15.9 per cent. These figures for rates of unemployment can now be compared to those provided in table 1 (chapter 2), thus giving table 18.

What this table clearly demonstrates is that since 1985 unemployment has fallen much faster in the UK as a whole than in Northern Ireland, and that therefore the difference between the mainland and Northern Ireland is greater now than it was in 1977. In short, while it is possible to argue that the recession has ended in Britain, the same claim can hardly be made for Northern Ireland.

Figures for the duration of male unemployment spells, recorded in table 19, present a very striking picture of the persistence of long-term unemployment in Northern Ireland. These show that while total unemployment in the Province has fallen since 1985, long-term unemployment (defined as being out of work for more than one year) has actually increased from 56.5 per cent to 60.6 per cent of the total of unemployed people. Moreover, this increase is not due to a preponderance of the

Table 18. *Rates of unemployment
(percentages) for United Kingdom and
Northern Ireland for three selected
years*

	1977	1985	1989
Northern Ireland	10.5	21.0	15.9
United Kingdom	5.8	13.5	7.0
Ratio of NI to UK rates of unemployment	1.81	1.55	2.27

older unemployed (over fifty years of age), since of the 18,268 registered as having been without work for over five years in April 1989 very nearly 13,000 are between the ages of twenty-five and forty-nine.

A final piece of evidence will help to give a more complete description of the unemployment situation in Northern Ireland. While figures for unfilled vacancies at job centres in many parts of the south of England have begun to outstrip the number of unemployed people available for work, the picture remains much bleaker in Northern Ireland. The number of unfilled job-centre vacancies (one-fifth to one-third of all vacancies) has shown little change. In April 1985 there were 1,200, In April 1987 there were 2,000, and in July 1989 there were 3,200, this latter figure representing one vacancy for every twenty-five unemployed men.

It is in the context of continuing recession that new training schemes and social security legislation must be understood. I shall take the former subject first.

Employment-training schemes are not new to the late 1980s; many of the present schemes are based on previous ones that have been in place for a decade or more. What is new is the pressure exerted on unemployed people to take up a training place or other kind of option.

In regard to pressure, several new moves have been introduced and old regulations tightened up. There is an ever-growing number of fraud investigators to root out the 'working' unemployed; there is a stricter test of 'availability for work', which is designed to remove the 'malingerer' and the 'scrounger'; there are increased penalties for 'voluntarily' leaving a job or getting the sack; and there are reduced social security benefits for the under-25s, to sharpen their incentive to

Table 19. *Duration of male unemployment spells for Northern Ireland, for the years 1985 and 1989*

	April 1985	April 1989
0–6 months	24,201	20,563
6 months–1 year	14,319	10,735
1 year–2 years	16,025	11,904
2 years–3 years	11,115	7,371
3 years–4 years	7,330	6,102
4 years–5 years	6,682	4,406
over 5 years	9,271	18,268
Total	88,943	79,349
Percentage unemployed more than 1 year	56.5	60.6

Source: Employment Gazette, June 1985; Employment Gazette, June 1989.

take low-paid jobs. These latter are on the increase, partly because of the progressive de-regulation of the labour market brought about by, amongst other things, the abolition of the official Wages Councils which protected the wages of young workers.

Under earlier employment schemes, unemployed people had generally been left to decide for themselves whether or not they wished to take advantage of Employment Service schemes. However, in recent years the government has seen fit to introduce a greater degree of coercion. Thus, for example, the new social security legislation no longer provides school leavers and those aged sixteen to seventeen with a general entitlement to benefit. Those not in work and those who reject a place on the Youth Training Scheme (Youth Training Programme in Northern Ireland) are now denied benefit unless they can prove 'severe hardship'. Since the YTS is now a two-year programme, this group of youngsters has been almost completely removed from the unemployment register. The government presumably also hopes that these youths will no longer be led astray by their unemployed elders into a 'welfare-dependency' culture.

Under the Restart programme, which commenced in 1986 and which is targeted at those over eighteen and unemployed for more than six months, unemployed individuals are called in for interviews at their local job centres. On offer to them is a menu of options. They can go to a

Job Club to learn how to look for jobs more efficiently ('looking for a job can be hard work' so the slogan goes), and to find out about interview techniques; they are also allowed free use of newspapers, type-writers, stationery, stamps, photocopying, etc. There is the further possibility of self-employment under the Enterprise Allowance Scheme; the option, under Jobstart Allowance, to take a job paying less than £90 a week and thus to receive a top-up benefit of £20 a week for six months; and finally one can opt for a place on the new Employment Training Scheme (Job Training Programme [JTP] in Northern Ireland). The ETS (which also subsumes several older schemes) is hoped eventually to provide some 600,000 places either in practical training with an employer or in directed training. Everyone on ET receives a training allowance of £10 a week more than their benefit payment. It is also possible to be reimbursed for travel costs exceeding £4 a week and child-care costs of up to £50 a week.

The level of compulsion associated with Restart and ETS is very difficult to assess. This is mostly because of the gap between sanctions theoretically available and the way they are actually used in practice. Moreover, the manner in which sanctions are used may well be linked to varying employment conditions both over time and in different regions. One sanction that is available is that those called to Restart interviews can have their benefit stopped if they fail to show up on three occasions (Digby, 1989: 113). What is not yet clear is the extent of pressure exerted on clients during the interviews (the use of the euphemistic term 'clients' rather than the derogatory term 'claimants' is deliberate – it conjures up a picture of the service as governed by market forces and which must therefore woo its customers, who in theory can take it or leave it, with an attractive and valuable product). It is hoped that Restart counsellors will be able to secure the agreement of clients to take up one of the various options open to them. Refusal to take anything may result in the client's availability for work coming under suspicion, and this can carry a penalty of withdrawal of benefit. Whilst this has always been the case in regard to availability, the regulations have been considerably tightened up (Child Poverty Action Group, 1988: 4). Moreover, the government is to introduce further new legislation in October 1989 under which the burden of proof of availability for work will shift from the officials to the claimants, thus making benefit disallowance somewhat easier. Alternatively such clients can be referred to a claimant advisor, whose role is to give help with 'benefit problems'. Since the category of 'unemployability' is now no longer acceptable to the government, clients who refuse to take up any of the Restart options cannot any longer be deemed unemployable.

It seems that one tactic claimant advisors can use in these situations is to persuade such people to switch from unemployment benefit to sickness benefit, thus removing another group from the unemployment register (Hillyard and Percy-Smith, 1988: 222).

Finally the notion of 'suitable' job is being redefined. Previously a 'suitable' job was a job in one's own usual occupation, paying similar wages to past jobs and located within reasonable distance. The new form (UB 671) for testing availability now asks claimants to consider taking jobs other than in their usual occupation; whether they will start work immediately irrespective of personal and family circumstances; whether they are prepared to work weekends, travel greater distances to a job, and take wages lower than those in a previous job (Child Poverty Action Group 1989: 4–5). In the light of all this, it is little wonder that there is considerable controversy over whether the government's main objective is to see the unemployed back in work in reasonably paid, safe, and productive jobs or whether it is simply to reduce the unemployment figures, regardless of any personal cost to the individuals concerned.

To what extent have the new schemes been successful? The explicit aim of ETS, according to the government's glossy advertising campaign, is to train the workers without jobs to do the jobs without workers. This suggests that success is to be defined in terms of how many people are eventually placed in real jobs. The figures so far are not very encouraging. Even in Britain the ETS has not been conspicuously successful. Early reports recorded that only one in twenty people interviewed under the Restart scheme went on to training, and that a mere one in two hundred used this as a path into regular work (Digby, 1989: 115). More recent figures suggest that the scheme is now expanding, since as of March 1989 around 150,000 were in training places, of whom 61 per cent were single and 71 per cent were males (*Employment Gazette*, April 1989).

As far as the situation in Northern Ireland is concerned, going on figures supplied to me personally by the Department of Economic Development, by August 1987 some 1,240 people were on placement in the Job Training Programme, of whom 350 are residents of Belfast. Moreover, it is roughly estimated that of these up to 70 per cent are under twenty-five years of age. In other words the training schemes in Belfast have so far had very little effect on the age group twenty-five to fifty years, the group which is the primary focus of this book.

The trouble with the slogan about jobless workers and workerless jobs is that it is just that, a slogan. It gives a ridiculously optimistic and simplistic picture of the situation, and one which pays scant regard to the demographic distribution of unemployment and available jobs. Most unemployment is of unskilled men and women and it is disproportionately located in areas where few openings exist. Where there is a shortage of labour, mainly in the south of England, it is a shortage of skilled labour. Not only would the unskilled unemployed from other areas find it difficult to fill such vacancies; they are also prevented from moving because of the costs of resettlement, the massive regional differentials in the price of housing, and the lack of cheap rented accommodation. The fact that a major job-hunting resource of unskilled people is the informal network of friends and contacts in which they are locally embedded is a further limitation on their mobility.

All of these obstacles perhaps apply with greater force to the unemployed in Northern Ireland than they do to those in Britain. Although Belfast is a less blighted area than other parts of the Province, there are still, as already noted, a great many unemployed for every unfilled vacancy, and while of course there is a long tradition of migration from Ireland, during my research I encountered very few married men who considered such migration as a real option to continued unemployment. Unless the general economy of Northern Ireland considerably expands, or unless there is a major change in the number of people active in the labour force (due to changes in the age structure of the population), employment training schemes can have but a marginal and very limited impact. Even if they really do provide effective training (and there is a great deal of controversy about that) the problem of matching people to vacancies remains.

Returning to the issue of sanctions, it is one thing to apply these to unemployed individuals in an area of good employment opportunities, but something else again to do so in a depressed economy, and Belfast has such a depressed economy. In such a context, what does 'availability' for work mean, when people cannot persistently look for jobs that do not exist, or will not look for jobs in areas where they have a legitimate fear for their personal safety?

Given the base line of so few real jobs (and if the economy is severely depressed it is unlikely to be able to generate enough employment training places for even a fraction of the unemployed), sanctions against the unemployed can only have highly deleterious consequences, either forcing them into the black economy or into crime, or shifting responsibility for the problem of poverty and disadvantage from the state and industry on to the local community which can ill afford it. Informally, I have been told that in Northern Ireland sanctions have not been applied rigorously on the unemployed (in relation to Restart and the JTP) as it is recognized that it is unrealistic to do so.

In regard, then, to 'assistance' to the unemployed to get them back into work or to help them look for work or obtain new skills, there are few grounds for arguing that the situation has perceptibly changed between 1985 and 1989. And if the formal labour markets have not much improved, there is also no reason to think that my analysis of doing the double needs modification.

I now turn to a brief description of the changes in social security legislation. In April 1988 the SB scheme was replaced by IS. Although the basic calculation, 'requirements less resources' (with requirements being a needs level determined by Parliament) remains the same, there are significant differences in the way that people's requirements are calculated. Basically, the SB long-term rates, the differential between householder and non-householder and the additional requirement provisions (ARs for heating, special diets, laundry costs, etc.) have all been abolished. These normal and additional requirements have been replaced by personal allowances and 'client group premiums'. Most personal allowances remain at levels similar to those of the short-term SB rates. However, single childless people under the age of twenty-five now receive a proportionately lower benefit than they did under the SB scheme. There are premiums for families, lone parents, pensioners, disabled people, and children on either attendance allowance or mobility allowance. It is these premiums which substitute for the long-term rates and additional requirements (ARs) of SB.

There have also been changes which affect housing requirements. Thus water rates, house insurance, up to 20 per cent of general rates, and half of mortgage interest for the first six months, have now all to be met from the personal allowances. Although the earnings' disregard has been increased to £5, work expenses and child-care costs can no longer be offset against earnings.

As far as this study is concerned the other major change is the abolition of the single-payments provisions. These have been replaced by the social fund. Single payments were disbursed as grants in accordance with legally binding, parliamentary regulations; the budget was theoretically unlimited and claimants had a right of appeal to an independent body. The social fund administers mainly loans from a cash-limited budget (the limit set at a figure well below that which was spent in the last years of the single-payments scheme); the loans, to be repaid by direct deductions from benefit, are at the discretion of social fund officers (although guidance on priorities is available), and there is no right of appeal to an independent body. Finally, the social fund now covers far fewer items than did the single-payment scheme.

In relation to the social fund, there now appears to be something of a catch-22 built into the system. Those who most need loans are likely to be the very poorest with the highest levels of existing debts. If social fund officers decide that a claimant cannot realistically repay the loan (because of the competing demands on the weekly benefit income), then the loan cannot be made. Instead, such claimants can be offered 'money advice' and be pointed in the direction of charities, relatives, and money-lenders. This is yet further evidence of the unloading of responsibility for maintaining the poor onto the local community.

But it is not just the new social security rates that need to be considered in evaluating the overall changes in income distribution. There have also been important changes in housing benefit, income tax, and the rating system. The effect of these reforms on net income has been calculated by Esam and Oppenheim. They note that, of the losers and gainers, the former are concentrated at the bottom end of the income scale and the latter at the top. Their conclusion is that 'Overall the reforms are highly regressive' (1989: 81).

This shift in the balance of national resources from the poor to the rich has now being going on for a ten-year period (Hills, 1988). While thus the government's stated aim has been to target resources on those who most need them, its policies have succeeded in achieving the very opposite. It is in fact a case, to use John Moore's apt phrase, of 'perverse targeting' (Rt. Hon. J. Moore, MP, *House of Commons Hansard*, 27 October 1988, cols. 456–7). In summary, then, of the millions of people subsisting on IS, more are now worse off than they were prior to the recent changes.

Clearly this situation is likely to have an adverse impact on conditions in social security offices. Although there is as yet very little information to go on, what there is points to increased tension between claimants and officers. Of course basic IS, which accounts for the lion's share of benefit, is paid in much the same way as before and this appears to be running reasonably smoothly. It is the administration of the social fund which is causing the trouble. According to one social fund officer, 'we had more abuse in three months [since April 1988] than at any time in the previous thirteen years' (Craig, 1988: 15). Moreover, some people who need loans in fact refuse them when they discover the repayment conditions (Craig, 1988: 16). Craig further reports that many social fund officers feel they cannot in practice use their theoretically available discretionary powers. This is for two reasons. First, because the cash-limited budget 'rules, regardless! Discretion ought to go two ways, yes and no, but in practice we're only going one way, to *not* give grants' (Craig, 1988: 16; italics in original). Second, because the existence of a kind of league table, combining priority claimant groups with priority items of need, designed to be used as guidance in making discretionary decisions is in some offices being turned into a directive enforced on officers by their managers. In one office, 'payment of a medium priority item is seen as a bad decision by management and the word is "low priority" should not get loans or grants at all' (Craig, 1988: 16). Yet in other offices 'any slack at the end of the month was taken up by giving [grants] to medium priority claims' (Craig, 1988: 16). It is not unlikely then that the system is reverting to a pre-1980 situation, in which the practical use of discretion varied widely in different parts of the country.

As regards the categories 'deserving' and 'undeserving', there is simply not enough solid and reliable information to tell how these are being used at the local level. However, before I close this section let me make the following two points. Under the SB system many officers denied that they made discretionary decisions, arguing instead that they disbursed single payments in line with regulations and official guidance. However, it was demonstrated in chapter 5 how notions of deservingness intervened to produce an informal process whereby attempts were made to victimize one set of claimants (the so-called undeserving). In the new scheme, although discretion has been formally re-introduced, some officers deny that they can employ it both because the small size of the budget makes it impossible and because they are being forced to adopt a *de facto* rule-bound system. There is, therefore, in this sense at least, a certain practical similarity in the two systems (although I would not wish to push this too far), which makes it likely that ideas of deservingness will play their part in social fund decisions.

My second point is that in those offices in which managers allow social fund officers to use their discretionary powers, such discretion will almost certainly be infected by ideas of deservingness. This is because, although there are differences between SB and IS, there is also continuity in the officials running them, in the beliefs and values they hold, and in the wider public context in which welfare schemes have to be administered. After all, preoccupations with targeting, deservingness, and fraud and abuse figured centrally in the government's thinking when it drew up the new legislation. It would be naive to think that this has not had a substantial impact on many of those who run the schemes.

What I am claiming then, and in my view it is not much of a claim, is that, despite obvious differences between the old and the new systems, ideas of deservingness are bound to continue to play a significant role, just as they have done for the past 400 years. On the other hand, it is not any part of my argument that these ideas and stereotypes will be applied in exactly the same way as they were in the SB system. How they manifest themselves in the context of IS is a topic other researchers will have to look into.

Finally, I want to say a few words about the so-called culture of welfare dependency. For several hundred years, governments and the middle class have agonized about the persistent problem of poverty, and there have always been two sides to the dilemma. On the one hand, it has always been recognized that many poor people are committed to the values and institutions of main-stream society and hence deserve assistance to better themselves. On the other hand, poverty has equally always been viewed as a problem of social order and control: the poor are a seed-bed of revolution, a potentially disruptive force that must be pacified and neutralized. State policies in relation to poverty have often exhibited this two-edged approach, and some (George, 1973, along with Marxist analyses) have argued that assistance is itself a form of social control. By making available a steady stream of small material rewards, the poor are given a stake in society which they will not willingly surrender. On this view, benefits are a sop to keep the poor quiescent. Behind both of these aims is the further objective of maintaining a well-disciplined and healthy labour force, without which the economy, and hence the better off, could not thrive. Throughout this book, I have tried to demonstrate how our society attempts to deal with some of its more unfortunate and disadvantaged citizens by means of a combination of barely adequate financial subventions and pervasive social control.

But there is still another aspect to the problem of poverty. Given that society has always acknowledged that some forms of adversity and misfortune are outside one's personal control and hence require external help, the difficulty remains, first, of how to discriminate between the truly eligible and the 'cheats' and 'loafers', and second, how to circumvent the supposed deleterious consequences of such assistance. To provide aid without requiring a return of some kind has generally been thought to exacerbate the dependency it is designed to eliminate and thus to stifle self-reliance, thrift, and initiative. It is indeed true that uni-directional gift giving can involve both political and economic dependency. But does the case of welfare benefits to the unemployed in an industrial, capitalist economy, in which a job is the only survival strategy, really fit this pattern? I would argue that it does not. If what is meant by a culture of dependency is that recipients prefer to rely on state benefits when they could in fact make private provision for themselves, then this study provides a great deal of evidence to counter such a view. What welfare benefits do induce is not a psychological or cultural dependence, but rather stigma and humiliation, not for every-one but for a great many. What unemployed welfare recipients want to do is not remain on the dole in a loathsome subservient position that betokens a barren future; rather, they want to work for their living, give a return for what they receive, lock themselves into society via whole sets of exchange relationships. The last thing they desire is to be isolated, housebound, and fearful of what their friends, neighbours, and relatives think of them.

There is no *culture* of dependency; the work ethic with its associated values, practices, and institutions is too great an antidote. What there really is is an *economics* of dependency. Without jobs poor people are forced to depend on benefits; they have no other choice. But it is because they despise this dependency and the stigma attached to it that they look for jobs, or doubles, with more persistence than perhaps we have a right to expect (given that if they are successful the jobs they obtain are not particularly enviable). In short, with the partial excep-tion of the idle rich, unemployment is not, and probably never has been, an eligible status.

The 'culture of dependency' is part of that complex of ideas that, along with others, I have denoted as individualism. Individualism, which incorporates notions of deservingness, is a powerful ideology. It reflects a commonsensical understanding of the everyday world at the same time as it hides many of the real causes of disadvantage and inequality. Because it is so widespread and entrenched, it inevitably finds itself being used as a basis for the formulation of social policy. The implementation of such policies throws up many anomalies which are in turn interpreted by recourse to individualistic explanations, thus com-pleting the vicious circle. Only within the terms of reference of such a one-sided rhetoric, in which inherent contradictions pass by unnoticed, could it possibly be argued that the rich need ever larger slices of the national cake whilst the poorest can make do with progressively smaller ones. It is often argued that government social policies combine a stick-and-carrot approach, and certainly this is true; but it is only within the framework of the ideology of individualism that the carrot is offered to the better-off whilst the stick remains the lot of the poor.

In the interests of a saner and more civilized society, can we not remember what Richard Tawney told us over fifty years ago, that the problem of poverty is not that there are poor people, but that there are rich people? If not, we will continue to punish the poor for their poverty, despite the fact that the causes of their misfortune and disad-vantage originate elsewhere; and we will continue to make sure that, in the doleful words of that old song, 'it's the poor wot gets the blame'.

Notes

1 Introduction

1 Female unemployment, which unfortunately this book is not concerned with, poses greater problems of definition than does male unemployment.

2 The 'genuinely seeking work' test placed the burden on the claimant to demonstrate materially that he was doing everything in his power to find work. In practice, administrators often allowed benefit conditional on unemployed people travelling long distances on the basis of the merest rumours that jobs might be had elsewhere.

3 In general there is a considerably more varied literature in the 1980s. There are, for example, several community studies (Port Talbot in South Wales; Falkirk; the Isle of Sheppey; and other places) which have been completed or are still going on. In addition there are some collections which are diverse in their interests (for example, Roberts et al., 1985; Allen et al., 1986; Fineman, 1987). In this material there is much more concern to treat unemployment as a process and to look at issues such as unemployment and the construction of gender, unemployment and the work ethic, unemployment and the social relations of domestic life. Where pertinent, reference will be made to these works.

4 I prefer to maintain the present tense when writing about SB. This is because, although there are important differences between the old and new schemes, I will argue (ch. 9) that the administration and claiming of IS involves social processes very similar to those I describe for SB. Reverting to the past tense could give the misleading impression that the analysis of these processes is no longer valid.

2 The political economy of Northern Ireland and the anthropology of sectarianism

1 The SB scale rates in Northern Ireland and Great Britain were identical. However, evidence clearly suggests that the cost of living in Northern Ireland (particularly the cost of fuel) is higher than in Great Britain, and that therefore 'parity in benefits has not meant the provision of a similar standard of living for claimants [in Northern Ireland]' (Evason, 1985: 12).

2 The SB scheme had many other features and limiting conditions, and on these see Lynes (1981) and chapter 5.

3 The 1971 Payments for Debt (Emergency Provisions) Act (Northern Ireland) allows money to be deducted at source from the benefits of people in arrears to public bodies. When the Housing Benefit scheme was introduced in 1984, Housing Executive tenants in receipt of supplementary benefit could no longer opt to have their rent deducted at source; it became compulsory. Given the very high prices for fuel, most claimants of SB found great difficulty in meeting their bills. 'In essence' as Eileen Evason so clearly argues, 'the Payments for Debt Act has been used since the latter part of the 1970s to ensure that the province's rising rents and fuel prices result in private hardship rather than in public debt' (1985:8).

3 Doing the double in Belfast: the general picture

1 The earnings' disregard was set at £4 in 1975; in 1985 it rose to £5. Had it risen in line with inflation it would have been £9 in 1984. When IS was introduced in 1988 the disregard remained at £5.

2 This sounds implausible, but unusual conditions prevailed at the time which made this possible.

3 See O'Dowd et al. (1980, particularly chapters 1 and 2), Cormack and Osborne (1983), Darby (1983), and Boal and Douglas (1982), for modern treatments of how sectarian politics influences most aspects of social and economic life in the province. For further information on the history of industrialization and the labour movement in Ireland, see Lyons (1973), Berresford Ellis (1985), and Gray (1985).

4 On the social significance of territorial prerogatives in Northern Ireland, see for a case study, O'Dowd and Tomlinson (1980), Tomlinson (1980) and Singleton (1982); and also Boal (1969).

5 Using survey data collected in 1973 and 1974, Miller (1983) has argued that the information on social mobility in Northern Ireland indicates a 'widening, not shrinking or stable, disparity in the occupational distributions of Protestants and Catholics', and that therefore it would be 'inaccurate and foolish to assume that present-day inequities are only legacies from the past that will somehow fade into oblivion of their own volition. On the contrary the assumption must be that present-day inequities will most likely remain or even intensify'. This is a conclusion which this chapter endorses.

4 Doing the double or doing without

1 I cannot generalize these findings beyond the areas concerned in the research because other surveys analysing perceptions of job-centre services have produced different findings. It is worth pointing out, however, that even in 1979, when unemployment in Northern Ireland was about half what it is now, there were fifty-five unemployed for every unfilled vacancy

at the job centres whereas the corresponding figure for Great Britain was five (Trewsdale, 1980: 32–3).

2 There is a growing literature, largely economistic, on the subject of work incentives and the unemployment and poverty traps. Parker (1982b: 110) has estimated that in 1982 about five-and-a-half million adults were being affected by these traps. Both Kay, Morris, and Warren (1980) and Atkinson and Flemming (1978) argue that at the heart of this problem is the very badly integrated system of taxation and benefits which can on occasion result in some people being better off unemployed. However the authors of these two articles concur that whilst there might be justifiable concern about incentives in the short term this is, for the most part, confined to those at the very bottom of the income ladder, and that prolonged unemployment for the vast majority is financially devastating. This assessment is, I think, more correct for England, where wages are higher than in Northern Ireland, prices are lower, and benefits the same. This means that the unemployed of the Province are financially worse off both in unemployment and in work than their English counterparts. Since only very-low-paid jobs are presently available, and very few of these, it also means that the problem of incentives is posed in a more acute fashion in Northern Ireland. Evidently what the unemployed themselves say on this topic quite clearly reflects the predicament they face.

3 Frazer (1968: 273) has said that one of the supreme conflicts of life in a modern industrial society is both the desire and need for work, and the detestation of the work done. Anthony remarks, more pithily, 'work demoralizes; the loss of work demoralizes' (1977: 164). The descriptions people give of their jobs, recorded by Frazer (1968, 1969) and by Terkel (1975), are a disturbing testimony to this paradox. In addition, the work of industrial sociologists has shown that workers are not so much satisfied with their jobs, as resigned to them. They respond to them by accepting the reality of life in a factory, on a site, in an office or shop, by attempting to make the best of it. Studies have demonstrated that beneath the vague expressions of satisfaction there lurks a good deal of dissatisfaction, frustration, anger, envy, and resistance (see, especially, Goldthorpe et al., 1968; Beynon and Blackburn, 1972; Mann, 1973: 28–29; Beynon, 1975; and Nichols and Beynon, 1977).

However, there is, as Kumar (1979: 13) points out, the humanist definition of work as 'the first moral category'. In this tradition, work is integral to our very being, it enables us to transform the world, to enhance our sense of being alive (Berger, 1964). With the advance of industrial society, work is increasingly identified with a 'job' in the formal economy, and from there status and identity are in large measure defined and evaluated by what type of job. The irony, of course, is that at the very point at which work becomes narrowly focused and separated socially and physically from the home, its ability to fulfil and satisfy disappears and in fact for some commentators, following Marx, becomes alienating and degrading (e.g. Braverman, 1974). On the other hand while the tasks may well be boring, repetitive and dehumanizing, there are many latent functions of work, created by the same processes which define work as factory employment (R.E. Pahl, 1984), which when removed by the loss of a job have the alarming and distressing consequences so familiar to many of the unemployed (Jahoda, 1979; 1982). It is little wonder then that many people have such ambivalent attitudes to work. For further discussion of many of these points see R.K. Brown (1985), Carr-Hill (1985), and Kelvin (1980, 1981).

4 Here 'work' is being defined, narrowly, as 'employment', consistent with the literature cited in the previous note.

5 This is a very crude stereotype of the Northern Ireland working-class male, but even though there are, empirically, many exceptions, it is nevertheless a dominant image which shapes attitudes and actions. For example, not a few of the research subjects referred disparagingly to the unmanly activities of some of their neighbours: pushing prams, going shopping, doing housework, etc; and the latter themselves saw this as demeaning and in conflict with what they considered the normal male role. The majority of the unemployed in the samples do perform some household duties, but what they do is determined by a scale of preferences shaped by this image. For data on other parts of the UK, see Morris (1984a, 1984b, 1985), McKee and Bell (1985, 1986) and Laite and Halfpenny (1987).

6 See Parker (1982b: 26–7) for information on the advantages and disadvantages of different methods of calculating replacement ratios. The method chosen in this work is slightly different to Parker's but is free of most of the usual drawbacks. For England Kay, Morris, and Warren (1980) and Davies, Hamill, Moylan, and Smee (1982) have produced figures to show that RRs drop to around 50 per cent for about half the unemployed (after about six months out of work) and hardly rise above 70 per cent for the rest. The RR figures from the present study are higher than this, which again demonstrates that Northern Ireland wages are lower (since benefits are identical) and that incentives to take low-paid jobs must be weaker.

7 Murie (1974) provides data showing that although the take-up rate of FIS in Northern Ireland, at 70 per cent of those eligible, is higher than in Britain, where the figure is 50 per cent, the benefit is not sufficient to raise the low-paid out of poverty.

8 See Press (1979: 239–41) for data on similar practices in the construction industry in Seville, Spain.

9 There is of course a vast literature concerning the relationships between social welfare, the economy, poverty, and equality. In addition to the references cited in the text see, for example, George and Wilding (1976), Gough (1979), Jordan (1976, 1981), and Wilensky (1975).

5 The 'deserving' and the 'undeserving': administrative practice in a social security office

1 The office in question, selected by the DHSS, served an almost entirely Protestant clientele and, except for a few isolated remarks, there was no

'religious' aspect to day-to-day interaction between staff and claimants.

Circumstantial evidence allows me to feel reasonably confident that the processes described in this chapter are also at work in those SSOs which cater for a largely Catholic claimant population. First, the Catholic claimants of Mallon Park speak in very much the same way, concerning the offices they are registered at, as do those in Eastlough. Frequently they use identical language to couch their complaints, not only about personnel but also about the system in general. Second, at one point in the research, I spent a week in an SSO in Catholic west Belfast and engaged many of the staff in brief conversation. What was most notable was the similarity of views and ideas about claimants to those I encountered in east Belfast. Officers spontaneously remarked on the need to discriminate between the 'genuinely' poor and the scroungers; on the 'fact' that many unemployed are actually working; on the cupidity of many claimants who must be restrained; on the band-wagon effect – that when someone discovers the availability of a particular type of claim, others quickly find out and submit claims irrespective of 'real' need – which means that staff have to be circumspect with regard to how they allocate information about the scheme: and so on. Third, the accumulated literature on the administration of supplementary benefit indicates that while there might well be variations, linked to local circumstances, in the degree to which such processes are found, the overall picture is one which is shaped by much more general factors: widespread ideas concerning the categories of the deserving and the undeserving; resource constraints; emphasis on the prevention of fraud and abuse; and so forth.

2 Legislation in Northern Ireland is almost identical to that in Great Britain. The Regulations are laid down by Parliament, frequently up-dated, and deal with the minutiae of the scheme.

3 All figures quoted in this chapter were those current in the summer of 1982.

4 A complete analysis would need to look at the history of the SB scheme, the influence of peer-group pressures, the impact of different types of performance measures, and so on.

5 It should be noted that in many cases the collection of personal data is not a simple matter; it is surprising how often a claimant cannot even remember dependants' dates of birth. Moreover, the failure to bring various pieces of documentation is a cause of frustration to both staff and claimants.

6 There is an argument, frequently invoked, that work on fraud detection eliminates the scrounger and thereby creates a better service for the genuine claimant. This might be true if it were possible to identify unequivocally those making fraudulent claims. However, for a variety of reasons, many claims are unwittingly fraudulent (Weightman, 1981). Moreover, it is very difficult to obtain unambiguous evidence of fraud in a large proportion of cases, because of the problem of establishing intent (M. Hill, 1969: 82). Finally many cases of fraud involve small amounts and/ or claimants who are obviously pathetic. Such cases rarely get to court, because not only are they expensive but they also show the Department in

an unflattering light. In general, only cases which involve large amounts of money or organized fraud find their way to court. If this gives rise to the idea that social security abuse regularly entails excessive sums, it may further fuel public indignation.

7 There has been some criticism of the tactics of fraud officers over the past few years. P. Moore (1981) and Robinson and Wainwright (1981) have alleged that, in default of the kind of evidence that would hold up in a court of law, such officers sometimes bully suspected fraud cases into withdrawing their claims. However, there is no way of knowing whether those who withdrew their claims were committing fraud or were simply frightened off. Similar worries concerning the Unemployment Review Officers have been voiced by P. Moore (1981) and Sinfield (1981: 15–16). If such allegations are true, then methods of fraud procedure, rather than promoting an improved service, are likely instead to generate a service which is both harsher and more stigmatizing.

8 Some SSOs store leaflets in racks in the public waiting areas.

6 Claimants and the claiming process: the reluctant claimant

1 Stevenson is probably wrong on this point; for a shift in the balance of power to occur requires that procedural rights be effectively (practically) translated into substantive rights (Adler and Asquith, 1981: 17; Page, 1984: 138).

2 By acceptance I mean that many claimants agree on the 'rules of the game', that is, on the validity of the classifications used by SSO staff, not necessarily that they themselves have been correctly labelled and stereotyped.

3 In England, before 1983, newly unemployed people had to register at the local job centre, at the unemployment benefit office, and if they needed to claim SB, at the local SSO as well. Since then, registration at the job centres has been discontinued and unemployment benefit offices and SSOs have, in many places including Northern Ireland, been amalgamated into what are called integrated local offices (Rayner Report, 1981).

4 This is of course an ideal-type construction (cf. R.E. Pahl, 1984: 131–5), but I again use the argument that whilst the empirical facts may deviate considerably from this model, the latter is the representation which a very large majority of working-class married men and women in Belfast, and presumably elsewhere, use to evaluate the propriety of particular, existent, divisions of labour and work strategies.

8 The employed and the unemployed: conflict, discourse, and ideology

1 According to Anthony Cohen (1986:9) symbolic boundaries 'are most starkly manifest when those on either side of them explicitly attribute different or contrasting meanings to the same objects and symbols'. We will see how important this is in the present study.

2 Ideally the unemployed should obtain less in benefits than the employed do

in wages. This entails that life-styles and consumption practices should be curtailed to fit the new circumstances. It is by no means difficult, however, for many employed to argue that there is very little material difference between themselves and the unemployed. In chapter 4, data were provided to show that RRs are very high. Given that some unemployed do the double, there are bound to be those who are better off than some in work. Many employed extrapolate from the jobless they do see who are not apparently in abject penury to the general mass of the unemployed.

3 It is not being argued that the employed use precisely these words to express their distaste for some of the unemployed, but these are the implications of what they do say. It is noteworthy in this context how those holding ideas of the deserving and the undeserving when referring to particular people often remark on how these are similar or different to themselves, and about how they are unable to fathom the reasons for certain forms of behaviour: 'He's just like me, he's breaking his neck to get a job, desperate for work . . . But there's others, you always get them, they just don't seem to care, what makes them tick I don't know . . . can't understand it' (Tony Madden); 'You can see he wants to work, keeps asking me to get him a job in the Council, but he's no chance. He's always walking round the estate, he just can't sit. I'd be the same if I was unemployed . . . [but of someone else] I never see him, he seems content to lie in his bed, I think he's just bone idle . . . never was much of a worker . . . his kids are just the same, no interest in working. Me I can't lie on, I'm always one of the first at work' (John Duffy).

4 Of course such models are used in concrete situations and hence must be flexible and adaptable to a variety of contexts. Clearly, a general, representational, model of unemployment must take account of ideas guiding behaviour in other contexts. In this sense any particular social situation has a configuration which draws on several models, and it is this which constitutes the complexity of everyday life. On such theoretical issues see, for example, Caws (1974), Holy and Stuchlik (1981), and McFarlane (1986).

5 I should make it clear that the D model does include the idea that obtaining jobs is partly dependent on factors like skill, age, sex, possession of useful contacts, etc. The point, however, according to this view, is that if a person remains unemployed, then whatever the talents and contacts he may have he has failed to make efficient use of them. Despite being old and unskilled, there are examples of such people securing jobs, and therefore what differentiates those who do from those who do not must be differences in levels of desire, initiative, motivation, and willingness. Alan Martin, for example, remarked that he was old and his skills (HGV, class 1 lorry driver) no longer of use, but he still managed to get a job without too much trouble, 'so there's no reason why others can't', and if they do not it is because 'they're just lazy buggers'. In short, while the D model incorporates structural explanations for certain aspects of unemployment, these play second fiddle to individualistic explanations.

6 It is not part of my argument that individuals espouse one of these views to the total exclusion of the other. While there is sufficient evidence to claim that many people consistently use the same interpretive framework across a variety of situations, it is also true that accounting for unemployment can be situationally specific. In such cases it is more appropriate to see the two models as available cultural resources which can be drawn upon as context and purpose require. The parent who, at a general level, classes most of the unemployed as scroungers might well explain the unemployment of a child in much more sympathetic terms. The man who claims that all the unemployed want to work can find it irresistible to question the motives and interests of long-term jobless individuals whom he sees in receipt of large grants from the benefit system. Clearly, then, there is always a need to distinguish general accounts of unemployment from accounts tactically applied to specific individuals.

7 Let me be very clear here. In private, both the employed and the jobless will freely castigate specific others. In public arenas this happens more rarely. Rather, the unemployed are discussed in general terms (some are genuine, others are not). In such circumstances any unemployed man can never know into which category he is deemed to be included. Even if he is told 'Oh, I don't mean you', he can never be sure of this. Moreover, he becomes stigmatized by association, for despite the fact that he is being excluded from the undeserving group, he cannot do anything there and then to demonstrate that such classification is merited. To engage in tactics of impression management, which many do in such situations, is in fact evidence that this exclusion cannot be taken at face value.

References

Abel-Smith, B. and P. Townsend. 1965. *The poor and the poorest*. London: G. Bell and Sons Ltd

Abercrombie, N. 1980. *Class, structure and knowledge*. Oxford: Basil Blackwell

Abercrombie, N., S. Hill, and B.S. Turner. 1980. *The dominant ideology thesis*. London: George Allen & Unwin

Adler, M. and S. Asquith (eds.). 1981. *Discretion and welfare*. London: Heinemann Educational Books

Albeson, J. and R. Smith. 1984. *We don't give clothing grants any more*. London: Child Poverty Action Group

Allen, S., A. Waton, K. Purcell, and S. Wood (eds.). 1986. *The experience of unemployment*. London: Macmillan

Anthony, P.D. 1977. *The ideology of work*. London: Tavistock

Ashley, P. 1983. *The money problems of the poor: a review of the literature*. London: Heinemann Educational Books

Atkinson, A.B. 1969. *Poverty in Britain and the reform of social security*. Cambridge: Cambridge University Press

Atkinson, A.B. and J.S. Flemming. 1978. Unemployment, social security and incentives. *Midland Bank Review*, Autumn, 6–16

Atkinson, A.B. and C. Trinder. 1981. Pride, charity and the history of take-up. *New Society*, 13 August

Aunger, E.A. 1975. Religion and occupational class in Northern Ireland. *Economic and Social Review*, 7, 1–23

  1983. Religion and class: an analysis of the 1971 census data. In R.J. Cormack and R.D. Osborne (eds.), *Religion, education and employment: aspects of equal opportunity in Northern Ireland*. Belfast: Appletree Press

Bakke, E. Wight. 1933. *The unemployed man: a social study*. London: Nisbet

Bardon, J. 1982. *Belfast: an illustrated history*. Belfast: Blackstaff Press

Barnes, B. 1982. *T.S. Kuhn and social science*. London: Macmillan

Barrit, D.P. and C.F. Carter. 1962. *The Northern Ireland problem: a study in community relations*. London: Oxford University Press

Barth, F. 1969. Introduction. In F. Barth (ed.), *Ethnic groups and boundaries*. Boston: Little Brown and Co.

Beales, H.L. and R.S. Lambert. 1934. *Memoirs of the unemployed*. London: Victor Gollancz Ltd

Beckett, J.C. 1979. *A short history of Ireland: from earliest times to the present day*. London: Hutchinson

Berger, P.L. 1964. Some general observations on the problem of work. In P.L. Berger (ed.), *The human shape of work*. London: Macmillan

Berger, P.L. and T. Luckmann. 1967. *The social construction of reality*. Harmondsworth: Penguin Books

Berresford Ellis, P. 1985. *A history of the Irish working class*. London: Pluto Press

Berthoud, R. 1984. *The reform of supplementary benefit*. London: Policy Studies Institute

Beveridge Report. 1942. *Social insurance and allied services*. London: HMSO, Command 6404

Beveridge, W. 1931. *Unemployment – a problem of industry*. London: Longmans Green

Beynon, H. 1975. *Working for Ford*. Wakefield: EP Publishing Ltd.

Beynon, H. and R.M. Blackburn. 1972. *Perceptions of work*. Cambridge: Cambridge University Press

Black, B., J. Ditch, M. Morrissey, and R. Steele. 1980. *Low pay in Northern Ireland*. London: Low Pay Unit

Blackburn, R. and M. Mann. 1979. *The working class in the labour market*. London: Macmillan

Blacking, J., L. Holy, and M. Stuchlik. 1978. *Situational determinants of recruitment in four Northern Irish Communities*. Social Science Research Council (Economic and Social Research Council): British Lending Library

Blau, P.M. 1963. *The dynamics of bureaucracy*. Chicago: University of Chicago Press

1964. *Exchange and power in social life*. New York: John Wiley & Sons

Bloor, D. 1976. *Knowledge and social imagery*. London: Routledge & Kegan Paul

Boal, F.W. 1969. Territoriality on the Shankill–Falls Divide, Belfast. *Irish Geography*, 6, 30–50

Boal, F.W., P. Doherty, and D.G. Pringle. 1974. *The spatial distribution of some problems in the Belfast Urban Area*. Belfast: Northern Ireland Community Relations Commission

Boal, F.W. and J.N.H. Douglas (eds.). 1982. *Integration and division: geographical perspectives on the Northern Ireland problem*. London: Academic Press

Bond, N. 1975. Knowledge of rights. In R. Holman and E. Butterworth (eds.), *Social welfare in modern Britain*. London: Fontana

Bostyn, A. and D. Wight. 1984. From coal to dole: ethnography of an ex-mining village in central Scotland. *Proceedings of the Association for Scottish Ethnography*, 1, 47–69

Bourdieu, P. 1977. *Outline of a theory of practice*. Cambridge: Cambridge University Press

Bradshaw, J. 1985. Tried and found wanting: the take-up of means-tested benefits. In S. Ward (ed.), *DHSS in crisis*. London: Child Poverty Action Group

Braverman, H. 1974. *Labour and monopoly capital: the degradation of work in the twentieth century.* New York: Monthly Review Press

Briar, K.H. 1977. The effect of long-term unemployment on workers and their families. *Dissertation Abstracts International,* 37 (9-A), 6062

Briggs, E. and A.M. Rees. 1980. *Supplementary benefits and the consumer.* London: Bedford Square Press

Brook, E. and D. Finn. 1978. Working class images of society and community studies. In *On ideology,* Centre for Contemporary Cultural Studies, University of Birmingham. London: Hutchinson

Brown, P. 1987. *Schooling ordinary kids: inequality, unemployment and the new vocationalism.* London: Tavistock

Brown, R.K. 1985. Attitudes to work, occupational identity and industrial change. In B. Roberts, R. Finnegan, and D. Gallie (eds.), *New approaches to economic life.* Manchester: Manchester University Press

Buchanan, R.H. 1982. The planter and the Gael: cultural dimensions of the Northern Ireland problem. In F.W. Boal and J.N.H. Douglas (eds.), *Integration and division: geographical perspectives on the Northern Ireland problem.* London: Academic Press

Buckley, A.D. 1982. *A gentle people: a study of a peaceful community in Ulster.* Ulster Folk Museum: Cultra

Bufwak, M.S. 1982. *Village without violence: struggles in a Belfast community.* Cambridge, Mass.: Schenkman

Burghes, L. 1980. *Living from hand to mouth.* London: Child Poverty Action Group

Burton, F. 1978. *The politics of legitimacy: struggles in a Belfast community.* London: Routledge & Kegan Paul

Carr-Hill, R. 1985. Whither (research on) unemployment? In B. Roberts, R. Finnegan, and D. Gallie (eds.), *New approaches to economic life.* Manchester: Manchester University Press

Caws, P. 1974. Operational, representational and explanatory models. *American Anthropologist,* 76, 1–10

Chambers, G. 1987. *Equality and inequality in Northen Ireland: the workplace.* London: Policy Studies Institute

Child Poverty Action Group. 1988. Further crack down on the unemployed. *Poverty,* 69, 4–5

Clark, M. 1978. The unemployed on supplementary benefit. *Journal of Social Policy,* 7, 385–410

Clayre, A. 1974. *Work and play: ideas and experience of work and leisure.* London: Weidenfeld & Nicholson

Coates, K. and R. Silburn. 1981. *Poverty: the forgotten Englishmen.* Harmondsworth: Penguin Books

Coffield, F., C. Borrill, and S. Marshall. 1983. How young people try to survive being unemployed. *New Society,* 2 June

1986. *Growing up at the margins.* Milton Keynes: Open University Press

Cohen, Abner. 1969. *Custom and politics in urban Africa.* London: Routledge & Kegan Paul

Cohen, Anthony (ed.). 1986. *Symbolising boundaries: identity and diversity in*

British cultures. Manchester: Manchester University Press

Cohen, H. 1965. *The demonics of bureaucracy*. Iowa: Iowa State University Press

Cohen, Max. 1945. *I was one of the unemployed*. London: Victor Gollancz

Colin, J. 1974. *Never had it so good*. London: Victor Gollancz

Collman, J. 1981. Postscript: the significance of clients. *Social Analysis*, 9, 103–12

Compton, P. 1981. Demographic and geographical aspects of the unemployment differential between Protestants and Roman Catholics in Northern Ireland. In P. Compton (ed.), *The contemporary population of Northern Ireland and population-related issues*. Belfast: Queen's University of Belfast, Institute of Irish Studies

Cooper, S. n.d. *Observations in supplementary benefit offices*. London: Policy Studies Institute

Cormack, R.J. and R.D. Osborne (eds.). 1983. *Religion, education and employment: aspects of equal opportunity in Northern Ireland*. Belfast: Appletree Press

Cormack, R.J., R.D. Osborne, and W.T. Thompson. 1980. *Into work? Young school leavers and the structure of opportunity in Belfast*. Belfast: Fair Employment Agency for Northern Ireland

Craig, G. 1988. Nightmare lottery of the Social Fund. *Social Work Today*, 24 November

Crick, B. (ed.). 1981. *Unemployment*. London: Methuen

Daniel, W.W. 1974. *A national survey of the unemployed*. London: Political and Economic Planning

   1981. *The unemployed flow: stage 1 interim report*. London: Policy Studies Institute

Darby, J. 1983a. The historical background. In J. Darby (ed.), *Northern Ireland: the background to the conflict*. Belfast: Appletree Press

   (ed.). 1983b. *Northern Ireland: the background to the conflict*. Belfast: Appletree Press

Davies, R., L. Hamill, S. Moylan, and C. Smee. 1982. Incomes in and out of work. *Employment Gazette*, 237–43

Deacon, A. 1976. *In search of the scrounger*. London: G. Bell and Sons Ltd

   1978. The scrounging controversy. *Social and Economic Administration*, 12, 120–35

   1981. Thank you God for the means-test man. *New Society*, 25 June

Deacon, A. and J. Bradshaw. 1983. *Reserved for the poor: the means test in British social policy*. Oxford: Martin Robertson

Dennehy, C. and J. Sullivan. 1977. Poverty and unemployment in Liverpool. In F. Field (ed.), *The conscript army*. London: Routledge & Kegan Paul

Devlin, P. 1981. *Yes we have no bananas: outdoor relief in Belfast 1920–39*. Belfast: Blackstaff Press

Digby, A. 1989. *British welfare policy: workhouse to workfare*. London: Faber and Faber

Dilnot, A.W., J.A. Kay, and C.N. Norris. 1984. *The reform of social security*. London: Institute for Fiscal Studies

Dilnot, A.W. and C.N. Norris. 1981. What do we know about the black economy? *Fiscal Studies*, 2, 58–73

Ditch, J. 1984. *Hard terms: unemployment and supplementary benefit in Northern Ireland*. Northern Ireland Consumer Council

Ditton, J. 1977. *Part-time crime: an ethnography of fiddling and pilferage*. London: Macmillan

Doherty, P. 1981. The unemployed population of Belfast. In P. Compton (ed.), *The contemporary population of Northern Ireland and population-related issues*. Belfast: Queen's University of Belfast, Institute of Irish Studies

  1982. The geography of unemployment. In F.W. Boal and J.N.H. Douglas (eds.), *Integration and division: geographical perspectives on the Northern Ireland problem*. London: Academic Press

Donnan, H. and G. McFarlane. 1983. Informal social organisation. In J. Darby (ed.), *Northern Ireland: the background to the conflict*, Belfast: Appletree Press

  1986a. *Social anthropology and the sectarian divide in Northern Ireland*. London: Royal Anthropological Institute Occasional Papers, no. 41

  1986b. 'You get on better with your own': social continuity and change in rural Northern Ireland. In P. Clancy, S. Drudy, K. Lynch, and L. O'Dowd (eds.), *Ireland: a sociological profile*. Dublin: Institute of Public Administration

Douglas, J. 1980. The view from the local office. In J. Coussins (ed.), *Dear SSAC . . .* London: Child Poverty Action Group

Eisenberg, P. and P.F. Lazarsfeld, 1938. The psychological effects of unemployment. *Psychological Bulletin*, 35, 358–90

Epstein, A.L. 1978. *Ethos and identity: three studies in ethnicity*. London: Tavistock

Esam, P. and C. Oppenheim, 1989. *A charge on the community: the poll tax, benefits and the poor*. London: Child Poverty Action Group and Local Government Information Unit

Evans-Pritchard, E.E. 1937. *Witchcraft, oracles and magic among the Azande*. Oxford: Clarendon Press

Evason, E. 1976. *Poverty: the facts in Northern Ireland*. London: Child Poverty Action Group

  1978. *Family poverty in Northern Ireland*. London: Child Poverty Action Group

  1980. *Ends that won't meet*. London: Child Poverty Action Group

  1985. *On the edge: a study of poverty and long-term unemployment in Northern Ireland*. London: Child Poverty Action Group

Fair Employment Agency for Northern Ireland, 1978. *An industrial and occupational profile of the two sections of the population in Northern Ireland*. Belfast: Fair Employment Agency for Northern Ireland

Farrell, M. 1976. *Northern Ireland: the Orange state*. London: Pluto Press

Feige, E.L. 1981. The UK's unobserved economy: a preliminary analysis. *Economic Affairs*, 1, 205–12

Field, F. 1979. Scroungers: crushing the invisible. *New Statesman*, 16 November

1981. *Inequality in Britain: freedom, welfare and the state*. London: Fontana

Field, F. (ed.). 1977. *The conscript army*. London: Routledge & Kegan Paul

Field, F., M. Meacher, and C. Pond. 1977. *To him who hath*. Harmondsworth: Penguin Books

Fineman, S. (ed.). 1987. *Unemployment: personal and social consequences*. London: Tavistock

Fisk, R. 1975. *The point of no return: the strike that broke the British in Ulster*. London: Deutsch

Flett, H. 1979. Bureaucracy and ethnicity: notions of eligibility to public housing. In S. Wallman (ed.), *Ethnicity at work*. London: Macmillan

Foster, P. 1983. *Access to welfare*. London: Macmillan

Fraser, C. 1980. The social psychology of unemployment. In M. Jeaves (ed.), *Psychology Survey No. 3*. London: George Allen & Unwin Ltd

Fraser, D. 1973. *The evolution of the British welfare state*. London: Macmillan

Frazer, R. 1968. *Work*. Harmondsworth: Penguin Books

1969. *Work 2*. Harmondsworth: Penguin Books

Fryer, D. and R. Payne, 1983. Towards understanding proactivity in unemployment. Medical Research Council/Economic and Social Research Council Social and Applied Psychology Unit, Sheffield University, mimeo 540

Fryer, D. and P. Ullah. 1987. Editors' introduction. In D. Fryer and P. Ullah (eds.), *Unemployed people: social and psychological perspectives*. Milton Keynes: Open University Press

Garraty, J.A. 1978. *Unemployment in history: economic thought and public policy*. New York: Harper and Row

Gellner, E. 1983. *Nations and nationalism*. London: Unwin Books

George, V. 1973. *Social security and society*. London: Routledge & Kegan Paul

George, V. and P. Wilding. 1976. *Ideology and the welfare state*. London: Routledge & Kegan Paul

Gershuny, J.I. 1977. Post-industrial society: the myth of the service sector. *Futures*, 10, 103–14

1978. *After industrial society: the emerging self-service economy*. London: Macmillan

1979. The informal economy: its role in industrial society. *Futures*, 11, 3–15

Gershuny, J.I. and R.E. Pahl. 1979–80. Work outside employment: some preliminary speculations. *New Universities Quarterly*, 34, 120–35

1980. Britain in the decade of the three economies. *New Society*, 3 January

Gibson, N. and J. Spencer, 1981. Unemployment and wages in Northern Ireland. In B. Crick (ed.), *Unemployment*. London: Methuen

Giddens, A. 1976. *The new rules of sociological method*. London: Hutchinson

1979. *Central problems in sociological theory*. London: Macmillan

Glasscock, R.E. 1967. The growth of the port. In J.C. Beckett and R.E. Glasscock (eds.), *Belfast: the origin and growth of an industrial city*. London: British Broadcasting Corporation

Glazer, N. and D.P. Moynihan. 1963. *Beyond the melting pot*. Cambridge, Mass.: Harvard University Press

Goffman, E. 1968. *Stigma: notes on the management of spoiled identity*. Harmondsworth: Penguin Books

1971. *The presentation of self in everday life*. Harmondsworth: Penguin Books

Golding, P. and S. Middleton. 1982. *Images of welfare: press and public attitudes to poverty*. Oxford: Martin Robertson

Goldthorpe, J.H., D. Lockwood, F. Beckhofer, and J. Platt. 1968. *The affluent worker: 1. industrial attitudes and behaviour*. Cambridge: Cambridge University Press

Gough, I. 1979. *The political economy of the welfare state*. London: Macmillan

Gould, P. and J. Kenyon. 1972. *Stories from the dole queue*. London: Temple Smith

Gray, J. 1985. *City in revolt: James Larkin and the Belfast dock strike of 1907*. Belfast: Blackstaff Press

Grillo, R.D. 1980a. Introduction. In R.D. Grillo (ed.), *'Nation' and 'State' in Europe: anthropological perspectives*. London: Academic Press.

1980b. Social workers and immigrants in Lyon, France. In R.D. Grillo (ed.), *'Nation' and 'State' in Europe: anthropological perspectives*. London: Academic Press

1985. *Ideologies and institutions in urban France: the representation of immigrants*. Cambridge: Cambridge University Press

Gudeman, S. 1986. *Economics as culture*. London: Routledge & Kegan Paul

Gurney, R. and K. Taylor. 1981. Research on unemployment: defects, neglects and prospects. *Bulletin of the British Psychological Society*, 34, 349–52

Hakim, K. 1982. The social consequences of high unemployment. *Journal of Social Policy*, 11, 433–67

Hannerz, U. 1969. *Soulside: inquiries into ghetto culture and community*. New York: Columbia University Press

1974. Ethnicity and opportunity in urban America. In Abner Cohen (ed.), *Urban ethnicity*. London: Tavistock

Harris, R. 1972. *Prejudice and tolerance in Ulster: a study of neighbours and strangers in a border community*. Manchester: Manchester University Press

Harrison, R. 1976. The demoralising experience of prolonged unemployment. *Department of Employment Gazette*, April, 339–48

Hartley, J.F. 1980. Psychological approaches to unemployment. *Bulletin of the British Psychological Society*, 33, 412–14

Hartley, J.F. and D. Fryer. 1984. The psychology of unemployment: a critical appraisal. In G.M. Stephenson and J.H. Davis (eds.), *Progress in applied psychology*, vol. II. London: John Wiley and Sons

Hawkins, K. 1979. *Unemployment: facts, figures and possible solutions for Britain*. Harmondsworth: Penguin Books

Hayes, J. and P. Nutman. 1981. *Understanding the unemployed: the psychological effects of unemployment*. London: Tavistock

Henry, S. 1978. *The hidden economy: the context and control of borderline crime*. London: Martin Robertson

Henry, S. (ed.). 1981. *Can I have it in cash: a study of informal institutions and unorthodox ways of doing things*. London: Astragal Books

Henry, S. and G. Mars. 1978. Crime at work: the social construction of amateur property theft. *Sociology*, 12, 245–63

Hepburn, A.C. 1983. Employment and religion in Belfast, 1901–1951. In R.J. Cormack and R.D. Osborne (eds.), *Religion, education and employment: aspects of equal opportunity in Northern Ireland*. Belfast: Appletree Press

Higgins, J. 1978. *The poverty business*. Oxford: Basil Blackwell

Hill, J.M. 1977. *The social and psychological impact of unemployment: a pilot study*. London: Tavistock Institute of Human Relations

Hill, M. 1969. The exercise of discretion in the National Assistance Board. *Public Administration*, 47, 75–90

  1976. *The state, administration and the individual*. London: Weidenfeld & Nicholson

  1981 *Understanding social policy*. Oxford: Martin Robertson

Hill, M., R. Harrison, A. Sargeant, and V. Talbot. 1973. *Men out of work*. Cambridge: Cambridge University Press

Hills, J. 1988. *Changing tax: how the tax system works and how to change it*. London: Child Poverty Action Group

Hillyard, P. and J. Percy-Smith. 1988. *The coercive state: the decline of democracy in Britain*. London: Fontana

Holman, R. 1978. *Poverty: explanations of social deprivation*. Oxford: Martin Robertson

Holy, L. and M. Stuchlik (eds.). 1981. *The structure of folk models*. London: Academic Press

  1983. *Actions, norms, and representations: foundations of anthropological inquiry*. Cambridge: Cambridge University Press

Howe, L.E.A. 1983a. Unemployment in Belfast: some findings from a pilot project. Final Report to the Economic and Social Research Council

  1983b. The unemployed are different. Paper delivered to the Northern Ireland branch of the British Psychological Society, Stranmillis College

  1984. The unemployed on supplementary benefit. *Scope*, 76, 12–14

  1985. The 'deserving' and the 'undeserving': practice in an urban, local social security office. *Journal of Social Policy*, 14, 49–72

  1989. Social anthropology and public policy: aspects of unemployment and social security in Northern Ireland. In H. Donnan and G. McFarlane (eds.), *Social anthropology and public policy in Northern Ireland*. Aldershot: Avebury

Hutson, S. and R. Jenkins. 1989. *Taking the strain: family, unemployment and the transition to adulthood*. Milton Keynes: Open University Press

Jahoda, M. 1979. The impact of unemployment in the 1930s and the 1970s. *Bulletin of the British Psychological Society*, 32, 309–14

  1982. *Employment and unemployment: a social-psychological analysis*. Cambridge: Cambridge University Press

Jahoda, M., P.F. Lazarsfeld, and H. Zeisel. 1972. *Marienthal: the sociography of an unemployed community*. London: Tavistock

Jackson, P.R. and S. Walsh. 1987. Unemployment and the family. In D. Fryer and P. Ullah (eds.), *Unemployed people: social and psychological perspectives*. Milton Keynes: Open University Press

Jefferson, C.W. and J.V. Simpson. 1980. *The cost of living in Northern Ireland*. Belfast: Northern Ireland Consumer Council

Jenkins, R. 1978. Doing the double. *New Society*, 20 April

   1982. *Hightown rules: growing up in a Belfast housing estate*. Leicester: National Youth Bureau

   1983. *Lads, citizens and ordinary kids: working-class youth life-styles in Belfast*. London: Routledge & Kegan Paul

   1984. Understanding Northern Ireland. *Sociology*, 18, 253–63

   1986. *Northern Ireland: in what sense 'religions' in conflict?* Royal Anthropological Institute Occasional Paper, no. 41

Jenkins, R. and P. Harding. 1986. *Informal economic activity in Northern Ireland: a review of the literature*. Swansea: University College of Swansea, Department of Sociology and Anthropology

Johnson, P. 1980. *Ireland: a concise history from the twelfth century to the present day*. London: Granada

Jordan, Bill, 1974. *Poor parents: social policy and the cycle of deprivation*. London: Routledge & Kegan Paul

   1976. *Freedom and the welfare state*. London: Routledge & Kegan Paul

   1981. *Automatic poverty*. London: Routledge & Kegan Paul

Kay, J.A., C.N. Morris, and N.A. Warren. 1980. Tax, benefits and the incentive to seek work. *Fiscal Studies*, 1, 8–25

Kelvin, P. 1980. Social psychology 2001: The social psychological bases and implications of structural unemployment. In R. Gilmour and S. Duck (eds.), *The development of social psychology*. London: Academic Press

   1981. Work as a source of identity: the implications of unemployment. *British Journal of Guidance and Counselling*, 9, 2–11

Kelvin, P. and J. Jarrett. 1985. *Unemployment: its social psychological effects*. Cambridge: Cambridge University Press

Kennedy, D. 1967. The early eighteenth century. In J.C. Beckett and R.E. Glasscock (eds.), *Belfast: the origin and growth of an industrial city*. London: British Broadcasting Corporation

Kincaid, J.C. 1975. *Poverty and equality in Britain*. Harmondsworth: Penguin Books

Kumar, K. 1979. The social culture of work: work, employment and unemployment as ways of life. *New Universities Quarterly*, 34, 5–47

   1984. Unemployment as a problem in the development of industrial societies: the English experience. *Sociological Review*, 32, 185–233

Laite, J. and P. Halfpenny. 1987. Employment, unemployment and the domestic division of labour. In D. Fryer and P. Ullah (eds.), *Unemployed people: social and psychological perspectives*. Milton Keynes: Open University Press

Larsen, S.S. 1982. The two sides of the house: identity and organisation in Kilbroney, Northern Ireland. In A.P. Cohen (ed.), *Belonging: identity and social organisation in British rural cultures.* Manchester: Manchester University Press.

Lewis, O. 1966. *La Vida: A Puerto Rican family in the culture of poverty – San Juan and New York.* New York: Random House

Leyton, E. 1974. Opposition and integration in Ulster. *Man,* 9, 185–98

1975. *The one blood: kinship and class in an Irish village.* St. John's, Newfoundland: Institute of Social and Economic Research, Memorial University

Lipsky, M. 1981. *Street-level bureaucracy.* New York: Russel Sage Foundation

Lister, R. 1974. *Take-up of means-tested benefits.* London: Child Poverty Action Group

1980. Discretion: getting the balance right. In J. Coussins (ed.), *Dear SSAC . . . .* London: Child Poverty Action Group

Lloyd, P. 1974. Ethnicity and the structure of inequality in a Nigerian town in the mid-1950s. In Abner Cohen (ed.), *Urban Ethnicity.* London: Tavistock

Lynes, T. 1981. *The Penguin guide to supplementary benefits.* Harmondsworth: Penguin Books

Lyons, F.S.L. 1973. *Ireland since the famine.* London: Fontana

Macafee, K. 1980. A glimpse of the hidden economy in the national accounts. *Economic Trends,* February, 81–7

McFarlane, G. 1979. 'Mixed' marriages in Ballycuan, Northern Ireland. *Journal of Comparative Family Studies,* 10, 191–205

1986. 'It's not as simple as that': the expression of the Catholic and Protestant boundary in Northern Irish rural communities. In A. Cohen (ed.), *Symbolising boundaries.* Manchester: Manchester University Press

McKee, L. and C. Bell. 1985. Marital and family relations in times of male unemployment. In B. Roberts, R. Finnegan, and D. Gallie (eds.), *New approaches to economic life.* Manchester: Manchester University Press

1986. His unemployment, her problem: the domestic and marital consequences of male unemployment. In S. Allen, A. Waton, K. Purcell, and S. Wood (eds.), *The experience of unemployment,* London: Macmillan

McLaughlin, E. 1987. In search of the female breadwinner: gender and unemployment in Derry City. Seminar paper delivered at Queen's University of Belfast

1989. In search of the female breadwinner: gender and unemployment in Derry city. In H. Donnan and G. McFarlane (eds.), *Social anthropology and public policy in Northern Ireland.* Aldershot: Avebury

MacLeod, J. 1987. *Ain't no makin' it: levelled aspirations in a low income neighbourhood.* London: Tavistock

Mann, M. 1973. *Consciousness and action among the western working class.* London: Macmillan

Mars, G. 1982. *Cheats at work: an anthropology of workplace crime.* London: George Allen & Unwin Ltd

Marsden, D. 1969. *Mothers alone.* Harmondsworth: Penguin Books

1982. *Workless.* London: Croom Helm

Mathews, K. 1983. National income and the black economy. *Journal of Economic Affairs,* 3, 261–7.

Meakin, D. 1976. *Man and work. Literature and culture in industrial society.* London: Methuen

Millar, D.W. 1978. *Queen's rebels: Ulster loyalism in historical perspective.* Dublin: Gill and Macmillan

Miller, R.L. 1978. *Attitudes to work in Northern Ireland.* Belfast: Fair Employment Agency

    1983. Religion and occupational mobility. In R.J. Cormack and R.D. Osborne (eds.), *Religion, education and employment: aspects of equal opportunity in Northern Ireland.* Belfast: Appletree Press

Miller, R.L. and R.D. Osborne. 1983. Religion and unemployment: evidence from a cohort survey. In R.J. Cormack and R.D. Osborne (eds.), *Religion, education and employment: aspects of equal opportunity in Northern Ireland.* Belfast: Appletree Press

Mills, C.W. 1970. *The sociological imagination.* Harmondsworth: Penguin Books

Mingione, E. 1985. Social reproduction of the surplus labour force: the case of southern Italy. In N. Redclift and E. Mingione (eds.), *Beyond employment: household, gender and subsistence,* Oxford: Basil Blackwell

Moore, B., J.R. Rhodes, and R. Tarling. 1978. Industrial policy and economic development. *Cambridge Journal of Economics,* 2, 99–114

Moore, P. 1980. Counter-culture in a social security office. *New Society,* 10 July

    1981. Scroungermania again at the DHSS. *New Society,* 22 January

Morris, L. 1984a. Redundancy and patterns of household finance. *Sociological Review,* 32, 492–523

    1984b. Patterns of social activity and post-redundancy labour-market experience. *Sociology,* 18, 337–52

    1985. Renegotiation of the domestic division of labour in the context of male redundancy. In B. Roberts, R. Finnegan, and D. Gallie (eds.). *New approaches to economic life.* Manchester: Manchester University Press

Morrissey, M., T. O'Connor, and B. Tipping. 1984. Doing the double in Northen Ireland. *Social Studies,* 8, 41–54

Murie, A. 1974. Family Income Supplement and low incomes in Northern Ireland. *Social and Economic Administration.* 8, 22–42

National Consumer Council, 1976. *Means-tested benefits.* London: NCC

Nelson, S. 1984. *Ulster's uncertain defenders.* Belfast: Appletree Press

New Society, 1980. Paying for tax fiddlers. 6 November

Nichols, T. and H. Beynon. 1977. *Living with Capitalism.* London: Routledge & Kegan Paul

Northern Ireland Assembly. 1984. *Social security fraud.* Belfast: HMSO (2 vols.)

Northern Ireland Economic Council. 1983. *Economic assessment: April 1983.* Belfast: Northern Ireland Economic Development Office

    1984. *Economic assessment: April 1984.* Belfast: Northern Ireland Economic Development Office

Northern Ireland Housing Executive. 1976. *Northern Ireland household survey. 1975,* Belfast: Northern Ireland Housing Executive

    1979. *Belfast household survey. 1978,* Belfast: Northern Ireland Housing Executive

O'Dowd, L. 1980. Regional policy. In L. O'Dowd, B. Rolston, and M. Tomlinson, *Northern Ireland: between civil rights and civil war*. London: CSE Books

    1982. Regionalism and social change in Northern Ireland. In M. Kelly, L. O'Dowd, and J. Wickham (eds.), *Power, conflict and inequality*. Dublin: Turoe Press

O'Dowd, L., B. Rolston, and M. Tomlinson. 1980. *Northern Ireland: between civil rights and civil war*. London: CSE Books

O'Dowd, L. and M. Tomlinson. 1980. Urban politics in Belfast: two case studies. *International Journal of Urban and Regional Research*, 4, 72–95

Osborne, R.D. and R.J. Cormack. 1983. Conclusions. In R.J Cormack and R.D. Osborne (eds.), *Religion, education and employment: aspects of equal opportunity in Northern Ireland*. Belfast: Appletree Press

Osborne, R.D. and R.C. Murray. 1978. *Educational qualifications and religious affiliation in Northern Ireland*. Belfast: Fair Employment Agency

Outer Circle Policy Unit, 1980. *Measuring the hidden economy*. London: Outer Circle Policy Unit

Page, P. 1984. *Stigma*. London: Routledge & Kegan Paul

Pahl, J. 1983. The allocation of money and the structuring of inequality within marriage. *Sociological Review*, 31, 237–62

Pahl, R.E. 1980. Employment, work and the domestic division of labour. In M. Harloe and E. Lebas (eds.), *City, class and capital*. London: Edward Arnold

    1984. *Divisions of labour*. Oxford: Basil Blackwell

Pahl, R.E. and C. Wallace. 1985. Household work strategies in economic recession. In N. Redclift and E. Mingione (eds.), *Beyond employment: household, gender and subsistence*. Oxford: Basil Blackwell.

P.A. Management Consultants. 1977. *Survey of employment problems and practices in the Northern Ireland construction industry*. Belfast Federation of Building and Civil Engineering Contractors

Parker, H. 1982a. Social security foments the black economy. *Journal of Economic Affairs*, 3, 32–5

    1982b. *The moral hazards of social benefits*. London: Institute of Economic Affairs

Parkin, F. 1972. Class inequality and political order. London: Granada Publishing Ltd

Patterson, H. 1980. *Class conflict and sectarianism: the Protestant working class and the Belfast labour movement 1868–1920*. Belfast: Blackstaff Press

Piachaud, D. 1987. The growth of poverty. In A. Walker and C. Walker (eds.), *The growing divide: a social audit 1979–1987*. London: Child Poverty Action Group

Pilgrim Trust, 1938. *Men without work*. Cambridge: Cambridge University Press

Pinnaro, G. and E. Pugliese. 1985. Informalization and social resistance: the case of Naples. In N. Redclift and E. Mingione (eds.), *Beyond employment: household, gender and subsistence*. Oxford: Basil Blackwell

Pound, J. 1971. *Poverty and vagrancy in Tudor England*. London: Longman

Press, I. 1979. *The city as context: urbanism and behavioural constraints in Seville, Spain*. Urbana, Ill.: University of Illinois Press

Prottas, J.M. 1979. *People processing*. Lexington, Mass.: Lexington Books

Rayner Report. 1981. *Payment of benefits to unemployed people*. London: Department of Employment and Department of Health and Social Services

Rein, M. 1983. *From policy to practice*. London: Macmillan

Ritchie, J. and P. Wilson. 1979. *Social security claimants*. London: Office of Population, Censuses and Surveys

Roberts, K., R. Finnegan, and D. Gallie (eds.). 1985. *New approaches to economic life*. Manchester: Manchester University Press

Robinson, A. and S. Wainwright. 1981. Specialist claims control: a local experience. *Poverty*, Child Poverty Action Group, 49, 8–14

Robinson, P. 1982. Plantation and colonisation: the historical background. In F.W. Boal and J.N.H. Douglas (eds.), *Integration and division: geographical perspectives on the Northern Ireland problem*. London: Academic Press

Rose, R. 1983. *Getting by in the three economies*. Glasgow: University of Strathclyde, Centre for the Study of Public Policy

Rubin, M. 1983. *Charity and community in medieval Cambridge*. Cambridge: Cambridge University Press

Rutter, R. and N. Madge. 1976. *Cycles of disadvantage*. London: Heinemann Educational Books

Ryan, W. 1976. *Blaming the victim*. New York: Random House

Sandford, C., C. Pond, and R. Walker (eds.). 1980. *Taxation and social policy*. London: Heinemann Educational Books

Saunders, P. 1979. *Urban politics*. Harmondsworth: Penguin Books

Schlozman, K.L. and S. Verba. 1979. *Injury to insult: unemployment, class and political response*. Cambridge, Mass.: Harvard University Press

Seabrook, J. 1982. *Unemployment*. London: Quartet Books

Shepherd, G. 1983. Poverty in *Piers Plowman*. In T.H. Ashton, P.R. Cross, C. Dyer, and J. Thirsk (eds.), *Social relations and ideas*. Cambridge: Cambridge University Press

Showler, B. 1981. Political economy and unemployment. In B. Showler and A. Sinfield (eds.), *The workless state*. Oxford: Martin Robertson

Showler, B. and A. Sinfield (eds.). 1981. *The workless state*. Oxford: Martin Robertson

Sinfield, A. 1970. Poor and out of work in Shields. In P. Townsend (ed.), *The concept of poverty*. London: Heinemann Educational Books

1978. Analyses in the social division of welfare. *Journal of Social Policy*, 7, 128–56

1981. *What unemployment means*. Oxford: Martin Robertson

Singer, H.W. 1940. *Unemployment and the unemployed*. London: Victor Gollancz

Singleton, D. 1982. Poleglass: a case study of division. In F.W. Boal and J.H.N. Douglas (eds.), *Integration and division: geographical perspectives on the Northern Ireland problem*. London: Academic Press

Smith, A. 1981. The informal economy. *Lloyds Bank Review*, 141, 45–61

Smith, A.D. 1981. *The ethnic revival*. Cambridge: Cambridge University Press

1986. *The ethnic origins of nations*. Oxford: Basil Blackwell

Smith, D.J. 1980. How unemployment makes the poor poorer. *Policy Studies*, 1, 20–6

1987a. *Equality and inequality in Northern Ireland: employment and unemployment*. London: Policy Studies Institute

1987b. *Equality and inequality in Northern Ireland: perceptions and views*. London: Policy Studies Institute

Stevenson, O. 1973. *Claimant or client?* London: George Allen & Unwin

Stone, R. and F. Schlamp. 1971. *Welfare and working fathers*. Lexington, Mass.: D.C. Heath

Supplementary Benefits Commission, 1978. *Annual Report*. London: HMSO

1978. *Take-up of supplementary benefits*. London: HMSO

Swartz, B. 1974. Waiting, exchange and power: the distribution of time in social systems. *American Journal of Sociology*, 79, 841–87

Tawney, R.H. 1964. *Equality*. London: Unwin Books

Terkel, S. 1975. *Working*. London: Wildwood House

Tierney, B. 1959. *Medieval poor law: a sketch of canonical theory and its applications in England*. Berkeley: University of California Press

Titmuss, R. 1958. The social division of welfare. In R. Titmuss, *Essays on the welfare state*. London: George Allen & Unwin

Commitment to welfare. London: George Allen & Unwin

Tomlinson, M. 1980. Housing, the state and the politics of segregation. In L. O'Dowd, B. Rolston, and M. Tomlinson (eds.), *Northern Ireland: between civil rights and civil war*, London: CSE Books

Townsend, P. 1976. The scope and limitations of means-tested social services in Britain. In P. Townsend, *Sociology and social policy*. Harmondsworth: Penguin Books

1979. *Poverty in the United Kingdom*. Harmondsworth: Penguin Books

Trewsdale, J. 1980. *Unemployment in Northern Ireland, 1974–1979*. Belfast: Northern Ireland Economic Council

Turner, R., A. Bostyn, and D. Wight. 1985. The work ethic in a Scottish town with declining employment. In B. Roberts, R. Finnegan, and D. Gallie (eds.), *New approaches to economic life*. Manchester: Manchester University Press

Valentine, C. 1968. *Culture and poverty: critique and counter proposals*. Chicago: University of Chicago Press

Wadel, C. 1973. *Now whose fault is that? The struggle for self-esteem in the face of chronic unemployment*. St Johns, Newfoundland: Institute of Social and Economic Research, Memorial University

1979. The hidden work of everyday life. In S. Wallman (ed.), *Social anthropology of work*. London: Academic Press

Walker, C. 1983. *Changing social policy*. London: Bedford Square Press

Wallace, C. and R.E. Pahl. 1986. Polarisation, unemployment and all forms of work. In S. Allen, A. Waton, K. Purcell, and S. Wood (eds.), *The experience of unemployment*. London: Macmillan

Walsgrove, D. 1987. Policing yourself: social closure and the internalisation of stigma. In G. Lee and R. Loveridge (eds.), *The manufacture of disadvantage.* Milton Keynes: Open University Press

Warner, W.L. and L. Srole. 1945. *The social system of American ethnic groups.* New Haven: Yale University Press

Warr, P. 1983. Work, jobs and unemployment. *Bulletin of the British Psychological Society*, 36, 305–11

Watson, I. 1985. *Double depression: schooling, unemployment and family life in the eighties.* Sydney: George Allen & Unwin

Weber, M. 1964. *The theory of social and economic organization.* Edited with an introduction by Talcott Parsons. New York: The Free Press

Weightman, G. 1978. Under the grille. *New Society*, 5 January

White, M. 1984. *Unemployment and labour markets.* London: Policy Studies Institute

Wiener, R. 1975. *The rape and plunder of the Shankill.* Belfast: Notaems Press

Wilensky, H.C. 1975. *The welfare state and equality: structural and ideological roots of public expenditure.* Berkeley: University of California Press

Willis, P. 1977. *Learning to labour: how working class kids get working class jobs.* London: Saxon House

Index

assertive claimants: *see* claimants

battle of the Boyne (1690), 20, 28
Belfast
    distribution of jobs in, 19–24, 51, 70–6
    growth of population of, 20–1
    industrial development in, 19–24, 69–70,
        237 n.3
    origin of, 19–20
    unemployment in, 24–6, 52, 56–9, 66–7,
        224
benefits, 2–3, 7, 17, 42–4, 83–91, 146–7, 161,
    166–8, 193–9
    social security: *see* social security benefits
    see also claimants; doing the double; means
        test; poverty; Supplementary Benefit
        scheme; supplementary benefit staff
        practice
Beveridge, W., 42, 205
Beveridge Report, 42
black economy, 39, 44, 48
    as a route into the formal economy, 99–100
    differences between Catholics and
        Protestants in, 47–105, *see also* Catholics
        and Protestants
    getting into the, 97–9
    unemployment and, 14, 39–40, 44, 47–105
    unemployed Catholics in: *see* doing the
        double
    unemployed Protestants in: *see* doing the
        double
bureaucracy, 106–7, 136, 138, 140, 158
    office culture in: *see* office culture
    see also claimants; Supplementary Benefit
        scheme; supplementary benefit staff
        practice

Catholics, 34–7
    as claimants, 168–74
    black economy and: *see* doing the double
    stereotypes of, 55, 70, 73, 168, 199
    unemployment among, 24, 56, 66
    see also Catholics and Protestants; doing
        the double; sectarian divide
Catholics and Protestants
    differences between, 21, 23, 27–8, 30,
        66–76, 144, 167–8, 172–3, 199, 209–10
    similarities between, 30–1, 44–6, 210
    see also Catholics; Protestants
Child Poverty Action Group, 109
claimants, 108–84
    assertive, 15–16; 160–84
    characterizations of, 120–1, 122–5, 129–34,
        163–5
    learning to be, 136–40, 163–5
    practical problems and, 154–8
    relations between bureaucrats and, 107,
        112–36, 138, 140–1, 153–4, 183–4
    reluctant, 15–16, 141–60, 169
    typology of, 123–5, 129–34, 140, 163,
        165–7
    see also deserving and undeserving; social
        security office; Supplementary Benefit
        scheme; supplementary benefit staff
        practice
Cohen, Anthony, 16, 187
construction industry, malpractice in, 60–3

debt, 44, 79, 155–8, 174, 177, 182, 211; *see*
    also means test; poverty
Democratic Unionist Party (DUP), 70, 168
Department of Health and Social Security
    (DHSS), 36, 41, 55, 63, 70–1, 96, 99, 108,
    110, 125–6
deserving and undeserving
    administrative use of distinction between,
        3, 15, 106–35, 183–4, 233
    claimant dispositions and distinction
        between, 165–84
    criteria distinguishing between, 1–2,
        122–5, 188–9
    development of distinction between, 4–6

deserving and undeserving (*cont.*)
  disagreement over the classification of
    people as, 2, 188, 194–5
  factual basis of distinction between, 1–2,
    188
  ideology of, 1–6, 9–11, 191–2
  ideology of individualism and, 10–11, 145,
    162, 166–84, 191–2, 210–12, 220–2, 235
  reproduction of distinction between, 4,
    108, 112, 129–35, 141, 167, 183–4, 195
  social use of distinction between, 1–4, 108,
    129–35, 165–84, 188
  see also claimants; Supplementary Benefit
    scheme; supplementary benefit staff
    practice
discretion, 107, 109–11, 115, 232–3
discrimination
  individual, 33–4
  institutional, 33–4
  Northern Ireland state and, 33, 69–76, 171
  sectarian divide and, 21, 28, 33, 69–76
  unemployment and, 33–4, 69–76, 169–70
distancing, 16–18, 55, 86, 159, 165–6, 168,
    170, 172–3, 176, 187, 190, *see also*
    symbolic boundaries
doing the double, 47–105
  advantages of, 61, 90–1
  attitudes to, 58, 65, 68; *see also* stereotypes
  benefit to employers of, 60–4, 104
  Catholics and, 59–66, 80–3
  claiming grants and, 64, 173
  disadvantages of, 63, 64, 104–5
  evaluation of, 58, 60, 64–5, 68
  fraud and, 47, 62–3, 108, 122
  income from, 61, 64, 90–7, 100–1
  Protestants and, 53–58, 79
  sectarian divide and, 70–6
  social networks and, 77, 97–9
  welfare benefits and, 56, 58, 63–8, 76
  see also black economy; deserving and
    undeserving; employment;
    unemployment; unemployed people
domestic organization, and unemployment,
    87–90, 93, 144–5, 161, 171–2, 239 n.5
Donnan, H., 31–2, 72–4

Eastlough, 16, 34–42
economy, cultural mediation of, 50–1, 68–76
  see also black economy; doing the double;
    informal economy; local economies;
    Northern Ireland economy; UK economy
employers, 62–3, 76, 85–6, 104, 203, 205–6
employment
  benefits of, 16–17, 84, 145, 185, 190, 205,
    215, 220
  costs of, 16, 85, 93, 187, 190, 238 n.3
  differences between Catholics and

  Protestants in patterns of, 20–7, 33–4,
    51–3, 59–61, 66–76
  histories of: *see* working record
  ideology of, 16–17, 56, 58, 67–8, 87–8,
    145, 187–9, 200, 208, 212, 215, 220–3
  see also doing the double; job centre; job
    hunting; jobs; work
Employment Training Scheme (ETS), 226,
    228–30
Enterprise Allowance Scheme, 206, 228
Epstein, A.L., 29
exceptional needs payments (ENP), 109–10

Fair Employment Act (Northern Ireland), 34
Fair Employment Agency for Northern
  Ireland, reports of, 23–4
fraud and abuse: *see* doing the double; fraud
  investigators; Supplementary Benefit
  scheme
Fraud Investigator's Guide, 123
fraud investigators, 55, 60, 63, 70, 91, 122,
  182, 241 n.7

genuinely seeking work test: *see*
  unemployment
Gershuny, J.I., 49
Giddens, A., 12–14
Goffman, E., 2, 139, 146, 164–5
Grillo, R.D., 38, 107

Harland and Wolff ship yard, 51, 224
Hayes, J., 7, 146, 215
hidden economy: *see* black economy;
  informal economy

identity
  ethnic, 29, 145
  occupation and, 86, 145–6, 184, 200–1, 238
    n.3
  unemployment and, 90, 145–6, 166, 168,
    200, 220, 223
ideology, 191, 210–12, 220–3, 235; *see also*
  deserving and undeserving;
  employment; individualism
impression management
  strategies of, 2, 15, 16–17, 90, 146, 159,
    164, 166, 171, 181, 188–9, 195, 203,
    218–21
Income Support (IS), 43, 106, 141, 231–2, 236
  n.3, 237 n.1
  differences from Supplementary Benefit
    scheme, 231–4
  social fund: *see* social fund
individualism
  definition of, 9
  explanations of unemployment in terms of:
    see unemployment

ideas of deservingness and: *see* deserving
    and undeserving
ideology of, 9–11, 210–12, 220–2, 235
informal economy, 48–50,
    demand side of, 98–9
    see also black economy; doing the double
Irish National Liberation Army (INLA), 33
Irish Republican Army (IRA), 33, 36–7, 60,
    62, 73

Jahoda, M., 7–8, 84, 90, 185, 239 n.3
Jenkins, R., xii, 9–10, 13, 27, 32–4, 50
job centre, 26, 78–9, 180, 200, 202–3, 226,
    237 n.1
job-hunting, 53, 78–9, 86, 180–1, 187,
    199–208, 212
    doing the double and, 77, 97–100
    importance of personal networks in, 77,
        98, 201, 230
    skill level and, 78, 200–1, 205–6
Job Training Programme (JTP), 228–30
jobs
    argument between employed and
        unemployed over, 199–208
    incentives and: *see* work incentives
    latent functions of, 84, 90–1, 185, 220, 238
        n.3
    low pay and, 83–97, 175, 187, 191, 210,
        212
    social security benefits and, 83–97, 226–7
    status and, 86, 184, 200–1, 238 n.3
    see also doing the double; employment;
        work
Jobstart Allowance, 228

Kelvin, P., 8, 90, 124, 140, 145, 152, 165,
    201, 208, 215, 239 n.3

labelling
    in terms of deserving and undeserving,
        2–3, 10, 129–34, 165, 187–90
    social processes of, 2–3, 10, 13, 55, 70,
        73–4, 124, 129–34, 158–9, 166, 169, 172,
        181, 183, 223
    see also stereotyping
labour markets, 71–2, 86, 161, 203–4
    local, 72
Lipsky, M., 107, 111, 136–7, 141, 153
local economies, 50, 72–6
    in Catholic west Belfast, 59–60, 66–8
    in east Belfast, 54, 56, 66–7
low pay: *see* jobs; work incentives

McFarlane, G., 31–2, 72–4
malingering: *see* unemployment, scrounging
    and
Mallon Park, 16, 34–42

managerial ideology, 10
marital relations, unemployment and: *see*
    domestic organization
Marsden, D., 42, 77, 103, 142
means test
    administration of, 5–6, 15, 43–4, 106–35,
        141–2
    deficiencies of, 42, 118
    harshness of, 6; *see also* debt; poverty
    justice in, 136
    poverty and, 42, 44, 121, 125
    stigma of: *see* stigma
    take up of, 121, 126, 141–3, 239 n.7
    see also deserving and undeserving;
        poverty; Supplementary Benefit scheme;
        supplementary benefit staff practice;
        unemployed people

National Assistance, 42, 137, 142
Northern Ireland economy
    Belfast's position in, 20, 69; *see also* Belfast
    development of, 19–27, 69
    sectarian nature of, 21, 23–5, 69–76; *see*
        also discrimination
    unemployment in, 24–7, 224–6
    see also black economy; doing the double;
        local economies; sectarian divide
Northern Ireland state, 27
    contested legitimacy of, 33–4, 73, 75,
        209–10
    direct rule in, 27
    discrimination in, 21, 33–4, 69–76, 171
    establishment of, 27
    Protestant control of, 20, 28, 30, 69–70,
        209–10
    sectarian nature of: *see* sectarian divide
Nutman, P., 7, 146, 215

office culture, 112, 124, 132–3; *see also*
    bureaucracy; supplementary benefit
    staff practice
Official Unionist Party (OUP), 70
Orange Order, 21, 27, 69, 72

Pahl, R.E., xii, 49–50, 56, 97, 99, 239 n.3, 241
    n.4
partition of Ireland, 27, 33
Payments for Debt Act (Northern Ireland),
    237 n.3
plantation of Ireland, 19, 28, 33
policy process, 107, 111
Poor Law Amendment Act of 1834, 6, 108
Poor Laws, 5–6, 108, 110, 141–2
poverty, 4–6, 11, 21, 42–4, 68, 104, 113, 121,
    125, 156, 208, 234–5; *see also* debt;
    means test; Poor Laws; unemployment
principle of less eligibility, 6

Protestants, 37–8
  as claimants, 174–83
  black economy and: *see* doing the double
  stereotypes of, 73–4, 199
  unemployment among, 24, 51–3, 56–8
  see also Catholics and Protestants; doing
    the double; sectarian divide

redundancy, 26
  payments for, 207
reluctant claimants: *see* claimants
replacement ratios, 91–96, 239 n.6
Restart programme, 227–30

scrounging: *see* unemployment
sectarian divide, 27–34, 36
  all-embracing nature of, 27–8
  anthropological research into, 31–3
  discrimination and, 28, 33, 69–76
  ethnic nature of, 29–31
  Northern Ireland economy and, 21, 23–5,
    69–76, 237 n.3
  see also black economy; Catholics;
    Catholics and Protestants; doing the
    double
self-employment, 206–8
Short Brothers, 51, 71–2, 79, 224
single mothers, 109, 113, 123–4
Sinn Fein, 33, 37, 70, 117
Social Democratic and Labour Party (SDLP),
  70
social division of welfare, 101–3
social fund, 231–3
social policy
  black economy and, 39–40
  bureaucracy and, 107
  ideologies of deserving and undeserving
    in, 3, 235
  unemployment and, 5–6, 234
  see also Supplementary Benefit scheme
social security benefits
  abuse of, 47, 63, 101–3, 108, 122–5
  jobs and, 83–97, 204–5
  reforms of, 3, 109–11, 227, 231, 241 n.3
  social division of welfare and, 101–3
  take up of: *see* means test
  wages and, 83–97, 204–5
  work incentives and, 7, 64–5, 83–7, 96,
    175, 196–8, 204–5, 226, 238 n.2, 239 n.6
  see also claimants; doing the double;
    Supplementary Benefit scheme;
    unemployed people
Social Security (Northern Ireland) Order
  1980, 110
social security office (SSO), 108, 111, 136, 239
  n.1, 241 n.3

conditions in, 112, 119–21, 140
queueing in, 120–1, 137–40
staff practice in: *see* supplementary benefit
  staff practice
violence in, 120–1
waiting in, 120–1, 137–40
see also bureaucracy; claimants;
  Supplementary Benefit scheme
stereotyping, 55, 70, 73–5, 131, 168, 199,
  214, 223
see also Catholics; labelling; Protestants
stigma
  by association, 139, 213, 243 n.7
  Erving Goffman's theory of, 164
  unemployment and, 3, 56, 144–5, 160, 162,
    165–7, 200, 204, 235
  welfare benefits and, 122, 128, 130–1, 142–5
  see also unemployed people
supplementary benefit: *see* claimants; social
  security benefits; Supplementary Benefit
  scheme; supplementary benefit staff
  practice
Supplementary Benefit (SB) scheme
  abuse of, 47, 108, 122–5, 240 n.6
  additional requirements (ARs) in, 43, 109,
    112, 119, 152, 231
  development of, 109
  distinction between deserving and
    undeserving in, 15, 108, 122–5, 129–35
  interviewing officers (IO) in, 113–16, 139
  knowledge of claimants about, 117–19,
    126–7, 143, 151, 162
  long-term scale rate (LTSR) of, 108, 113,
    118, 231
  non-voluntary nature of, 112, 141, 153
  provision of information about, 111–14,
    116–19, 126–7, 162
  provisions of, 43, 109, 152
  resource constraints on, 111, 119–122
  single payments in, 43, 109–12, 119, 121,
    152, 196–9, 231
  visiting officers (VO) in, 113–18, 149–51
  see also bureaucracy; claimants; deserving
    and undeserving; doing the double;
    Income Support; means test; poverty;
    social security benefits
supplementary benefit staff practice, 108–35
  deserving and undeserving and: *see*
    deserving and undeserving
  deviation from official policy of, 111–13,
    116, 125, 128
  effects on claimants of, 15, 112–13, 128–
    31, 140, 148
  ideals of, 110
  moral classification of claimants and: *see*
    deserving and undeserving

response of claimants to, 15, 112, 131–3, 140, 167
see also Supplementary Benefit scheme
Supplementary Benefits Commission (SBC), 44, 109, 142
symbolic boundaries, 16–18, 124, 134, 177, 187–90, 194, 241 n.1; *see also* distancing

Tawney, R.H., 189, 235
Titmuss, R., 101–3

unemployed people
  activities of, 12, 45–6, 188, 215–16
  as claimants: *see* claimants
  black economy and: *see* black economy; doing the double
  choices open to, 12, 14
  deserving and undeserving: *see* deserving and undeserving
  domestic organization and: *see* domestic organization
  employed's expectations of, 186, 188–90, 199, 203, 209, 213–16
  employed's views of, 185–223
  feelings of shame amongst, 89, 128, 144–5, 160, 162, 167
  friends and, 77, 79, 82, 98–9, 108, 160–2, 170–3, 188, 201–4, 213–14
  identity and: *see* identity
  interaction with the employed, 185–90, 193, 195–6, 201–2, 216–19
  isolation of, 3, 45–6, 162, 166, 188–9, 215, 223
  job-hunting and: *see* job-hunting
  kin and, 44, 77, 79, 98, 156, 160–2, 170–1, 174, 188, 195–6, 213–14, 216, 243 n.6
  life-style for, 213–19, 241 n.2
  means-tested benefits and, 42, 83–97, 113, 116–19, 193–99; *see also* means test
  stigmatization of, *see* stigma
  variation amongst, 11, 44–5, 58, 66–7, 77, 84, 163–84, 191, 212
  see also Catholics; Protestants; Supplementary Benefit scheme; unemployment
unemployment
  early research into, 6–7
  effects of, 11, 45–6, 145–6, 185, 208–9
  explanations of, 11, 74, 161, 168–84, 186–7, 191–2, 209–10, 217–22, 242 n.5

genuinely seeking work test and, 6, 141, 226–9, 236 n.2
  in Belfast, 21, 24–6, 56–8, 66, 224
  in Northern Ireland, 24–7, 224–6
  in United Kingdom, 24–7, 224–7
  jobs and: *see* jobs
  modern research into, 7–12, 236 n.3
  political economy of Northern Ireland and, 19–27
  poverty and, 11, 42–3, 152–8, 208–9, 234–5
  social density of, 162, 169–70
  scrounging and, 78, 86, 88, 108, 122, 133, 147–9, 161, 169, 181, 187, 189, 199, 205, 211–12, 214, 222, 226
  sectarian divide and: 19–27; *see also* sectarian divide; doing the double
  stage (phase) theory of, 7–8
United Irish Movement, 20
United Kingdom economy, 22–5, 224–5

Wadel, C., 17, 121, 147, 164, 185–6, 218
wages
  domestic organization and, 87–9
  perception of, 87–9
  see also employment; jobs; low pay; work
Weber, M., 106, 164
welfare dependency
  culture of, 3, 227, 234–5
  supposed effects of, 3–7
  see also deserving and undeserving; social policy
work
  as an activity, 84, 90–1, 238 n.3
  ethic of, 17, 23, 68, 84–5, 123, 146, 198, 200, 212, 235; *see also* employment, ideology of
  identity and: *see* identity
  paid work: *see* employment; jobs; low pay
  wages and: *see* wages
workhouse test, 6
work incentives, 7, 64–5, 83–7, 96, 175, 196–8, 204–5, 226, 238 n.2, 239 n.6; *see also* jobs; means test
work role, 16–17, 185; *see also* doing the double; employment, ideology of; jobs; unemployment
working record, 187, 218

Youth Training Scheme (YTS), 227